Native American Verbal Art

NATIVE AMERICAN VERBAL ART

Texts and Contexts

William M. Clements

The University of Arizona Press
Tucson

Publication of this book is made possible in part by the proceeds of a permanent endowment created with the assistance of a Challenge Grant from the National Endowment for the Humanities, a federal agency.

The University of Arizona Press
Copyright © 1996
The Arizona Board of Regents
All rights reserved
♾ This book is printed on acid-free, archival-quality paper.
Manufactured in the United States of America
01 00 99 98 97 96   6 5 4 3 2 1

Library of Congress Cataloging-in-Publication Data
Clements, William M., 1945–
Native American verbal art : texts and contexts / William M. Clements.
  p. cm.
Includes bibliographical references (p.   ) and index.
ISBN 0-8165-1659-6 (cloth : acid-free paper). —
ISBN 0-8165-1658-8 (pbk. : acid-free paper)
1. Indian literature—North America—Translating—History and criticism.   2. Indians of North America—Languages—Translating.
3. Indians of North America—Languages—Texts.   I. Title.
PM218.C54   1996
897—dc20

96-10026
CIP

British Cataloguing-in-Publication Data
A catalogue record for this book is available from the British Library.

Selections from *Shaking the Pumpkin: Traditional Poetry of the Indian North Americas*, edited by Jerome Rothenberg, are reprinted by permission of Sterling Lord Literistic, Inc. Copyright © by Jerome Rothenberg.

Title-page photograph: Mountain Chief, a Blackfeet Indian, translating a tribal song into sign language for the ethnologist Frances Densmore in 1916. (National Anthropological Archive, Smithsonian Institution, photo no. 55300)

For three generations:

Dorothy K. Clements

Frances M. Malpezzi

Evelyn R. Clements

CONTENTS

ACKNOWLEDGMENTS

Research for this study was conducted at these libraries: Dean B. Ellis Library, Arkansas State University; Library of Congress; Ohio State University Library; University of Arizona Library; and West Virginia University Library. I am grateful for the assistance of the staffs of these institutions, especially the members of the Interlibrary Loan Department of the Dean B. Ellis Library. Time, of course, is as important a resource as the material housed in libraries. I am indebted to the following for helping me allocate this precious resource to this project: Charles R. Carr, Chair of the Department of English and Philosophy at Arkansas State University; Lawrence Boucher, C. Calvin Smith, and Richard McGhee, deans of ASU's College of Arts and Sciences; and Robert Culbertson and Robert Hoskins, successive academic vice presidents at ASU.

Some of the research was carried out while I was a participant in a National Endowment for the Humanities Summer Seminar at the University of Arizona. I appreciate the assistance and advice of Roger Nichols, the seminar director, and the other participants.

I am grateful to the readers and staff of the University of Arizona Press for their advice. Several of the chapters included here were previously published as essays and received helpful criticism from editors and readers for the journals and collections in which they originally appeared. I also appreciate the comments offered by members of the audiences at professional meetings where some of this material was presented orally.

"Papago: Elegy Dream Song" from *The Magic World: American Indian Songs and Poems*, edited by William Brandon, is reprinted by permission of The Ohio University Press/Swallow Press. Natalie Curtis's translation of a Hopi song, which originally appeared in *Harper's* 107 (1903), is reprinted by permission of Harper's Magazine Foundation.

Finally, I am obligated in too many ways to name to Frances Malpezzi.

INTRODUCTION

Europeans and Euroamericans have been making written records of the spoken words of Native North Americans since at least the early 1600s. During the four centuries that have elapsed, they have made literally thousands of records of those words and descriptions of how they were expressed. Two diametrically opposed views on the value of those records—especially the ones produced before the insights of ethnopoetics, total translation, and other recent developments in such record-making became available—provide the impetus for this study. Some commentators (particularly in the past) have uncritically assumed that these records provide absolutely reliable information about the nature of American Indian oral expression, even its esthetic qualities. Meanwhile, many modern students have dismissed these records as utterly worthless. I take a middle ground between these positions. While I recognize the limitations of the older records, I am interested in why they are limited in the particular ways that they are and in possibly recovering something from them despite their limitations. In many cases, they represent all we have from an entire verbal heritage; in most cases, they are all that we have of particular heritages at certain points in history. To use them indiscriminately is foolish; not to use them at all seems foolish also. But admittedly they are not always what they claim to be. Consider what has become a classic instance of such record-making.

In January 1835 the *North American Review* ran a largely favorable review of the autobiographical *Life of Ma-ka-tai-me-she-kia-kiak or Black Hawk,* which had been published the previous year. Although the reviewer—apparently journalist W. J. Snelling—expressed his certainty of the work's authenticity, he had one doubt about the volume: "The only drawback upon our credence is the intermixture of courtly phrases, and the figures of speech, which our novelists are so fond of putting into the mouths of Indians. These are, doubtless, to be attributed to the bad taste of Black Hawk's amanuensis" (1835: 69). Perhaps Snelling was reacting to a passage such as the following from the Sauk leader's dedication of his autobiography to Brigadier General Henry Atkinson:

> The changes of fortune, and vicissitudes of war, made you my conqueror. When my last resources were exhausted, my warriors worn down with long and toilsome marches, we yielded, and I became your prisoner. . . . The changes of many summers, have brought old age upon me,—and I cannot expect to survive many moons. Before I set out on my journey to the land of my fathers, I have determined to give my motives and reasons for my former hostilities to the whites, and to vindicate my character from misrepresentation. (Black Hawk 1834: 7)

Black Hawk continues in the same vein before invoking the blessing of the "Great Spirit" on his former adversary and dating his words "*10th Moon, 1833*" (1834: 8).

This English translation of the dedication accompanies the same material spoken by Black Hawk in the Algonquian language, apparently dictated to Antoine LeClair, the highly regarded government interpreter for the Sauks, whom Black Hawk had approached, LeClair claimed, with "a great desire to have a History of his Life written and published" (Black Hawk 1834: n.p.). Presumably the Sauk leader, who had recently returned to his people in the Midwest following imprisonment and a tour of the East after his defeat in the fifteen-week Black Hawk War in 1832, told his life story in Algonquian to LeClair, who made a rudimentary translation into English. Probably because English was not his first language, the interpreter turned the translation over to John B. Patterson, editor of the Galena, Illinois, *Galenian*, who reworked the manuscript and, according to one modern critic, "actually wrote the history of Black Hawk's life" (Krupat 1985: 45). But even if the material is genuine, LeClair's translation accurate, and Patterson's editing less intrusive than Krupat believes, readers illiterate in Algonquian who rely upon the English version of the words attributed to Black Hawk might wonder what manner of Indian spoke them. On one hand, he uses vocabulary that LeClair or Patterson has rendered with such Latinate diction as "vicissitudes," "hostilities," and "vindicate." His syntax achieves periods, which, if not exactly Ciceronian, resemble the constructions absorbed by generations of students whose writing and public speaking styles were shaped by exposure to the oratorical patterns employed by Roman senators.

On the other hand, Black Hawk uses some stereotypically "Indian" terminology. He reckons time by "moons" (yet plugs this concept into the Euroamerican calendar), describes death as a "journey to the land of my fathers," and calls upon a deity referred to as the "Great Spirit." In his review of the volume, Snelling calls special attention to its frequent use of the term "pale faces," which was "never in the mouth of any American savage, excepting in the fanciful passages of Mr. Cooper." Snelling concludes his brief consideration of the language in Black Hawk's autobiography by remarking, "There are many more phrases and epithets of the like nature, and we only mention them, because we think it is time that authors should cease to make Indians talk sentiment" (1835: 70).

When Black Hawk's *Life* was reissued in 1882, editor Patterson recalled, "After we had finished his [the Sauk leader's] autobiography the interpreter read it over to him [in English?] carefully, and explained it thoroughly, so that he might make any needed corrections, by adding to, or taking from the narrations; he did not desire to change it in any material manner" (quoted in Krupat 1985: 46). This testimony suggests that the objection raised a half century earlier by Snelling amounted to a minor quibble. After all, if the text created by Patterson represented accurately *what* Black Hawk intended, what difference did it make how it was presented? As representative of the perspective (somewhat distinctive in published form in the 1830s) of a Native American, the *Life* served its documentary purpose. Questions of style pertained to literary art, a term that could not be applied to Black Hawk's autobiography.[1]

The same could be said about other utterances by Native Americans encountered by Euroamericans—the songs, orations, ritual discourse, and narratives (both traditional myths and tales and accounts of personal experience similar to Black Hawk's life story). Knowing what Indians were saying had practical, political import, but the artistic potential of such discourse was seldom acknowledged. Translating the words of Native Americans into English (or any other European tongue) required only a more or less accurate matching of content and whatever stylistic devices were necessary to render it accessible to Euroamerican readers. When esthetic features of American Indian verbal expression did receive attention, it was often only to note how Indians had to rely on figurative tropes in order to compensate for the absence of abstraction in their languages. For example, a commentator writing on "Indian Eloquence" in *The Knickerbocker* in 1836 opined, "We would anticipate eloquence from an Indian. He has . . . a poverty of language, which exacts rich and apposite metaphorical allusions, even for ordinary conversation" ("Indian Eloquence" 1986: 5).[2]

But when it came to being considered artistic from a Euroamerican perspective, American Indian discourse began with two marks against it. First, it was the speech of "savages," persons whose identity stemmed from direct antithesis to civilization—"the antiprinciple to humane existence" (Sheehan 1980: 38; see also Pearce 1988). Although attitudes toward Native North Americans varied from the sixteenth through the mid-nineteenth centuries, they were consistently defined in terms of what they lacked. If Indians were regarded as representing an early stage in the progress of humanity toward the ideal of European civilization, they were consequently perceived as lacking development in the components of that ideal, including literary artistry. If Indians were believed to represent a degeneration from an antediluvian state of high civility, they had now lost what their ancestors had possessed eons previously. Even if Euroamerican observers noted the force of "natural reason" in Indian societies and cultures, that force lacked the refinement that civilization could bring to it.

Second, Indian discourse suffered from being oral rather than written. Though the Romantic movement of the late eighteenth century had celebrated the unlettered bard, personified in Homer, Ossian, or the peasant balladmaker (Fairchild 1961: 461), the rhapsodies of these oral poets achieved their identity as literature in written forms—for example, the Homeric translations of Chapman celebrated by Keats, the Ossianic collations of McPherson, or the ballad collections of Percy, Scott, and a host of others (Friedman 1961). Part of the appeal of the oral was its place in the developmental history of literature and its potential as an inspiration for writers. Homer, Ossian, and the balladmakers had esthetic descendants who produced real literature (Hodgen 1964: 340–343). The savages of America had no such descendants, no one to demonstrate the literary potential of their discourse. Consequently, even though what they said might occasionally represent a "pre-literature," little evidence existed that anything truly artistic could follow from it. The juxtaposition of "oral" with "literature" simply had not occurred to a sufficient number of Euroamericans to encourage attention to esthetic qualities in Native American discourse.

The notion that Native American discourse at best amounted to a pre-literature characterized the views of most Euroamericans throughout the nineteenth century and well into the twentieth. As long as it persisted, concerns about the translation of Black Hawk's diction and style remained minor issues, secondary to matters of content. But as commentators have begun to recognize inherently "literary" qualities in Native American verbal art, those concerns have loomed larger. Literary analysis of American Indian "texts" (a term to which I will return below) requires careful attention to the implications raised by the "only drawback" to W. J. Snelling's "credence" in Black Hawk's *Life:* the strange verbal mixture of the stereotypically Indian with the highly formal Euroamerican—a product of the nearly inevitable collaboration between a Native American speaker and a Euroamerican interpreter/ translator (Krupat 1985: 7; Murray 1991). From that situation arises the often-expressed caveat that what readers encounter as Native American "literature" in print distorts the nature of its original realization. Among the many who have expressed this caveat was Margot Astrov, whose anthology of Native American "poetry" (usually, songs without the music) originally published in 1946 remains one of the more successful of such inherently limited volumes (see chapter 9): "One might be inclined to consider the fact that he [the translator] is likely to color somehow the oral expression of the native in a way that may seriously impair the authentic value of the document. This may or may not be the case. It quite depends on the quality—shall we say poetic quality—of the translator. For translation is, if not creative, then re-creative work" (1946: 4–5). I will suggest, however, that more is involved than the translator's "poetic quality," whatever Astrov means by that.

Astrov's admonition, which could (and will) be illustrated with many specific examples, leads to the assumption that drives this study: careful examination of the processes that yield particular representations of Native American verbal art must accompany critical evaluation of published Native American "literature" (another term I will treat below). Such examination will seldom reveal any representation as either totally without merit or completely satisfactory. But it can draw attention to what is useful in specific representations by identifying how and why the decisions that shaped them probably came about. As Arnold Krupat has noted, "[W]e need to be acutely aware of the mode of production of Native American texts, taking into account the varying contributions of Native performers, informants, interpreters, and the like, as well as those of non-Native editors. Whatever understanding of traditional Native American literature may currently be achieved, it will have to take into account the role Euramericans have played in its textual production. This is only one price of our history of domestic

imperialism" (1989: 129n). In exploring that role, this study is both an
expose of and an apologia for domestic imperialism in the realm of
esthetics. It emerges from a set of propositions about the relationship
between texts and oral expressions and about how to evaluate manifestations of that relationship.

"Texts" continue to be central to the study of Western literature,
their availability constituting a "prerequisite for interpretation" (Clifford 1988: 38). Even for those theoretical approaches that argue against
"foregrounding" texts by concentrating on readers' responses and that
question such fundamental notions of earlier critical doctrines as textual authenticity, texts nevertheless remain the point of departure.
Krupat notes that a necessary condition for the development of literary
criticism in the Western sense is a corpus of texts (1992a: 175–176). In
fact, some schools of criticism have emerged from the idea that the text
is *all* that one effectively needs. Simply put, for the study of literature,
the text is the thing.

In cultures without written literary traditions, texts in the sense the
term is used by students of literature, of course, do not exist. In what
Walter Ong calls "primary oral cultures" (1982: 1), verbal artistic expression becomes manifest as an event rather than as object. Like other
events, a verbal art event consumes a period of time, happens in a specific spatial context, and involves specific participants as speakers and
listeners. A verbal art event is also nonrepeatable; it is "historically
situated speech" (Asad 1986: 160). Unlike a written text, it cannot be
reexamined or enjoyed again. Whatever is said and how it is said exist
only during the span of the event—during the act of discourse. As Ong
suggests, "[S]ounded words are not things, but events: a sounded word
can never be present all at once, as things are. In saying 'nevertheless,'
by the time I get to the latter part of the word, '-theless,' the first part
of the word, 'never-,' has passed out of existence" (1988: 265). This
discourse-centered approach to verbal artistic expression assumes that
art exists only as it is expressed, not as a rarefied abstraction in the
realm of the ideal (cf. Urban 1991). Verbal artistry has being only in
specific verbalizations. In a primary oral culture (or, in fact, in any
social situation where oral artistry occurs), the event is the thing. Verbal art in such milieus "never exists as text, but only as act" (Kroeber
1983: 106).

What, then, is the relationship between texts—required by Western
literary study and available, as far as Native North American verbal

artistry is concerned, since at least the early seventeenth century—and oral expression? I believe that one represents the other. But clearly, that is no easy matter. "In living speech," Ricoeur writes, "the instance of discourse has the character of a fleeting event, an event that appears and disappears. That is why there is a problem of fixation, of inscription. What we want to fix is what disappears" (1973: 93) No text, despairs another commentator, "can re-create a living voice" (Staub 1991: 449). Moreover, texts are characterized by their "dissociation" from the intentions of the speaker and by their being directed at a wider, more diverse audience than the original expression (Ricoeur 1973: 105), entailing that texts inevitably distort what they seek to represent. Nevertheless, I believe that the goal of text production (elusive though it may be) can be simply to record oral expression as an event. Consequently (and idealistically), a text should reproduce that expressive event as accurately and comprehensively as possible—an especially significant charge when Native American verbal art is involved, since most of us will come to that art only through texts. This belief grounds this study.

The concept of "text"—fundamental to Boasian anthropology, anthropological linguistics, folklore studies, and literary criticism (all disciplines relevant to this study)—has become more expansive recently. Traditionally straightforward definitions of "text" equate it simply with a written (or printed) record of the linguistic component of discourse (i.e., "language-event or linguistic usage" [Ricoeur 1973: 92]) in an indigenous language: "material dictated or recorded by a native speaker and member of the culture in the native language," according to the Boasian view (Codere 1966: xiv). But a broader, more complex perspective, shaped in part by the reflexive anthropology of the late twentieth century, sees "text" in terms of the process of textualization—in James Clifford's definition, the process "through which unwritten behavior, speech, beliefs, oral tradition, and ritual come to be marked as a corpus, a potentially meaningful ensemble separated out from an immediate discursive or performative situation." He adds, "In the moment of textualization this meaningful corpus assumes a more or less stable relation to a context" (1988: 38). Applied specifically to oral expression, textualization becomes what Bauman and Briggs call "entextualization": "the process of rendering discourse extractable, of making a stretch of linguistic production into a unit—a *text*—that can be lifted out of its interactional setting" (1990: 73). Texts result when an expressive event becomes a fixed "subject/object" for the enjoyment or study of Western readers (Krupat 1992a: 190). The purpose of the text is to record faithfully, to allow an event to become "an object of science . . . by virtue of a kind of objectification similar to the fixation which occurs in writing" (Ricoeur 1973: 98).[3]

According to this expanded definition, a text freezes expression, verbal or otherwise. It preserves an instant of behavioral dynamics in more or less permanent form, separating it from the ongoing flow of activity for purposes of analysis or appreciation. In this sense, the process of converting verbal expression into text resembles documentary photography. A sports photographer who takes a picture of a layup shot at a basketball game captures only an instant in the process of the executed maneuver (which, in turn, is part of a still larger event, the game), but in doing so makes a permanent record (at least as long as the negative and prints endure) of that instant. Most of the time the act of photographing does not interrupt the process. The shooter usually completes his layup without regard for the photographer, whose flashbulb becomes unnoticeable in the bright lights of the arena.

A text of verbal expression likewise captures only an instant in the ongoing process of discourse in a speech community. But while the process of textualization does not *necessarily* affect the ongoing process of discourse, it *can* do so in two important ways. On one hand, a speaker who realizes that what he or she says is going to be textualized may very well adapt what is said to the particular situation. The expression may represent a pose assumed for the textmaker, much as if the basketball player shooting the layup winked at the photographer as he made his approach. Just as that wink may throw off the shooter's timing and cause him to miss the basket, the pose adopted by a speaker whose expression is being textualized may result in something other than the completely natural. Perhaps the expression will be richer, fuller, and more artistic since the expression is being preserved as a text for posterity (Niles 1993: 140), but consciousness of being textualized is just as likely to rob the expression of natural artistry. Moreover, while a text of an oral expression may have no effect on the ongoing expressive tradition (since it has been customary for texts of Native American verbal expression to be published in professional journals or museum series that are largely unavailable in the communities where the expressions originally occurred), sometimes texts do feed back into the tradition. The chasm between orality and literacy is not so great a divide as many theorists have suggested, and texts may often become major influences on an oral tradition. Oral expression and its textualization can, in fact, comprise a "durative, interactive system of representation" (Niles 1993: 141).[4] Just as the basketball player might study photographs to improve his form, the verbal artist may allow texts to influence how and what he or she says. But usually, as Albert B. Lord notes, even after their stories are written down, "storytellers continue to tell their stories as before" (1991: 24).

The sports photographer and the textmaker may have some motives in common. Both intend to re-create in another medium the firsthand experience of the moment for those who were not there. Someone who did not actually see the layup shot in person gets to experience it vicariously by looking at the photograph: a person who did not hear the verbal expression can read its text. Moreover, by making a moment in a process permanent, both sports photographer and textmaker create an archive of that moment for future examination and enjoyment.

However, both photographer and textmaker confront several obstacles to the successful attainment of these goals. The photographer may focus his camera incorrectly and obtain a distorted image. Likewise the textmaker's vision may be clouded by preconceptions about verbal expression and about the people whose expressions are being textualized, especially their language. Or the photographer may use a lens that is too narrow and fail to provide the necessary context for the moment in the process. The photograph, for example, might capture only the basketball player's face and upper body, omitting the footwork that is vital to his move. Similarly, the textmaker may concentrate exclusively on *what* was said in the expression and ignore other features of the event such as verbal style, paralinguistic features, kinesics, and audience responses in addition to the interactive situation that produced it. Only the careful photographer or textmaker may partially overcome these obstacles.

The "partially" suggests that inherent in both sports photography and textualization are two problems that may be almost unavoidable. The photograph of the layup shot, after all, does capture only a moment in one play in a complex game that involves nine other players as well as referees, coaches, and spectators. The context for the specific shot preserved by the photograph may be crucial for understanding its importance. At what point in the game did it occur? Was the shooter's team ahead? How did the shooter's teammates and the opponents figure into this particular shot? How does this shot represent the usual role of the shooter in the team's strategy? The text of a verbal expression may also be removed from its meaningful, informing contexts—those that were an immediate part of the expressive event ("context of situation") and those cultural attitudes and values that serve as the tacitly understood background for what is said and how it is said ("context of culture")

(Ben-Amos 1993: 215). Moreover, both photograph and text may come to stand for the entire process. One shot of a layup made by a mediocre player may no more reflect the art of basketball than one text recorded from the expression of a mediocre speaker may reflect the art of a community's discourse. With these inherent dangers in mind, though, the sports photographer and the textmaker are both striving for accuracy and completeness—even if neither one may be able to produce a product that on its own will achieve either goal.

Textualization may indeed share some features with documentary photography (an analogy offered primarily to emphasize the view advanced here that the text is not the primary object of study but only a representation thereof), but it even more clearly resembles translation, particularly if the latter is defined as "the transfer from one designative coherence to another" (Steiner 1975: 205), and with ethnography (Asad 1986). Considering textualization in terms of these two disciplines yields two ways of delimiting what is textualized. On one hand, a "linguistic" text represents only *what* is expressed. An "ethnographic" text places what is expressed in a specific expressive situation and in a general cultural context.

The most comprehensive investigation of linguistic textualization appears in Elizabeth Fine's *The Folklore Text*. There she defines textualization as a "hermeneutic act of translation" (1984: 8). Linguist Roman Jakobson has identified three types of translation (intralingual, interlingual, and intersemiotic), the last of which approximates textualization. Also called "transmutation," intersemiotic translation is, for Jakobson, the interpretation of verbal signs by means of a nonverbal sign system—for example, semaphore flags (1959: 233). This also describes textualization of verbal expression: the representation of oral and other behavioral signs by means of a visual sign system in either writing or print. The task of the textualizer is to find a method for representing oral expression in writing/print as accurately and as fully as possible. Ideally, this involves capturing every phoneme of the expression exactly as it was articulated. To replicate the oral expression as *oral*, though, requires representing not only its content but also how it was expressed as well as a multitude of variables both paralinguistic and kinesic—a task that continues to baffle those who work at the process of textualizing, and some of whose individual solutions I will examine below.

When verbal expressions in a Native American language become linguistic texts in English, "translation proper" (Jakobson 1959: 233), of course, occurs. Translation proper always involves an attempt to familiarize the linguistic Other. But the sense of Otherness, though varying in ways that shape the procedures of particular textmakers (see chapter 1), remains particularly strong in the translation of Native American materials, for just the identification of a linguistic text as "Lakota" or "Tlingit" or "Abnaki" or "Maidu" defamiliarizes it for readers of English in a way that similar identification of texts as "French," "German," or even "Arabic" does not. This is, after all, the product of an "Indian," historically considered the antithesis of civilization and civility, the principal avatar of the "primitive" antipode to high Culture for Euroamericans (Torgovnick 1990). So the transformation from oral expression to text is much more than the process that provides the principal focus for translation studies; it is also the anthropologist's task of "cultural translation," not just "a matter of matching sentences in the abstract, but of *learning to live another form of life* and to speak another kind of language" (Asad 1986: 149). Godfrey Lienhardt's contention that the ethnographer's responsibility is "largely . . . one of translation, of making the coherence primitive thought has in the languages it really lives in, as clear as possible in our own" (1954: 97) relates directly to the concerns of textmakers working with American Indian verbal expression. Moreover, since the writing of ethnography "translates experience into text. . . . [and] brings experience and discourse into writing" (Clifford 1988: 114), textualization should definitely be regarded as part of the ethnographic enterprise.

Translation theory has acknowledged the ethnographic dimensions of translation (e.g., Casagrande 1954; Myrsiades and Myrsiades 1983). In an essay published in *Translation Review*, R. Daniel Shaw stresses that translation involves the transfer of whole cultures, not just linguistic documents. Shaw notes that through translation "[t]he thoughts and ideas expressed in one context are presented in a different context where they take shape in a linguistic and cultural system other than that in which they were formed" (1987: 25). Effective translation, according to Shaw, should emerge from "a dynamic awareness of worldview differences" and have as its objective the serious representation of those differences (1987: 28). He posits a tripartite typology of world cultures and argues for establishing translation categories based upon the culture types to which the source, the receptor, and the translator belong. For example, most Native American textualization involves a source from Shaw's "kinship" culture type, a receptor from his "industrial" culture type, and a translator also from an "industrial" culture. It can thus be categorized as translation category T2: "The translation consists of either the source and receptor being of different culture

types while the translator is from the same type as the source or receptor, or the source and receptor are the same but the translator is from a
different type" (1987: 28).

Shaw's attempt to lay a foundation for translation as a cross-cultural
enterprise is commendable, but the specifics of his system demonstrate
the need for ethnographic input. For example, his tripartition of cultures into "kinship," "peasant," and "industrial" too patently recalls the
savagery-barbarism-civilization progression of nineteenth-century evolutionists. But his emphasis on perceived cultural differences—maybe
even "rankings"—as a factor in translation should be considered. Talal
Asad notes that "institutionally defined power relations" between cultures affect the nature of culture translation. As he "crudely" puts it,

> [B]ecause the languages of Third World societies . . . are "weaker" in rela-
> tion to Western languages (and today, especially to English), they are
> more likely to submit to forcible transformation in the translation pro-
> cess than the other way around. The reason for this is, first, that in their
> political-economic relations with Third World countries, Western na-
> tions have the greater ability to manipulate the latter. And, second,
> Western languages produce and deploy *desired* knowledge more readily
> than Third World languages do. (1986: 157–158)

Where cultural dominance is a factor, "the cultural translation is all
one-way and the penalty to the subordinate group is to cease to exist"
(Murray 1991: 6). Such translation situations result in "usurpation"
(Cheyfitz 1991: 72). For instance, the words of a Sauk telling his life
story (from a "kinship" level culture) will very likely assume the form
of Western prose when textualized and translated into English (the language of an "industrial" level culture). On the other hand, a similar bit
of discourse moving from English to an Algonquian language would
most likely require the readers of the translation to accommodate
English-based patterns and structures. Obviously, textualization can
involve the "domestic imperialism" mentioned by Krupat. Forgetting
its ethnographic dimensions can multiply occasions for that sin.

But to produce a fully realized ethnographic text—in the sense that
term is used here—requires much more than simply remembering the
Otherness of the original expression. It involves incorporating into the
representation of that expression a multitude of elements often dismissed as "context" (Briggs 1988: 4). As a model for an ethnographic
text, we might consider the desiderata for "good" ethnography recently
outlined by George E. Marcus and Michael M. J. Fischer. Such a repre-

sentation of human behavior "is one that gives a sense of the conditions of fieldwork, of everyday life, of microscale processes . . . ; of translation across cultural and linguistic boundaries (the conceptual and linguistic exegesis of indigenous ideas . . .); and of holism" (1986: 25). An ethnographic text of verbal expression should represent the linguistic component of the event (in a linguistic text which is as comprehensive as possible), the specifics of the situation when and where the event occurred (cf. "conditions of fieldwork, of everyday life, of microscale processes"), the placement of the event within the cultural contexts that inform it and to which it contributes (cf. "holism"), and the ideas, values, and attitudes that affect the event (cf. "exegesis of indigenous ideas"). The textmaker who operates ethnographically is aware of the complexity of the semiotic translation of what is expressed, but also realizes that representing oral expressions as the events that they are requires their being situated and contextualized as processes rather than compartmentalized as objects.

The idea that texts (linguistic or ethnographic) of verbal expression are of secondary significance to the expression itself need not deter literary critics from approaching texts from their own disciplinary perspectives. Though literary approaches to Native American texts may often involve ethnocentric imposition of interpretive tools developed in an alien context, some commentators have demonstrated that this is not inevitable (e.g., Ramsey 1983; Rice 1989). Moreover, the tools of literary and cultural criticism can be effectively employed as ways of appreciating texts as artifacts whose integrity need not depend entirely upon their situation of production (Krupat 1992a; Murray 1991). But I am less interested in texts' literary merits or demerits than in their documentary potential. Although trying to recover the oral expression that a text purports to represent may indeed be little more than "an idle and romantic gesture" (Niles 1993: 149), my concern here is with what texts can tell us about that expression.

Thus far, I have carefully avoided the term "oral literature," partly because domestic imperialism may arise even from the most basic terms we apply to the products of Native American verbal expression. William Bascom's term "verbal art" (1955) may, in fact, be more appropriate and less culturally determined than "oral literature" for naming the stories, orations, ritual utterances, and songs that have comprised the esthetic heritage in words of most Native American groups. "Oral literature" resurrects the eighteenth-century question of whether "literature" requires the use of "letters," as the word's etymology suggests, and, in fact, implies a static abstractness that is totally inappropriate to the dynamic process of oral expression. Moreover, separating off some portion of verbal expression in a culture as "literary" may be an etic imposition, the application of Western ways of looking at the verbal world to non-Western material and behavior. Joel Sherzer and Anthony Woodbury have refined Bascom's coinage by defining verbal art in terms of "a community's own conception of what in language use is aesthetically or rhetorically pleasing." According to this view, they claim, verbal art "can occur anywhere, from informal to everyday to formal and ritual discourse, and artistic forms, such as narratives, can be embedded in other forms, such as conversation, which in and of themselves might not be considered artistic" (Sherzer and Woodbury 1987: 8–9). Consequently, when referring to the esthetic expressions in words of Native Americans that have gone through the process of textualization, I will use "verbal art," not "oral literature."[5]

I also want to emphasize that not every verbal expression made by Native Americans merits that term, though I am not prepared to impose a Western touchstone for making such a distinction. More importantly for the terminology used here, not every Native American verbal expression should be denominated a "performance," a term that refers to a special way of expressing involving a community's emic criteria for verbal art (Bauman 1984: 7–14). Sometimes a speaker's expression will use few if any of the relevant performance variables. At other times, he or she may employ some of them. Every so often a speaker becomes a full-fledged "performer" by utilizing all or most of the community's recognized performance techniques (Hymes 1981: 80–86). To use "performance" generically to refer to all of these possibilities robs the word of the significance it has attained in folklore studies. Moreover, focusing exclusively on performance, even when it does occur, may blind the ethnographic textualizer to other dimensions of expressive dynamics, banishing them to context and other residual rubrics. Consequently, my generic term for a speech event will be "expression." I assume that not all textualizations attempt to capture performances, but all of them try to represent expressions.

The chapters that follow emerge, primarily and principally, from the assumptions that the text is always secondary to the oral expression and that the text's purpose is to represent in a different medium that expression as comprehensively and accurately as possible. While similar to translation, this process of representation is essentially an ethnographic enterprise informed—like all such enterprises—by its cultural and especially its intellectual contexts. Disclosing that context requires examining the intellectual climate in which textmakers worked, identifying any factors that *may* have shaped their ethnographic representation of Native American oral expression. It also requires an investigation of the situation in which the textmaker encountered the material that he or she recorded.

I begin in chapter 1 by introducing a structure by which efforts at textualization may be comprehended. The Identity-Difference continuum (borrowed from Fredric Jameson via Arnold Krupat) provides a general framework for the history of textualization of Native American oral expression, which I treat microcosmically by looking at the work of three textmakers on one oral expressive heritage (that of Zuni). This framework, though, is offered principally as a way of imposing some order on the three centuries' worth of texts and contexts that I treat later on. Chapter 2 treats what I believe to be the most crucial factor in evaluating a text's success at representing oral expression: the nature of the expressive behavior that has been textualized. To develop the point that the kind of expression a textmaker witnesses—whether "performance" or something less artistically realized—must shape the text, I present three examples from the nineteenth century and then apply what I derive from them to the work of Jerome Rothenberg, one of the most important contemporary textmakers.

Chapters 3–8 set forth a series of chronologically arranged case studies, which add up, I fear, largely to a history of failure in the crucial act of representation. My choice of cases to study reflects what I believe to be their importance in the history of the textualization of Native American oral expression. The Jesuits who missionized in New France during the seventeenth and eighteenth centuries, incidentally textualizing and theorizing about the verbal expressions (including art) of the Algonquians and Iroquoians among whom they were spreading Christianity, engaged in the first sustained ethnographic project in North America that yielded texts. Henry Timberlake's translation of a Cherokee war song in 1765 was probably the first printed English rendering of a Native American "poem." The early nineteenth-century textualizers and translators who saw in Native American verbal art a literature *manqué*, which they modified into a fully realized literature, represent a period of growing interest in the subject; Henry Rowe Schoolcraft, Indian agent and pioneer field collector of Native American verbal art, most fully developed this early nineteenth-century approach. The "scientific" textualizers who viewed Native American discourse as a source of data for historical, ethnographic, and especially linguistic information still exercise an influence on the work of anthropologists and linguists.

Concert pianist Natalie Curtis's field research among American Indians in the Southwest helped to launch a wave of interest in their verbal art by poets and literary critics that continues to the present. The concluding chapter examines anthologies, the format in which most nonspecialists encounter Native American texts. Failures—at least to measure up to rigorous standards of accuracy and thoroughness—abound in the efforts at textualization covered in these chapters. But from even the most abysmal failures something may be recovered. And the Epilogue notes some hopeful recent developments.

An unsigned note on "Indian Eloquence" that appeared in *The Ariel* in 1831 was undoubtedly correct in its evaluation of textualizations of Native American verbal expression: "The eloquence of the North American Indian has never appeared to full advantage, the interpreters generally employed being ignorant and illiterate persons" ("Indian Eloquence" 1831: 144). Unfortunately, though some notable exceptions do occur, the comment remains valid. Yet a history of textualization of Native American verbal expression need not merely lament what might have been done differently. Often it seems we can learn little about American Indian discourse from the work of past textualizers, much less than we could had those textualizers been as committed to a full ethnography of expression as we pretend to be today. But without their work we would know even less. An essay by Dell Hymes (1992) takes its title from a line by Kenneth Burke: "Use All There Is to Use." It offers Hymes a motto for his own work, which stresses the importance of considering every linguistic sign in an expression, performance, or linguistic text as one explores its artistry. Burke's line may also serve as a motto for a more generalized approach to the study of Native American verbal expression—one that attempts to use whatever is available to its fullest potential. Of course, in using a work such as Black Hawk's autobiography we risk putting too much faith in its accuracy in representing what the performer said and how he said it. While we may have become sophisticated enough to resist that danger, we may still succumb to another peril—the failure to use what discretion can show to be valuable material capable of adding to our knowledge of Native American verbal art, especially for periods when other documentation is unavailable.

CHAPTER ONE

"IDENTITY" AND "DIFFERENCE" IN THE TEXTUALIZATION OF ZUNI VERBAL ART

 Transformations of Native American oral expressions into European-language linguistic texts have reflected the translators' preconceptions about "the Indian" and about literature. For example, early nineteenth-century textmakers such as those treated in chapters 5 and 6 perceived in Native American oratory, narrative, and song the raw materials for "real" literature. As a result, they focused their translation efforts on the imagery from nature, figurative tropes, and patterns of rhythm that they believed inherent in Indian expression, embellishing and codifying these "very decided beginnings of a literature"—in William Gilmore Simms's phrase (1962: 137)—in whatever ways were necessary to produce stories and poems that met the Euroamerican literary conventions of their day. These translators' successors, the "scientists" treated in chapter 7, also operated with preconceptions about Native American verbal art; they emphasized its documentary function, its role as a source of data about language usage and other aspects of culture (e.g., Powell 1883: xx; Boas 1916: 393). Hence, they stressed the importance only of accurate preservation of Native-language originals, even their so-called "free translations" highlighting semantic correspondences and ignoring, for the most part, indigenous esthetic features. Early in the twentieth century, enthusiasts for Native Americana like Natalie Curtis (see chapter 8) and Mary Austin imposed still another preconception on their translations or interpretations, especially of American Indian oral poetry: the idea that this poetry represented the primitive phase in the evolution of true literature and that a genuine American literature must found itself

on aboriginal strivings toward verbal artistry in the Western Hemisphere (Castro 1983). Their translations portrayed Indians as primitive imagists, whose art anticipated modern trends in literature.

During the almost four centuries that Euroamericans have been translating Native North American verbal art, many preconceptions have colored their work, most of them emerging from a continuum anchored on one end by "Identity" and on the other by "Difference" (Jameson 1979: 43–45). The "peculiar, unavoidable, yet seemingly unresolvable alternation" between the poles of this continuum poses a dilemma whenever we confront alien cultural products, according to Fredric Jameson. If we perceive in these products that with which we identify—that which is accessible through "our own cultural *moyen du bord*"—we may overlook or minimize their otherness through what may become "little better than mere psychological projection." But if we focus on the alien cultural products' Difference, we truncate hopes of comprehension and appreciation (1979: 43).

Jameson examines one alternation between Identity and Difference by surveying contemporary responses to classical culture. Invoking the pole of Identity, we have found in the symmetrical formality of Greek classicism parallels not only to our own esthetic values but also to our sociopolitical ideals. Yet when, recognizing this view as an oversimplification, we turn to the pole of Difference, our perception of Greek antiquity as "a culture of masks and death, ritual ecstasies, slavery, scapegoating, [and] phallocratic homosexuality" is just as conditioned by preconceptions as the earlier perspective (1979: 44). Jameson's point is not that we should attempt to resolve conflicting views engendered by a perceived dichotomy between Identity and Difference, but that we should be aware that these poles of a continuum mediate between us and alien cultures.

Arnold Krupat has introduced Jameson's ideas into the discourse on Native American verbal art in a review of Karl Kroeber's *Traditional Literatures of the American Indian*. In terms of the ongoing Indian-Euroamerican encounter, Krupat notes, Identity and Difference reflect the varying, often contradictory responses of Euroamericans to contact with Native Americans. For the Puritans, Native Americans, subhuman denizens of "howling wilderness," epitomized Difference, since they were leagued with Satan in opposing the kingdom of God in New England. The eighteenth century also stressed ways in which Indians embodied Difference and placed investigations of their history, philology, and ethnology under the rubric of natural philosophy. On the other hand, the idealization of the Noble Savage generated a perception of

Native Americans in terms of Identity, as some Euroamericans saw in the Indian what they would themselves be without the trappings of civilization (Krupat 1983: 4).

By extending the pole of Identity to representations of Native American verbal art (Krupat 1992b), textmakers have assumed that they could render orations, narratives, and poems in ways that would make them readily accessible to Euroamerican readers—that adding rhyme and regularized meter to poetry or presenting oral narratives as paragraphed prose, for example, legitimately represented Indian verbal expression as art. Exponents of the Identity pole might cite Susan Hegeman's timely reminder, "If one did not acknowledge Anglo-American textual conventions to some extent, then there would be no translation" (1989: 20). As Krupat suggests, Identity becomes a matter of *"accessibility"* and seems to lie in the "disciplinary domain of art" (1992b: 4).[1]

Although the textualization/translation enterprise must at least acknowledge the pole of Identity, textmakers who recognize the alternative, Difference, have emphasized the dangers of using literary conventions of one culture to represent the true verbal artistry of another (especially when the cultures are often so diametrically distinct as Euroamerican and various American Indian cultures) and of transforming oral expression into written linguistic text. For them, Difference manifests itself in two ways, linguistic/cultural and semiotic—in the materials' languages and cultural matrices (Jakobson's "translation proper," informed by ethnographic perspectives) and in their media of expression ("transmutation"). Those leaning toward the Difference pole of the continuum would probably agree with Irving Goldman's caveat about textualization of Kwakiutl cultural expression: "As a matter of simple caution, we should assume that if the mode of thought of primitive peoples, as revealed by the ethnographic records, sounds all too familiar notes of recognition in the western academic mind, something is seriously wrong with the rendition" (1980: 334). The byword of Difference becomes *"authenticity,"* according to Krupat, and its disciplinary locus lies in social science (1992b: 4).[2]

The Identity-Difference continuum offers a heuristic framework for making sense of several centuries' work in linguistic and ethnographic textualization, translation, interpretation, and critical understanding of Native American verbal art. A reader can evaluate the usefulness of a particular representation at least partially in terms of its maker's choice of one pole or the other—whether he or she has decided to Navajoize English or to Anglicize Navajo, to oralize writing or to literacize speaking, to paraphrase Rudolf Pannwitz as quoted by Walter Benjamin

(1968: 80). Furthermore, the continuum provides a useful basis for comparing and contrasting texts, especially those representing the same Native heritage of verbal art. I want to demonstrate this latter function by examining linguistic textualizations of expression at Zuni, a pueblo in western New Mexico.

Since Frank Hamilton Cushing's residence of four and a half years beginning in 1879, Zuni has continued to attract anthropologists. James Stevenson, leader of the Smithsonian expedition of which Cushing was a member, also studied the community's culture. His wife, Matilda Coxe Stevenson, involved in the research from its inception, continued the work after her husband's death in 1888. Elsie Clews Parsons spent considerable time at Zuni between 1915 and 1930, A. L. Kroeber visited the pueblo during the summers of 1915 and 1916, Leslie Spier did archeological research nearby in 1916, Frederick Webb Hodge returned to Zuni periodically for almost forty years between 1886 and 1923, and Franz Boas was there briefly in 1920. Ruth Benedict and Ruth Bunzel came to Zuni in 1924, the latter returning for several subsequent summers (Pandey 1972). More recently, Omer C. Steward, John Adair, Stanley Diamond, Barbara Tedlock, Dennis Tedlock, and M. Jane Young among many others have done anthropological fieldwork at Zuni.[3]

While most of these researchers paid some attention to oral expression, many of them producing linguistic texts and/or translations, three stand out as representing the poles of Identity and Difference particularly well. At one extreme, Cushing's work adopts Identity, since his comments about Zuni verbal art and his translations suggest a belief that the material could legitimately be rendered according to Euroamerican literary conventions. Bunzel, on the other hand, gave the nod to Difference when she commented on her efforts at textualization. But her actual translations reflect Identity more than Difference. Tedlock has worked most consistently from the pole of Difference, since he has stressed not only the linguistic and cultural gap between Zuni and English, but also the distinction between oral expression and literature crafted within a tradition of writing.

Cushing published two major collections of translations of Zuni verbal art. "Outlines of Zuñi Creation Myths," brief cosmogonic and etiological narratives, appeared in 1896 in the *Annual Report* of the Bureau of American Ethnology (BAE). *Zuñi Folk Tales*, longer examples of what John Wesley Powell called "discredited mythology" (Cushing 1901: viii), came out posthumously in 1901. Though Cushing's published comments about his methods of textualization and translation are scanty, they reveal his acceptance of the principle of Identity. For example, in the introduction to "Outlines" he writes of the songs that appear in some of the myths: "In the originals these are almost always in faultless blank meter. . . . I do not hesitate . . . to tax to the uttermost my power of expression in rendering the meanings of them where I quote, clear and effective and in intelligible English" (1896: 374). Cushing found Zuni songs so like poetry in English that he could apply a generic term from the latter ("blank verse") to them. Moreover, he had no qualms about waxing literary in a Euroamerican mode when translating them. Powell's introduction to the folktale collection includes some telling comments about Cushing's "scriptorial wand," which the text-maker waved to make Zuni oral narratives "a part of the living literature of the world." Cushing was especially equipped to accomplish this since he could "think as myth-makers think, . . . speak as prophets speak, . . . [and] expound as priests expound" (Cushing 1901: ix). In other words, Cushing recognized Identity between what he might express in English literary prose and what the Zuni storyteller verbalized in oral narration.

Cushing's devotion to the pole of Identity probably arose from two sources. The first was his deeply personal involvement in Zuni culture. While some may dismiss such antics as his signing correspondence as "First War-Chief of Zuñi" (Woodward 1939) and being photographed in Zuni dress as manifestations of Cushing's idiosyncratic personality, they do reveal his sense that the Zuni and he—a "civilized" Euroamerican—were not all that different, even though at disparate stages in the scheme of cultural evolution that he espoused. This scheme, a second source of the attraction of the pole of Identity for Cushing, enjoyed the support of most anthropologists during the late nineteenth century. Refined by Edward Burnett Tylor and Lewis Henry Morgan and field-tested by Powell's BAE, it posited human psychic unity (i.e., "Identity") and the notion that cultural forms at various evolutionary stages had genetic connections presupposing at least traces of Identity. Fieldworkers like Cushing might see cross-cultural equivalences, even when they were lacking, because of the force of evolutionary theory—hence, for example, Tedlock's criticism that Cushing's "metaphysical glossing" of his material stressed a monotheism indicative of "the theoretical preconceptions of nineteenth-century anthropology rather than Zuni belief" (1983a: 58).

Cushing's linguistic textualizations of the Zuni material are colored by his opinion that Zuni oral narrative resembled Victorian prose

closely enough to warrant his use of a contemporary Euroamerican
esthetic. For example, consider how he handles a description of the
twin war gods in a myth to which he assigned the title "The Origin of
the Twin Gods of War and of the Priesthood of the Bow":

> Lo! dwarfed and hideous-disguised were the two gods Ahaiyuta and Mat-
> sailema, erst Uanamachi Piahkoa or the Beloved Twain who
> Descended—strong now with the full strength of evil; and armed as war-
> riors of old, with long bows and black stone-tipped arrows of cane-wood
> in quivers of long-tailed skins of catamounts; whizzing slings, and death-
> singing slung-stones in fiber-pockets; spears with dart dealing fling-slats,
> and blood-drinking broad-knives of gray stone in fore-pouches of fur-
> skin; short face-pulping war-clubs stuck aslant in their girdles, and on
> their backs targets of cotton close plaited with yucca. Yea, and on their
> trunks, were casings of scorched rawhide, horn-like in hardness, and on
> their heads wore they helmets of strength like to the thick neck-hide of
> male elks, whereof they were fashioned. (1896: 422)

The initial interjection and reversal of word order suggest an attempt to
be "literary" according to Victorian standards. The interminable length
of the first sentence, though perhaps reflecting the formulaic quality
of oral *poetry* (which many contemporary translators consider Native
American oral narrative to be [e.g., Hymes 1981]), more likely draws
upon classical European epic literature, which Cushing could have
known in several Victorian translations. Cushing also adopts a stilted
formality in vocabulary, which, though it could be an attempt to replicate the mythopoeic diction of Zuni narrators, probably derives from
the fad for conscious archaizing that characterized Victorian literature
set in the past (Bassnett-McGuire 1980: 72–73).

Cushing translated poetic passages in myths into Victorian verse. For
example, he treated the words of one of the "Ancients" summoned to
assist the war gods in their maturation as follows:

> "Why call ye, small worms of the waters
> And spawn of the earth and four quarters,
> Ye disturbers of thought, lacking shame;
> Why call ye the words of my name?"
> (1896: 421)

The use of rhyme introduces a feature of English poetics absent from
Zuni. Bunzel, in fact, chided Cushing for this "inexplicable blunder" of

rendering Zuni poetry in "regular short-lined rhymed English stanzas" (1932b: 620).

Cushing's treatment of the final paragraphs of a folktale he entitled "The Maiden and the Sun" offers another example of his approach to textualization and translation:

> And ever since then [the events of the story], my children, the world has been filled with anger, and even brothers agree, then disagree, strike one another, and spill their own blood in foolish anger.
>
> Perhaps had men been more grateful and wiser, the Sun-father had smiled and dropped everywhere the treasures we long for, and not hidden them deep in the earth and buried them in the shores of the sea. And perhaps, moreover, all men would have smiled upon one another and never enlarged their voices nor strengthened their arms in anger toward one another. (1901: 474)

This lengthy summary and explicit, garrulous statement of the story's moral exemplify what Tedlock regards as the "most serious difficulty" with Cushing's folktale translations: his embroidery of the originals "with devices, lines, and even whole passages which are clearly of his own invention and not mere distortions" (1983a: 59). As Brian W. Dippie has noted, Cushing was "more adept at conveying a feeling for myth" than at recording it with exactitude (1982: 285), but his sense of the essential Identity between the Zuni and himself and between their verbal art and Euroamerican literary tradition granted him license to cast Zuni oral expression in a Victorian mode. Unlike some translators who transform what they perceive as exotic, esthetically remote verbal art according to the esthetic conventions of the target language in order to make it accessible to the reader, Cushing did not regard Zuni myths and folktales as remote. He converted them into Victorian literature because he sensed their Identity with it.

Ruth Bunzel, trained by Franz Boas and initiated into fieldwork by Ruth Benedict, had no use for the cultural evolutionism of Cushing's generation of anthropologists. Instead, she accepted her mentors' doctrines of cultural diversity and cultural relativism—in other words, of Difference and respect for Difference. Unlike Cushing, she recognized the obstacles in translating from Zuni into English, but like him she often chose vocabulary and stylistic constructions for her linguistic texts that made them immediately accessible to readers of English, thus representing them in terms of Identity. The major collections of Bunzel's translations are "Zuñi Origin Myths" and "Zuñi Ritual Poetry," both of which appeared in 1932 in the BAE *Annual Report*, and *Zuñi Texts*, published the following year by the American Ethnological Society.

"Zuñi Ritual Poetry" contains most of Bunzel's commentary on her textualization and translation procedures. While Cushing was confident that Zuni and English evinced the principle of Identity to such an extent that he could easily translate from one to the other, Bunzel noticed some very real difficulties. In vocabulary, for instance, she cited problems produced by the "obsolete or special" language used in ritual discourse (1932b: 620) and the abundant word play that it contained (1932b: 619). The latter included double entendres and deliberate verbal and grammatical ambiguity, but even ascertaining "how much is word play, how much metaphor, and how much is actual personification" sometimes mystified her (1932b: 619). Bunzel also identified grammatical differences between English and Zuni, the Native American language's reliance on inflection being most significant.

Other grammatical features of Zuni that caused translation problems for Bunzel included its use of long periodic sentences, its typical word order (subject, object, verb), and its use of participial or gerundive clauses to express temporal or causal subordination ("impossible in English," she lamented) (1932b: 618–619). She regretted her inability to carry these aspects of Zuni grammar over into English and the resulting loss of "effective stylistic feature[s]" (1932b: 619). Bunzel was also unable to retain the rhythm of Zuni ritual poetry in her English versions (though she could preserve "its irregularity, the unsymmetrical alteration of long and short lines" [1932b: 620]). Finally, she believed her translations suffered "greatly from loss of sonority and vigor" because of her inability to transfer Zuni patterns of accent into English (1932b: 620).

Clearly, then, Bunzel was only too aware of the effects of Difference. Yet she did not represent those effects in her texts. Perhaps she believed doing so would have rendered them inaccessible to English readers and, like many other translators, opted to sacrifice features of the source language original for the sake of target language readability (Bassnett-McGuire 1980: 23) or chose source material in which the effects of Difference she perceived were minimal.

Whatever the reasons, Ruth Bunzel created poetic translations that read—by her own assessment—more like the blank verse of Milton or the free verse of the King James version of the Psalms than Zuni oral poetry (1932b: 620).[4] Notice her treatment of the ending of one of the prayers of the War Cult:

On roads reaching to Dawn Lake
May you grow old;
May your roads be fulfilled;
May you be blessed with life.
Where the life-giving road of your sun father comes out,
May your roads reach;
May your roads be fulfilled. (1932b: 689)[5]

Aside from the references to "Dawn Lake" and to the "sun father," nothing in these lines suggests that they originated in the verbal art of a culture as removed from that of most readers of English as the Zuni. In fact, their stately measure and litany-like parallelism fulfill expectations, shaped by Judaeo-Christian scripture and liturgy, of what ritual poetry should be. Bunzel certainly has not added these features; they exist to some degree in the Zuni version published alongside her translation. But she has not translated the Zuni in a way that suggests the Difference her commentary recognizes.

Bunzel's translations of Zuni oral narrative assume the same approach. The first paragraph of her translation of "Tale Concerning the First Beginning" is a straightforward rendering that only hints at Difference:

Yes, indeed. In this world there was no one at all. Always the sun came up; always he went in. No one in the morning gave him sacred meal; no one gave him prayer sticks; it was very lonely. He said to his two children: "You will go into the fourth womb. Your fathers, your mothers, käeto•-we, tcu-eto•we, mu-eto•we, łe•-eto-we, all the society priests, society p̂ekwins, society bow priests, you will bring out yonder into the light of your sun father." Thus he said to them. They said, "But how shall we go in?" "That will be all right." Laying their lightning arrow across their rainbow bow, they drew it. Drawing it and shooting down, they entered. (1932a: 584)

Though they would realize this is a translation, of course, because of the terms left in Zuni and probably because of culture-specific references such as "society bow-priests," readers of English would again find nothing to indicate that this is a passage from *oral* expression (and perhaps poetry instead of prose) in a language whose structure differs substantially from the Indo-European. A clear sense of Identity emerges despite the translator's recognition of Difference.

Dennis Tedlock's translations of Zuni oral narratives—most of which were originally published in *Finding the Center* in 1972—reflect more clearly than Bunzel's their common sense of the Difference between Zuni and English. Tedlock also goes farther than either Cushing or Bunzel by stressing that an important distinction between the original performances and their translated textualizations involves the media in which they are realized. Difference figures prominently in Tedlock's handling of Zuni verbal art because it is Zuni and because it is oral. Influenced not only by the continuing emphasis in anthropology on Difference as represented by cultural pluralism and relativism, but also by the "ethnography of communication" that developed in the 1960s (Gumperz and Hymes 1964) and emphasized the complexity of communicative activity and the need to record all its aspects—not just the linguistic text—Tedlock has written extensively on the translation practices of his predecessors at Zuni and his own methods. Many of these writings were collected in the volume *The Spoken Word and the Work of Interpretation* in 1983.

Critical to Tedlock's assumption of Difference as a basis for representing Zuni verbal art in print is his statement, "Those who have sought to transform the spoken arts of the American Indian into printed texts have attempted to cross linguistic, poetic, and cultural gulfs much larger than those faced by translators who merely move from one Indo-European written tradition to another" (1983b: 31). Particular problems that Zuni presents when one attempts to transform narratives composed in it into English, according to Tedlock, include some of those identified by Bunzel: word order and use of special vocabulary, for instance (1972: xxvii–xxviii). He also notes (as Bunzel's translations show that she recognized) that some Zuni words—interjections, proper names, opening and closing tale formulas—defy translation into English (1972: xxviii–xxx). Moreover, he stresses how the pole of Difference affects the general perception of the stories he has translated. What Zunis "picture" when they perform or hear verbal art differs from what Euroamericans might visualize. Tedlock admits, "[N]othing I could do would make them experience . . . [verbal art] precisely as a Zuni does" (1972: xxxi).[6] Meanwhile, like Dell Hymes, Tedlock argues that prose translations of oral narrative obscure its nature: "[P]rose has no real existence outside the written page" (1972: xix). Consequently, he suggests Difference in medium of presentation by rendering Zuni oral narratives poetically, equating line breaks with pauses of one-half to three-fourths of a second.

Tedlock's translation of the conclusion of a folktale entitled "Coyote and Junco" offers a glimpse of his technique. The narrative picks up after a two- or three-second pause by storyteller Andrew Peynetsa:

Coyote said, "QUICK SING," that's what he told her [Junco].
She didn't sing.
Junco left her shirt for Coyote.
He bit the Junco, CRUNCH, he bit the round rock.
Right here (*points to molars*) he knocked out the teeth, the rows of teeth
     in back.
(*tight*) "So now I've really done it to you."
     "AY! AY!" that's what he said.
THE PRAIRIE WOLF WENT BACK TO HIS CHILDREN, and by
          the time he got back there his children were dead.
Because this was lived long ago, Coyote has no teeth
          here (*points to molars*).
          LEE——SEMKONIKYA. (*laughs*) (1972: 83)

In addition to the pacing of the oral performance, marked by line divisions, Tedlock's translation indicates precise features of how Peynetsa told the story through words completely in upper case (spoken more loudly), italicized comments in parentheses (tone of voice, gestures, audience reactions), and a long dash following a vowel within a word (lengthening of about two seconds). In other passages, Tedlock signals such lengthening by repetition of letters. He also uses typography to mark softening of voice (small type) and changes in pitch (superscripting and subscripting words or syllables).

While Difference in medium emerges from what amounts to typographic manipulation, Tedlock actually does little more than Bunzel to signal linguistic/cultural Difference. In this passage, he leaves the closing formula—which Cushing usually handled as "Thus shortens my story" (e.g., 1901: 92)—untranslated. Elsewhere, he does the same with opening formulas (Cushing's "In the days of the ancients" [e.g., 1901: 65]).[7] He also attempts to match the tone and level of Zuni diction by using the relatively formal "prairie wolf" for the penultimate occurrence of "coyote." Occasionally, Tedlock creates the same effect by translating Zuni interjections with English archaisms. The formulaic "that's what he told her [said]" also represents the Zuni phraseology (printed on facing pages in *Finding the Center* only for "Coyote and Junco") and may help to communicate Difference, but the major factor in creating this effect is the appearance of the linguistic text on the

printed page. Tedlock's translations do not look like most textualizations of oral narrative in paragraphed prose; they are poetry, but poetry
that incorporates constant reminders of the relevance of the principle of
Difference in the media of presentation.

At first glance, applying Fredric Jameson's Identity–Difference continuum to the linguistic textualization of Native American verbal art
may seem simply a restatement of the tension that has characterized
translation theory and practice for centuries. Every translator must decide if his or her completed work will preserve elements of the source
language (SL) original even when they are obscure and ineffective in the
target language (TL). The alternative is to sacrifice SL for the sake of
readability in TL (Bassnett-McGuire 1980: 68–72). Most translators
have taken the latter course and produced translations—like Alexander
Pope's rendering of Homer in heroic couplets—that their readers can
appreciate. But the Identity–Difference continuum involves more than
a choice of whether to favor SL or TL. For instance, in creating his texts
translated from Zuni that favored TL, Cushing—if his and John Wesley
Powell's published comments are sincere—did not believe he was sacrificing SL at all. He saw such Identity between Zuni and English that
there was no reason to indicate Difference. At the other extreme, Tedlock, who would seem to favor SL at the expense of TL, does not really
do so. His translations, though preserving some of the Difference he
perceived in Zuni oral narrative, were originally published by a trade
press and are readily accessible for readers willing to deal with the typographic manipulations, which are products of Difference in medium,
not of the translator's favoring SL or TL. Of the three translators treated
here, only Bunzel may have been influenced by the translator's conventional dilemma of favoring SL or TL. Like Pope, she recognized the
essential Difference between SL and TL and produced a translation that
favored the latter, but unlike him she may have done so because she
believed there could be no other way to bring the Zuni into English.

Moreover, of course, the Identity–Difference continuum also applies
to media of presentation. Neither Cushing nor Bunzel seemed to perceive that the orality of Zuni verbal art made it Different from written
prose and poetry, so neither did anything to suggest the original orality
in their textualizations. They decidedly favored target medium over
source medium. Only Tedlock recognized and marked media Difference in his translations.

Consequently, Identity and Difference—as extended from Fredric
Jameson's original conceptualization to the principles governing the
textualization and translation of Native American verbal art—offer a

handle for dealing with the ways textmakers have worked. The Zuni case study provides an illustration of what Krupat (1992b) suggests might be done on a larger scale with the entire history of Euroamerican textualizations and translations of American Indian oral expression. The choice of Identity or Difference is not simply a matter of dispassionate philology. It factors into the politics of cultural imperialism. Very often, selecting the pole of Identity repeats a recurrent theme in American foreign relations—the welcoming of "homogenization, but . . . only in the terms of the policy maker" (Cheyfitz 1991: 5). Rejecting the "dignity of difference" (Cheyfitz 1991: 75) fulfills the goal of domination of the Other by minimizing that Other's alterity (Sarris 1993: 56). Although stressing Identity may suggest a "faith in human universals" and "essential qualities and characteristics" shared across cultural boundaries, this admirable view can actually amount to presumptuous denial of the distinctiveness of cultures (Krupat 1989; Murray 1991: 6).

At the same time, though, looking at textmakers and their translations in terms of the continuum does not presuppose that those designated as adherents of Identity have necessarily produced less "authentic" texts than exponents of Difference, or vice versa. An advocate of Identity may err by forcing Native American material into Euroamerican conventions, but a textmaker emphasizing Difference may unnecessarily exoticize the material—one critique that has been directed at the ethnopoetics movement (Tyler 1985: 688; cf. Clifford 1988: 15). Also, the nature of the material being textualized and the situations where it was recorded—not the textmaker's privileging either Identity or Difference—should be the principal factor in the shape a text assumes. Incorporating an account of that situation into a textualization moves a linguistic text toward becoming an ethnographic text. Meanwhile, it suggests how fully the linguistic text itself can be expected to represent the full artistry of authentic oral performance.

CHAPTER TWO

SITUATIONS AND PERFORMANCES

"Very little consideration has been given to Indian poetry as poetry," lamented Alice Corbin Henderson in 1917. In a commentary upon her own "interpretations" of "aboriginal" poetry, she complained that one of the weaknesses of representations of Native American verbal art prepared by some of her contemporaries, the ethnologists whose work was appearing in BAE publications and in periodicals edited by Franz Boas such as the *Journal of American Folklore* and *Publications of the American Ethnological Society,* was that they "overlooked the literary significance of Indian songs" in their attempts to reproduce with scrupulous linguistic accuracy what was sung or recited (1917: 256). Henderson's dissatisfaction with the texts of Native American oral literatures made by linguistically oriented anthropologists represents an early articulation of a note that has been repeatedly sounded throughout the twentieth century. Writing in 1933, Herbert J. Spinden—to cite another example—stated, "As a rule professional linguists are prosaic: it seems that they pay attention merely to structures and to the denotation of words, neglecting the connotation. It is the old story of botanists not seeing the beauty of flowers" (68).

Probably the most thorough critique of the practices that characterized late nineteenth- and early twentieth-century translation of Native American verbal art came a generation after Spinden. Though focusing specifically on the handling of Zuni oral narratives such as those treated in chapter 1, Dennis Tedlock, in an essay originally published in 1971, carefully delineated some of the problems produced by relying totally upon "scientific" texts. For one thing, he noted, narratives translated by the Boasians tended to be "condensations of what a performer would tell in a normal, spontaneous conversation" (1983b: 38). Tedlock worried about the effects of the awkward literalness of the translations upon readers who would likely wonder "whether the original style of these narratives was as choppy and clumsy" as the translations seemed to suggest (1983a: 57). In fact, Tedlock questioned whether linguistic texts so produced should really be considered *translations*, since they constituted

> what professional translators would call a "crib" or a "trot"—not a true translation into literate English, but rather a running guide to the original text, written in an English that was decidedly awkward and foreign. If "faithful renderings" [the phrase is Boas's] were faithful to anything, they were faithful to a linguistic position that places so much importance on the differences among languages as to cast suspicion on the very possibility of translation. (1983b: 31)

More recently, Arnold Krupat has complained that the prosaically literal translations of anthropologists "usually obscured completely the dynamics of Indian performances and made it very difficult for anyone to discover a genuine poetry among Native peoples" (1989: 109). Dell Hymes has been one of the few ethnopoetically oriented translators and commentators to find much of value in these linguistic texts, partly because they are often the only available documentation of now-extinct verbal heritages, but also because he has been able to identify indigenous artistic features that have survived the process of textualization into the Native languages if not that of translation into English (1981: 339).

These criticisms of the approach to textmaking taken by linguistically oriented anthropologists are just one feature of an ongoing reevaluation of the extant printed records of Native North American verbal art. This reevaluation is an essential step in establishing a corpus of materials documenting this art, and the lament that most anthropological representations fail to reflect the full range of Native artistry is generally valid. But such a lament may ignore the fact that the original material as encountered by the anthropologist or linguist did not always evince that artistry itself. The poetics of performance cannot be reproduced in representations of decidedly unpoetic oral renditions. In fact, a necessary starting point for assessing the reliability of published Native American oral expressive materials is determining exactly what has been textualized and translated. Doing so requires identifying the conditions under which the textmaker encountered the oral source material. Was it a "performance" or some other kind of expression? Who besides the storyteller, singer, or orator and textmaker were present? What were the physical conditions for the rendering of the oral material? What generated the rendering? Answers to such questions suggest to what extent the artistry of natural performance was present in the material encountered by the textmaker, and should shape reader expectations of linguistic or ethnographic representation.

Central to recent developments in the study of verbal art is the concept of "performance" as a special way of speaking, which emerged from the sociolinguistically influenced ethnography of communication of the 1960s (e.g., Gumperz and Hymes 1964). It emphasized that orators or storytellers within a tradition of esthetic discourse might assume varying degrees of responsibility for shaping their discourse to fulfill relevant artistic criteria. In a succinct codification of thinking about verbal performance, Richard Bauman suggested that when the enunciation of a message demonstrates features of language and paralanguage beyond the purely referential, "performance" might be occurring. A "performer," according to Bauman, accepts responsibility for displaying communicative skill so that his or her listeners may enjoy the manner of the discourse, regardless of its matter (1984: 11). Dell Hymes, whose work has provided a foundation for performance-oriented studies of verbal art, especially that of Native Americans, has suggested further that performances can be graded on a scale from "desultory" (a spiritless, rote recitation of a memorized message) to "authentic" (a full realization of the artistic potentialities within the tradition) (1981: 80–86).

An example of potential variety in the linguistic dimension of expression may clarify these distinctions. Someone could relate the plot of "The Star Husband," a folktale known throughout much of North America, as follows:

Two girls . . . sleeping out . . . make wishes for stars as husbands . . . . They are taken to the sky in their sleep . . . and find themselves married to stars . . . , a young man and an old, corresponding to the brilliance or size of the stars . . . . The women disregard the warning not to dig . . . and accidentally open up a hole in the sky . . . . Unaided . . . they descend on a rope . . . and arrive home safely. (Thompson 1964: 449)

Someone else—a more proficient storyteller—might recount the same plot with considerably more detail, describing the living conditions of the stars' wives, dramatically displaying their yielding to the temptation of violating the interdicted digging, maybe even quoting some dialogue. The whole, though, might consist of set pieces, memorized and repeated without regard for the particular situation of the telling. A third person—or the same one again in another setting—might use the basic plot formulation of "The Star Husband" (something similar to Stith Thompson's "Ur-text" quoted above) to create an emergent narrative, one that responds to and reflects the presence of a specific audience, engaging them in the story by manipulating both what is said (the message) and the way it is said (for example, through vocal dynamics, facial expressions, and body placement). Within the tradition of storytelling in primary oral cultures, such as those of pre-contact Native American groups, only the last rendition approaches full artistic potentialities; it is the "authentic" performance in Hymes's terms. In fact, terms such as "report," "resume," or "telling" may be more appropriate for a summary recounting of a story.[1]

While readers of scrupulously realized textualizations of any of the three *might* learn something of the relevant verbal art tradition, they can be *assured* of doing so only by examining one that represents the last. The same would hold true for textualizations of any renderings of Native American verbal art. Only when the textmaker has encountered an authentic performance does he or she have the raw material from which to create a text that can represent the full artistic potentialities of the oral tradition, either linguistically or ethnographically. While some of these potentialities may exist in non-performance renderings of verbal expression, textualizations of those renderings will most likely not be as artistically complete as representations of performances (nor should we expect them to be). Considering some specific situations that have produced texts from the oral traditions of Native North Americans will illustrate the importance of knowing what was textualized before assessing their value.

In 1832, George Catlin and a couple of trappers canoed down the Missouri River from Fort Union in eastern Montana, where Catlin had spent several weeks after traveling upriver aboard the steamboat *Yellowstone*. Some two hundred miles below the fort, they came upon a Mandan community, where the artist spent some time enjoying Mandan hospitality, painting portraits of willing subjects, and observing the community's way of life. Among the events he witnessed that summer was a rainmaking ceremony, during which several "medicine-men" in succession stood atop one of the earthen lodges and tried to summon the rain *"je-bi"* through the power of their magic and the strength of their oratorical skills. After observing several failed attempts, Catlin heard and recorded the oration of Wak-a-dah-ha-hee, who succeeded in calling forth a downpour. Catlin carefully described Wak-a-dah-ha-hee's appearance and noted several features of his delivery style—for example, his technique of "stamping his foot over the heads of the *magi*, who were involved in the mysteries beneath him" (apparently within the lodge on whose roof the orator was standing).

Presumably Catlin relied upon James Kipp, the agent for the American Fur Company stationed among the Mandans, for a translation of the oration, which he presents in its apparent entirety. Before beginning his speech, Wak-a-dah-ha-hee threw a feather into the air to determine the wind direction. Then he addressed the Mandan community:

My friends! people of the pheasants! you see me here a sacrifice—I shall this day relieve you from great distress, and bring joy amongst you; or I shall descend from this lodge when the sun goes down, and live amongst the dogs and old women all my days. My friends! you saw which way the feather flew, and I hold my shield this day in the direction where the wind comes—the lightning on my shield will draw a great cloud, and this arrow, which is selected from my quiver, and which is feathered with the quill of the white swan, will make a hole in it. My friends! this hole in the lodge at my feet, shows me the medicine-men, who are seated in the lodge below me and crying to the Great Spirit; and through it comes and passes into my nose delightful odours, which you see rising in the smoke to the Great Spirit above, who rides in the clouds and commands the winds! Three days they have sat here, my friends, and nothing has been done to relieve your distress. On the first day was Wah-kee (the shield), he could do nothing; he counted his beads and came down—his medicine was not good—his name was bad, and it kept off the rain. The next was Om-pah (the elk); on his head the raven was seen, who flies *above* the storm, and he failed. War-rah-pa (the beaver) was the next, my friends; the beaver lives *under* the *water*, and he never wants it to rain. My friends! I see you are in great distress, and nothing has yet been done; this shield belonged to my father the White Buffalo; and the lightning you see on it is red; it was taken from a black cloud, and that cloud will come over us to-day. I am the white buffalo's hair—and I am the son of my father. (Catlin 1841: 1:136)

In 1841 Rufus B. Sage began a several-year tour of the West for the sake of adventure, health, and topics for the lecture circuit. He fell in with a group of traders at Westport, Missouri, and their trail took them northwestward to the White River in Dakota Territory, where they hoped to establish a base of commercial operations in the vicinity of the winter quarters of the Brulé. While there, Sage and his colleagues enjoyed the companionship of Tahtunga-egoniska, "a head chief of the Brulé village," who came to the traders' camp with other Brulé. "Whenever the throng dispersed for a few moments," Sage recalled, "he would improve the opportunity for conversation with us. . . . We began to regard him with much deference, and felt quite at home in his company. He would frequently entertain us with anecdotes as occasions suggested" (1846: 89).

Sage was so impressed with the Brulé elder's stories that he included translations of four of them in the account of his travels published in 1846. He introduced each with a brief note about what occasioned it: a game of hand, interest in the Brulés' reasons for venerating a nearby mountain, an inquiry about a place name, and a question about the role of "medicine men" in Brulé society (1846: 90–96). Sage does not indicate whether Tahtunga-egoniska related the stories in Lakota or in English, but in each case the storyteller's primary audience was the contingent of Euroamericans who had come to trade.

The place-name story that Sage recorded from the narration of Tahtunga-egoniska represents a tradition that has become somewhat hackneyed in lore *about* Native Americans (De Caro 1986; Pound 1976: 79–92). Less often do we encounter "Lover's Leap" stories actually told by Indians themselves.[2] The site in question was a bluff on the White River known as "The Death Song." In response to Sage's inquiries, Tahtunga-egoniska began to narrate the reason for this name:

> Once, on a time, the Oglallas and Burnt-thighs [i.e., Brulés] held their encampment upon the river, opposite to the high point of which my son enquires. While there a dog-soldier [This is the title of those selected to superintend the civil affairs of a village. —Sage's note] of the Burnt-thighs received the offer of six horses from an Oglalla brave, for his only daughter—a sweet flower—such an one as oft pierces the warrior's heart with her charms, when the arrows of enemies fall harmless at his feet. The offer was quickly accepted—for the dog-soldier was poor. (1846: 94)

When the daughter, whose name was Chischille, heard this news, she was heartbroken, for she had already fallen in love with a warrior of her own people. In order to avoid the unwanted marriage, she and her lover escaped. Tahtunga-egoniska tells what happened next: "But, alas, for them! They were pursued, and overtaken. The life of the young warrior atoned for his temerity,—while Chischille was cruelly beaten and brought back to her father's lodge."

The next morning was to be her wedding to the Oglala suitor. After arraying herself in what appeared to be nuptial finery, Chischille ascended the precipice overlooking the river. Her people saw her seated there and heard her singing. When they realized that the song was her death song, several young men rushed to save her from destruction. As they approached, they could hear her song more clearly:

"Spirit of Death, set me free! Dreary is earth. Joyless is time. Heart, thou art desolate! Wed thee another? Nay. Death is thy husband! Farewell, oh sun! Vain is your light. Farewell, oh earth! Vain are your plains, your flowers, your grassy dales, your purling streams, and shady groves! I loved you once,—but now no longer love! Tasteless are your sweets,—cheerless your pleasures! Thee I woo, kind Death! Wahuspa calls me hence. In life we were one. We'll bask together in the Spirit Land. Who shall sunder there? Short is my pass to thee. Wahuspa, I come!"

Upon this she threw herself forward, as the warriors grasped at her; but, leaving her robe in their hands, she plunged headlong and was dashed to pieces among the rocks below! (Sage 1846: 94–95)

Tahtunga-egoniska concluded this sad tale by noting that Brulés still think of the young woman's death song whenever they see the distinctively named precipice.

About half a century later, on one of his summer ethnographic field trips to the Northwest Coast, Franz Boas began listening to stories told in the Kathlamet dialect of Upper Chinook. The storyteller was Charles Cultee, one of three remaining speakers of the dialect. More accustomed to speaking Chehalis, his wife's language which was used in their immediate family, Cultee had learned Kathlamet (the first language of his maternal grandmother) while living among its speakers in a community near present-day Astoria, Oregon. During the summers of 1890 and 1891 and in December 1894, Cultee dictated to Boas thirty-three traditional narratives, which the anthropologist punctiliously wrote down using the system of phonetic symbols he was developing for notation of Northwest Coast languages. Boas apparently did not understand Kathlamet at all, a fact that Cultee recognized, since all of their conversations occurred in the Chinook jargon, the lingua franca used by traders throughout the region. With Cultee's help, though, Boas was able to provide English translations of the stories from his phonetic textualizations (Boas 1901: 5–6). The first few sentences of a tale, told in 1894, that Boas entitled "Myth of the Swan" illustrates the English results of his work with Cultee:

> The people tried to buy a maiden, but her father did not give her away. Then the chief of the Swans bought her. They gave her to him. It became winter. Now the people had eaten all their provisions, and they became hungry. The Swan had a double dish. His mother gave him food. Dry broken salmon was in one dish, and pounded salmon bones were in the other. Then the Swan ate the dry salmon, and his wife ate the salmon bones. (1901: 34)

The story continues with the return of the Swan's wife to her home and her conjuration of smelts that her own people harvest, while they remain unavailable to the Swans. When they come to beg her for food to alleviate their hunger, she provides them with smoked smelt. However, they dislike the taste of the smoked fishes, and she drives them away with a curse.

Factors requisite for performance derive from culture-specific criteria (Bauman 1984: 13–14). The best and perhaps only way to determine how fully particular communicative events fulfill those criteria requires that one ascertain how communicators themselves perceive those events—an understanding that in cases such as these examples relies upon informed speculation. But it helps to know what generated the events and to what extent the generating factors were traditional stimuli for performance.

Wak-a-dah-ha-hee's rainmaking oration would presumably have been delivered whether or not George Catlin or any other Euroamericans had been present. The audience to whom he spoke included the Mandans who needed rain to water their maize crop as well as the supernatural agents who would provide that rain. The situation, completely natural for the oration, and the dramatic features of his delivery that Catlin noted suggest that Wak-a-dah-ha-hee "performed" in a way that fully reflected the appropriate esthetics of Mandan verbal artistry for the situation—an assessment reinforced by his success in producing the desired precipitation. While Catlin's presence may have affected how and what the orator performed (a manifestation of the "observer's paradox," the inevitable circumstance "that ethnographic situations are affected by the presence of an observer" [Urban 1991: 151]),[3] it was certainly not the primary constitutive factor in the event.

The conversations between Tahtunga-egoniska and the Rufus Sage party may be much less natural. Although Tahtunga-egoniska's status as elder would have given him some responsibility for communicating traditional lore, which might be couched in narratives, his usual audience would have been other Brulés, who, even if young, would bring to the exchange considerable knowledge of their own culture. Teaching that same lore to cultural outsiders like Sage, who probably did not even understand the Lakota language, forced Tahtunga-egoniska to fill in background that he could assume his usual audience would already possess. That burden might easily supersede many features of "authentic" performance artistry. In order to accommodate the ignorance of his Euroamerican listeners, Tahtunga-egoniska might have simplified plotlines and character development and augmented information about cultural setting. As Boas noted of the stories included in his monumental collection of Tsimshian myths, "It is not unlikely that some explanatory matter has been included . . . that in olden times would not have been present" (1916: 393). Moreover, Tahtunga-egoniska might have reduced the dramatic features in his delivery in order to present the material in as straightforward a manner as possible.

But before dismissing the Brulé elder's narrations as totally artificial, as less than authentic performance, we should note that Native Americans (Brulés and others) had been satisfying the curiosity of Euroamerican visitors for a couple of centuries before 1841, when Tahtunga-egoniska did the same for Sage. Even if Tahtunga-egoniska was not narrating under the most customary conditions or in response to the most familiar stimuli to perform, the situation may not have been totally unfamiliar to him. He may have drawn upon a traditional performance esthetic that responded to a situation in which outsiders comprised the principal audience. His rendering of the tales to Sage and his companions may have attained artistry within this esthetic.

Although the Cultee-Boas interchange shares the general interactive pattern of the one between Tahtunga-egoniska and Sage, it derived from a different kind of relationship. No casual visitor who heard stories by happenstance, Boas was an aggressive ethnographer whose primary interest in Kathlamet verbal art was the linguistic and other cultural data it could provide. One might view Cultee's narration as an example of what John D. Niles has called a *"folklore act"*: "a folkloric performance [or expression?] . . . that is commissioned and recorded by outsiders for the primary benefit of their own textual communities" (1993: 137). Though we cannot know how aware Cultee was of Boas's purposes, he certainly realized that Boas did not understand what he was saying as he narrated. Such a realization as well as the slow pace and frequent pauses involved in dictation may have reduced the storyteller's commitment to producing a fully developed performance.

But we should not too hastily dismiss the performance potential of Cultee's storytelling to Boas—or, in fact, of any situation that involves dictation. One point of view—that, in fact, articulated by Boas himself—holds that dictation invariably produces something less than natural expression. In an essay on the "stylistic aspects" of Native American verbal art originally published in 1925, Boas wrote that dictation usually "does not reach the standard of excellence of the native narrative," because the "difficulty of phonetic rendering of foreign languages requires such slowness of dictation that the artistic style necessarily suffers" (1940: 492). Dictation "almost always exert[s] an appreciable influence upon the form of the tale" (1940: 452). Yet another viewpoint—articulated by Albert Bates Lord among others—holds that dictation may produce the most artistically rich renderings. Several aspects of dictation may hinder the singer of tales (Lord's field experience involved epic performers in southeastern Europe): the lack of rhythmic assistance from a musical instrument, the inevitable pauses that occur while the scribe copies what has been expressed, and the absence of a traditional audience. But the slow pace of dictation also has advantages:

> The chief advantage to the singer of this manner of composition [during dictation] is that it affords him time to think of his lines and of his song. His small audience is stable. . . . He can ornament his song as fully as he is capable; he can develop his tale with completeness, he can dwell lovingly on passages that in normal performance he would often be forced to shorten because of the pressure of time or because of the restlessness of the audience. (1991: 46)

Moreover, Dell Hymes has demonstrated that dictated materials do effectively incorporate many verbal artistic features that can be restored through careful reexamination of the original language version (1981: 338). In fact, Hymes has shown how ethnopoetic analysis of the stories that Cultee dictated to Boas can uncover their Kathlamet verbal artistry (Hymes 1975; 1985a; 1985b). He notes that Cultee's "easy style" suggests the storyteller was quite comfortable with the dictation process and narrated naturally (Hymes 1994: 355).

The verbal artist's perception of the communicative event, the primary factor in determining whether the event produces an authentic performance, depends upon the motivations for the interaction. Moreover, the composition of the audience by age, gender, or nationality, its size, and the way its members respond to the communication contribute to what is said and how it is said. Greg Sarris, for example, has shown that the Pomo storytellers who narrated for Robert Oswalt during the late 1950s clearly shaped their renderings to the fieldworker's presence and to their assessment of his interests. Violet Parrish Chappell, daughter of one of these storytellers, told Sarris, " 'Mom just did it that way, for the language. He [Oswalt] wanted language. I heard those stories different—when Mom used to tell them when we kids were in bed' " (Sarris 1993: 21). Moreover, Sarris points out, the Pomo storytellers "were in the position of being asked to break taboo [against telling stories during the summer] and disregard an invasion of privacy" (1993: 22), both factors impacting how and what they narrated. In the case of the Kathlamet material, Charles Cultee's narration—no matter how comfortable he may have felt with the situation—to a single male European whose reaction to his stories involved careful linguistic notation and apparently negligible affective feedback would certainly differ from his telling of the same stories to a group of native speakers of Kathlamet whose values and worldview were bound up in the stories and who might respond verbally as he narrated. Moreover, even prosaic features of the communicative setting such as time of day, temperature, and acoustics—none of which we know for Cultee's telling (or for most other encounters that lead to textualizations of verbal art)—can affect the performance potential. In sum, though Cultee's rendering of Kathlamet oral narratives to Boas has some artistic qualities, those qualities probably did not *fully* represent what would occur in an authentic performance.

The three textualizations considered thus far—Catlin's presentation of a Mandan oration, Sage's recounting of several Brulé narratives, and Boas's handling of some Kathlamet stories—vary in the raw material upon which they are based. Consequently, even though the Kathlamet materials prepared by Boas represent the most scientifically accurate on a linguistic level, they may reveal less of the true artistry of oral expression, which includes paralinguistic and kinesic components as well as situational and contextual factors, than the Mandan and Brulé performances simply because that artistry may have been less prominent in what Boas encountered. If indeed performance artistry figured only at the linguistic level (if at all), criticizing Boas for not completely representing the oral poetic qualities of Kathlamet verbal art when he textualized and translated Cultee's stories misses the purpose of textualization and translation: to provide as accurate and complete a representation of what and how something *was* said, not what or how it *should* and *might* have been said under ideal performance conditions. At the opposite extreme, even though Catlin undoubtedly based his text of Wak-a-dah-ha-hee's rainmaking speech on an interpreter's rendering, he did witness a fully realized performance and therefore could have reported first-hand some of the components of natural verbal artistry precluded in the Cultee-Boas situation. In fact, though we may suspect the linguistic components of Catlin's textualization, his relatively full description of the expressive situation incorporates features necessary for a good ethnographic text. Sage may represent a sort of middle ground: even though he may have had as little access to Lakota as Catlin had to Mandan, his interpreter probably had more leisure to render an accurate translation of stories told in relatively casual circumstances than Catlin's interpreter could enjoy in the heat of ceremonial fervor. But Tahtunga-egoniska, the Brulé storyteller, was narrating as part of a cross-cultural interaction and probably did not draw as fully upon the indigenous performance esthetic as he might have when narrating to other Brulés. Nor did Sage describe the narrative situations for specific stories in much detail.

What we should expect from Catlin, then, is a textualization that represents authentic performance. That it fails linguistically to deliver up to its potential results from Catlin's lack of competence with Mandan and from the absence of a technology such as tape recording that would enable an accurate replication of the oration's content and some of the orator's paralinguistic devices. Yet Catlin did include invaluable information about some performance devices (for example, the tossing of the feather into the air) and about the ritual context of the performance. That information would not be available in a dictated oration permitting more linguistic accuracy. From Sage, we might expect a somewhat lesser degree of authentic performance. His highly literary translation, like Catlin's, signals his recognition that Tahtunga-egoniska's storytelling is artistic. Unfortunately, Sage followed most translators of Native American verbal art in representing its artistry in Euroamerican rather than Native terms—in terms of "Identity" rather than "Difference" (see chapter 5). From Boas, we should expect linguistic accuracy. Anything else would probably be the result of the collector's speculations rather than what Cultee actually said. Despite the linguistic detective work of Hymes, the sort of "poetry" desired by Henderson,

Spinden, Tedlock, and Krupat may not have figured prominently in the actual rendering that Boas heard.

The student of Native American verbal art who depends upon translated texts should evaluate them by first investigating exactly what they intend to represent. We can further illustrate this method by examining several texts that appear in an important anthology of Native American oral poetry, Jerome Rothenberg's *Shaking the Pumpkin*, now in its second edition. Rothenberg continues to be one of the most influential and provocative figures in ethnopoetics, "the study of pre-literate societies' modes of discourse, the formal complexity of which requires that they be understood as literature" (Kroeber 1989: 1). Rothenberg broke the ground for his own approach to this study in an important anthology of representations of oral poetry, his own and others. *Technicians of the Sacred* (1968) presented a "range of poetries" from Africa, Asia, Oceania, and the Americas. In 1969 Rothenberg published a description of his method for rendering Native American poetry in translation. His approach of "total translation" emerged from his recognition that oral poetry included many sounds (vocables, for instance) that could not be easily reproduced in straightforward written English. Instead of ignoring those sounds, as many earlier translators had done, Rothenberg aimed at responding to "*all* the sounds. . . . not only of the words but of all the sounds connected with the poem, including finally the music itself" (1983: 382). He intended "to account for all vocal sounds in the original but—as a more 'interesting' way of handling the minimal structures & allowing a very clear, very pointed emergence of perceptions—to translate the poems onto the page, as with 'concrete' or other types of minimal poetry" (1983: 385). Later Rothenberg would emphasize that total translation seeks "to develop special means for re-creating oral works within a literate culture" (1992: 70).

Rothenberg's commitment to foregrounding the full artistry of oral poetry so far as possible in the textualizations he produced and which he encouraged others to produce also found expression in his role as coeditor of the journal *Alcheringa/Ethnopoetics*, as editor of a symposium on ethnopoetics published by the journal in 1976, and as coeditor of *Symposium of the Whole* (Rothenberg and Rothenberg 1983), an eclectic anthology of source material for ethnopoetics. For present purposes, his most important ethnopoetic work has been the treatments of Native American poetry in *Shaking the Pumpkin*, whose first edition appeared in 1972.

Subtitled *Traditional Poetry of the Indian North Americas*, Rothenberg's anthology includes a wide variety of materials, representing culture areas from the Arctic circle to the Valley of Mexico. The poems themselves derive from several sources: translations from oral tradition by Rothenberg himself, often in collaboration with a Native speaker (for example, the Seneca poetic sequence that provides the book's title); ethnopoetic translations from oral tradition by others (such as Dennis Tedlock's use of "pause phrasing" in textualizing Zuni narrative poetry); "workings" or "versions" (that is, rewordings by Rothenberg without returning to a Native-language source of previous translations "that had failed to match the life of their sources" [1972: xxiii]); and workings by other poets (William S. Merwin, Edward Field, and James Koller, for example).

Shaking the Pumpkin appeared to generally favorable reviews in a wide range of periodicals. In the *Christian Science Monitor* for 20 April 1972, "V. H." effused, "Jerome Rothenberg's collection speaks to anyone interested in poetry. Naive, often repetitious, seldom obscure, American Indian poetry comes across in these modern translations as part of the seamless web of universal song." The nature magazine *Living Wilderness* suggested that *Shaking the Pumpkin* would be a "good book to take backpacking for a week in the woods" (Zahniser 1972: 36). *Library Journal* reported that Rothenberg's book was a "major effort" that succeeded in making evident the "total poetry" of oral performance (Demos 1972: 879). An unsigned review in *Choice* evaluated the book as "an important acquisition for all libraries; it is valuable from both a literary and an anthropological viewpoint" (Review of *Shaking the Pumpkin* 1972: 654–655). Professional publications related to Native American studies also praised *Shaking the Pumpkin*. In his review for *American Anthropologist*, Richard Howard Robbins hailed the anthology as a "masterpiece of translation and organization" (1973: 1062). Lawrence Evers, reviewing the book for the University of Nebraska's literary magazine *Prairie Schooner*, saw it as "far and away the most useful [book] of its kind presently available" (1973: 79–80). Even more positive was the assessment of John Bentley Mays, who called *Shaking the Pumpkin* "unquestionably the most stunning re-presentation of primitive literatures ever to appear in the English language" (1974: 41). To some extent, the volume has stood the test of time. Not only does the publication of a second edition (Rothenberg 1986) suggest this, but Paul Zolbrod's recently proposed framework for appreciating Native American "oral poetry" in print (1995) draws upon material from Rothenberg.

But some students of Native American verbal art have been uncomfortable with *Shaking the Pumpkin*, especially with the "workings" or versions reconstructed from previous translations. The most fully developed early criticism was that of William Bevis, who treated Rothenberg's book and several other anthologies in an essay published in 1974. Lamenting that "recently a number of 'editors' with little or no knowledge of Indian languages have rewritten older translations and published their revised versions as anthologies of Indian poetry," Bevis doubted "the quality of the material available to meet the growing demand for things Indian" (1974: 693). Other commentators took up the chase, including Anna Lee Stensland, who generalized that recent translators of Native American oral poetry, including Rothenberg, are primarily concerned with producing "a good English poem, not a truly Indian one" (1975: 46), a frequent criticism of translations of Native American verbal art since at least the mid-nineteenth century. Linguist William Bright had Rothenberg's work in mind when he wrote of the impositions that translators (and creators of "workings") tended to place upon Native American materials:

> We need to ask . . . whether a poetic structure exists in the original text, or whether it has been imposed by the English translator. In fact, although the translators have often been skilled poets, they have just as often been totally ignorant of the native languages concerned; their procedure has simply been to take literal English translations published by linguists and anthropologists, and to rewrite them in more poetic form. In such cases, we have no assurance that the native-language texts are in any way recognizable as poetry rather than prose. (1984: 83)

Other critics have suggested that the use of concrete, minimalist poetic forms smacks of gimmickry and may, in fact, rather create a distinctive visual experience for the reader than re-create the oral original. Often, so this critique goes, it is difficult to determine how a particular performance sounded based upon Rothenberg's total translation. Still another point of view argues that Rothenberg—and by implication other practitioners of ethnopoetics—devoted themselves to a "neoprimitive, exotic ideology" that shaped their reworkings of Native American oral poetry more than the relevant poetics did and that stressed "Difference" to the extent of creating what amounted to museum pieces (Wiget 1986: 1504). And Leslie Marmon Silko has seen in publications like *Shaking the Pumpkin* evidence of the continuing appropriation of Native American property by Euroamericans (1979: 211–216).

Clearly, *Shaking the Pumpkin* and Rothenberg's other work in ethno-

poetics have generated a mixed response. However, ignoring such issues as the theory and practice of total translation and the advisability
of passing off "workings"—at least three removes from an oral performance in a Native language—as legitimate representations of American
Indian verbal art, we can assess the book from the perspective introduced in the first half of this chapter by asking exactly *what* each text
in the document purports to replicate. Only those based upon what
Hymes calls "authentic performance" should lend themselves to all
that Rothenberg claims that total translation can do.

One of the most effective poems in *Shaking the Pumpkin* is "The
Killer (after A'yunini)." Designated as "Cherokee" and included in the
anthology's section called "A First Service," it is characterized as *"Jerome Rothenberg's working, after James Mooney"* (Rothenberg 1972:
62). The first seven lines of "The Killer" suggest a poetic power capable
of revealing Native American verbal artistry:

> Careful: my knife drills your soul
>   listen, whatever-your-name-is
>   One of the wolf people
> listen   I'll grind your saliva into the earth
> listen   I'll cover your bones with black flint
> listen   "   "   "   "   " feathers
> listen   "   "   "   "   " rocks
>   (1972: 62; 1968: 70)

Rothenberg's source for this poem is not his own contact with Cherokee
formulas in oral tradition. Instead, it is a paper by the anthropologist
James Mooney that appeared in the BAE *Annual Report* for 1885–1886,
"The Sacred Formulas of the Cherokees." Mooney there reproduces in
phonetic Cherokee and free translation a number of ritual incantations
preserved in the Swimmer Manuscript, a "small day-book of about 240
pages . . . about half filled with writing in the Cherokee characters" by
A'yunini ("The Swimmer") (Mooney 1891: 312).[4] Mooney's translation
of the incantation entitled "To Destroy Life," which Rothenberg presents as "The Killer," follows:

> Listen! Now I have come to step over your soul. You are of the (wolf)
> clan. Your name is (A'yu'nini). Your spittle I have put at rest under the
> earth. Your soul I have put at rest under the earth. I have come to cover
> you over with the black rock. I have come to cover you over with the
> black cloth. I have come to cover you with the black slabs, never to reap-
> pear. Toward the black coffin of the upland in the Darkening Land your

paths shall stretch out. So shall it be for you. The clay of the upland has come (to cover you. (?) [sic] Instantly the black clay has lodged there where it is at rest at the black houses in the Darkening Land. With the black coffin and the black slabs I have come to cover you. Now your soul has faded away. It has become blue. When darkness comes your spirit shall grow less and dwindle away, never to reappear. Listen! (1891: 312)

Rothenberg's working is certainly more poetic—at least from a Euroamerican perspective. But how poetic is the original upon which it is founded? Does the source material here constitute fully or even partially realized oral art? The answer must be in the negative.

The source for Mooney's Cherokee text is a document *written* in the Cherokee syllabary. Very likely that document was based on material that was orally performed, but the syllabary version, to which Rothenberg apparently did not have access, does not suggest much about how that oral performance might have been realized. Rothenberg's "The Killer," then, is a rewriting of a free translation of a phonetic rendering of a syllabary version of an orally performed incantation. It is four removes from an oral original about which we can know virtually nothing to suggest that Rothenberg's working comes anywhere near how it was rendered. We should not expect Mooney's translation to reflect oral performance esthetics since he was working from a written source. Even less should we expect Rothenberg's version to reflect those esthetics, which means that the poetry of "The Killer" must come from Rothenberg, not from the oral performances upon which A'yunini's syllabary text was based.[5]

The importance of the original verbal source in evaluating a textualization is also apparent in a series of four Winnebago "Peyote Visions," which are designated as *"Jerome Rothenberg's working, after Paul Radin"* (1972: 361). The source for the four poems in *Shaking the Pumpkin* is Radin's edition of *The Autobiography of a Winnebago Indian*, the forerunner of the famous autobiography *Crashing Thunder*. The earlier work was *written* in the Winnebago syllabary by Sam Blowsnake (alias Crashing Thunder, alias Big Winnebago). According to Radin, "The translation was made by the author [i.e., Radin himself] on the basis of a rendition by his interpreter" (1963: 2). The following is the apparent source of the first poem in Rothenberg's "Peyote Visions":

When I tried to drink coffee, I would spill it. When I lay down I would see big snakes. I would cry out and get up and then when I was about to go to sleep again, I would think that someone had called me. Then I would raise my cover and look around, but there would be nothing.

When the wind blew hard (I seemed) to hear singing. These (imaginary people) would spit very loudly. I heard them and I could not sleep. Just as soon as I closed my eyes, I would begin to see things. I saw things that were happening in a distant country.

I saw ghosts on horseback drunk. Five or six of them were on one horse and they were singing. I recognized them, for they were people who had died long ago. I head the words of their song, as they sang:

"I, even I, must die sometime, so of what value is anything, I think."

Thus they would sing and it made a good song. I myself learned it and later on it became a drinking song and many people learned it. I liked it very much. (1963: 40–41)

Rothenberg makes some major changes when he reworks this account of a personal experience to disclose its ethnopoetic artistry. The introductory lines of Rothenberg's "working" point the direction in which he takes the material from Blowsnake's autobiography:

> tried drinking coffee
>   i would spill it
> sleeping
> would see great snakes
>   would cry out & get up
>   raise my cover & look around
>   had someone called me?
>   (1972: 358)[6]

Clearly, the changes made by Rothenberg have no relationship to oral performance. No evidence suggests that Blowsnake ever recounted his vision orally, unless he did so when assisting Radin in translating his syllabary manuscript into English. The translation provided by Radin may or may not represent the written Winnebago accurately, but the original translators had no reason to reflect oral poetics, since they were not translating oral performance. Anything within a reworking such as Rothenberg's that points toward something other than written prose does not reflect the nature of the source.

Moreover, Rothenberg has erroneously identified that nature. Although this reworked poem appears as a "peyote vision" in *Shaking the Pumpkin*, it comes from a chapter in Blowsnake's autobiography entitled "I Get Delirium Tremens and See Strange Things," which describes the writer's problems with alcohol. Blowsnake's first encounter with peyote did not occur until several years after the events described in this chapter. Rothenberg's suggestion that the hallucinations of a drunken man constitute a peyote-induced visionary experience is especially unsettling when one considers the belief system of peyotism, which holds the peyote cactus as the embodiment of divine essence and the visions stimulated by its ingestion as sacred teaching or revelation. Moreover, the Peyote Way leads its followers strictly away from the use of alcohol.

Since he encountered the texts from A'yunini and Blowsnake in written sources remote from oral expression, Rothenberg should not have attempted to implement his program of total translation on them. But while his use of devices from concrete poetry may inadequately reflect the sound of the oral original and may produce texts that, in Andrew Wiget's felicitous phrase, are "utterly unutterable" (1986: 1504), Rothenberg has made some interesting attempts to replicate authentic performance in those texts that he has based directly upon oral performances. Because it does indeed reproduce the full range of sounds of its source, his most successful translation may be of the series of horse songs recorded by David McAllester from the performance of Navajo Frank Mitchell. The seventeen horse songs that Mitchell sang for McAllester are usually part of the Blessingway healing ceremony, whose efficacy may be invalidated by the presence of mechanical recording apparatus. Consequently, "a private recording session," apparently in 1961, provided the occasion for Mitchell's singing (McAllester 1983: 394; Frisbie and McAllester 1978: 3). Singing even for just one person is authentic performance, so we are probably safe in assuming that most of the relevant esthetic figured into Mitchell's renditions. Rothenberg himself listened to the songs on tape and was thus at two removes from a natural situation; nevertheless, he did hear all the sounds of the performance.

Shaking the Pumpkin includes Rothenberg's total translations of two of Mitchell's horse songs (the twelfth and the thirteenth) (1972: 350–353), and an excerpt from his work with the tenth song in the series appears in his methodological essay on total translation (1983: 391). The first three lines of "The 12th Horse-Song of Frank Mitchell" provide a taste of Rothenberg's approach to the material:

Some are & are going to my howinouse baheegwing
     hawuNnawu N nngahn baheegwing
Some are & are going to my howinouse baheegwing
     hawuNnawu N nngahn baheegwing
Some are & some are gone to my howinouse nnaht bahyee
     nahtgwing buhtzzm bahyee noohwinnnGUUH.

(1972: 350)

Rothenberg has been very forthcoming about how he translated this performance of Mitchell's and others (e.g., in Rothenberg 1992: 73–76), in which the singer manipulated Navajo sounds by distorting words and vocables. Trying to represent those distortions in translation meant selecting equivalent English distortions and vocables, which, of course, are not necessarily "meaningless" syllables but are often extensions of the sounds of morphemes. Rothenberg commented, "[A] total translation must distort words in a manner analogous to the original; it must match 'meaningless' syllables with equivalents in our very different English soundings" (1972: 466). In other words, he translated Navajo vocables and distortions of Navajo words into English vocables and distortions of English words. Using materials provided by McAllester (a tape of Mitchell's singing, transcriptions in Navajo with linguistic commentary, and literal translation of the actual words into English), Rothenberg created his own literary translation for meaning and then added expansions and distortions of the English words to produce the effect of the full range of sounds performed by Mitchell. Rothenberg saw his total translation onto the printed page as only a step in the whole process, which culminated with his own recording of an English version of the material in multiple voices that approximated what McAllester had suggested about the nature of the songs' performance in conventional situations.

As his critics have argued, the final product of Rothenberg's total translation of Mitchell's horse songs may reflect more of his own primitivistic esthetic than of the real artistry of the Navajo original. But in this case—unlike his workings of A'yunini's Cherokee formula and Sam Blowsnake's delirium tremens—Rothenberg is dealing with source material that approaches authentic oral performance. Consequently, his manipulations in the name of total translation, controversial though they be, reflect genuine attempts to do what Catlin, who also responded textually to authentic performance, did not do: represent not only what was said/sung but also how it was said/sung. To criticize Boas for not making a similar attempt misses the most fundamental point in the process of textualization, a point that Rothenberg apparently missed in his workings of the Cherokee and Winnebago material: one should only reflect in a textualization what was actually articulated in oral expression. If authentic performance did not figure into that expression, the textualization should not attempt to suggest what such performance might have been like had the circumstances of recording been different.

The student of Native American verbal art who depends upon translations should evaluate them initially by investigating exactly what they attempt to represent. Usually, one can expect to gain a full appreciation of indigenous artistry only from textualizations of authentic performances. Few translators, though, have been fortunate enough to encounter oral expressive culture in situations where such fully developed artistry is likely to occur; their presence alone may suffice to artificialize the communicative event. But even such events afford opportunities for some degree of verbal artistry, which textmakers may capture. Textualizations of events where performance does not occur certainly should not be dismissed, nor should they automatically be regarded as less valuable than records of authentic performance. That would mean rating relatively casual presentations of orations (the most usual kind of oral performance witnessed by Euroamericans in natural contexts) more highly than Boas's meticulous recording, transcribing, and textualizing of Cultee's stories. The complaints of Henderson, Spinden, Tedlock, Krupat, and others who have lamented the lack of artistry in translations made under the aegis of "scientific" linguistics and ethnography are justifiable, but the problem may have been more the circumstances of recording than the aims of the textmaker, who could and should have done no more than the material warranted. The goal of investigating the situation of encounter should be insight into what textmakers were working with and what we should consequently expect them to incorporate into their texts and translations. In this regard, our highest praise should go to those who have punctiliously described the situations where and when they heard the oral expressions they textualized. Not only have they provided a basis for evaluating the potential accomplishment of their linguistic texts, but they have included features of the expressive situation and context that must figure into fully realized ethnographic texts.

The expressive situations—and the presuppositions they brought with them to New France—informed the ways in which seventeenth- and eighteenth-century Jesuit missionaries regarded, textualized, and translated Native American verbal art. The next chapter examines their pioneering work in the study of artistic verbal expression by American Indians.

CHAPTER THREE

"NOT SO STUPID AS THEY MAY HAVE BEEN PAINTED"

The Jesuits and Native Canadian Verbal Art

May 24, 1633. Eighteen canoes of Ottawas had come down the St. Lawrence to Québec for their annual trading visit. Fortuitously, Samuel de Champlain, the French colonial governor, had also recently arrived from France. Fearing that the Ottawas might be going to visit the three English ships anchored near the river's mouth, Champlain met with them to provide assurances of his nation's friendship and support. After Champlain had finished a brief speech through an interpreter, the spokesman for the Ottawas—"*le capitaine*," as he is called in Jesuit missionary Paul Le Jeune's account of the proceedings—responded "with a keenness and delicacy of rhetoric that might have come out of the schools of Aristotle or Cicero" (Thwaites 1959: 5:205).[1] What he said and how he said it markedly impressed members of Champlain's party.

Le Jeune, superior for the Jesuit missions in New France, preserved a French translation of the Ottawa speaker's words in his *relation* of missionary activities for 1633. The Ottawa capitaine began by apologizing for his inadequacies as an orator. Then he restated and commented upon Champlain's expression of French affection for the Ottawas and the governor's claim that the French motive for moving into Ottawa territory was to offer protection to the Natives. The speaker noted that the French were welcome, a point that elicited Le Jeune's praise for its "discretion" (*JR* 5:207). Next *le capitaine* defended his people's trading of beaver skins to the English by claiming it was done to undermine the strength of their enemies, the Iroquois. He strongly asserted his lack of interest in further contact with the English but also noted his powerlessness in preventing others of his people—especially *"quelque ieune homme"* (*JR* 5:208)[2]—from intercourse with them. He also deplored the regrettable possibility that though the Ottawas and French might have the best intentions, misunderstandings leading even to violence could arise since *"tout le monde n'est pas sage"* (*JR* 5:210). Le Jeune's presentation of this speech, which he himself had not witnessed, includes one notice of a gesture made by *le capitaine,* an indication of the size of the buildings that the French would probably erect in the community they intended to establish among the Ottawas. The missionary also reported the appreciation of those who had heard the speech for how the Ottawa spokesman "raised his voice according to the subjects he treated, then lowered it with so much humility, and with such an attitude of submission, that he won the hearts of all who looked at him, though they did not understand him." Finally, Le Jeune concluded, "Those who think the Savages have dull and heavy intellects will recognize by this speech that they are not so stupid as they may have been painted" (*JR* 5:211).

Le Jeune's presentation of the translated text and context of this Ottawa orator's performance has considerable importance for the study of Native North American verbal art. For practical purposes, the textualization of Native North American oral expression begins with Paul Le Jeune and his colleagues, the Jesuit missionaries who arrived in New France early in the seventeenth century and maintained a precarious, intermittent presence there until the beginnings of British control of Canada in the late eighteenth century.[3]

By 1608, Henri IV had determined to send missionaries to Acadia. His confessor enlisted the Society of Jesus in this enterprise, and through the patronage of the Marquise de Guercheville, lady-in-waiting to the queen mother, the first Jesuits, Pierre Biard and Ennemond Massé, arrived in Acadia in 1611. Though a disagreement between local officials and the missionaries' French sponsors ended this mission in 1613, Jesuits returned to New France in 1625 and penetrated the North American wilderness as far as Québec, where they remained until 1629. In 1632, when Paul Le Jeune arrived, they assumed control of missionary activity throughout Canada (Kennedy 1950: 1–38; Moore 1982: 1–39).[4] Influenced by the missionary spirit that infuses Christianity in general (Hollis 1968: 73), by their founder Loyola's special emphasis on that spirit in his *Spiritual Exercises,* and by the *apologia* for colonialism that it provided a means for the conversion of the heathen (Bitterli 1989: 95), the Jesuits faced considerable hardships, witnessed behavior that they regarded as depraved and inhuman (even by the European standards of the day), and even suffered martyrdom as they worked their way westward through Huronia and the territory of the Iroquois all the way to the Mississippi River, where they arrived by the late seventeenth century.

Whether the Jesuits were successful in effecting significant conversions to Christianity became a point of contemporary controversy (Jaenen 1976: 66–69). And whether their whole enterprise should be hailed as pioneering the way for the benefits of "civilization" or condemned as the advance guard of a European invasion of North America certainly remains controversial. What is important for the study of North American Indian verbal art is that the Jesuit missionaries left a voluminous written record of their experiences that includes substantial descriptions of the Natives they encountered. Though these descriptions arose from the missionaries' need to understand Native life in order to expedite conversions (Jaenen 1976: 41–42), they nevertheless provide important and useful information for other purposes.

Most important among their writings were the *relations*, reports prepared by the superior of Québec. These documents not only recounted the experiences of the superiors themselves, but also drew upon reports from missionaries throughout New France. Complementing these publications were other documents, especially letters to relatives and other clerics. Taken as a whole, the writings of the Jesuits in New France represent the earliest extensive ethnographic material on the indigenous peoples of North America, primarily the Algonquian-speaking groups who stretched from the Atlantic shore to west of the Great Lakes and the Iroquoians who lived in what is now southern Ontario and western New York state. Among the ethnographic data reported by the Jesuits are numerous materials relevant to verbal art, including descriptions of the situations where and when performances might occur and of some performance components, representations of what might be said or sung in those situations (mostly translated into French, but occasionally in attempted depictions of the Native tongues), and summaries of Native belief systems.

The Jesuit materials, more than almost anything else written about Native North Americans, record pre-contact oral behavior. Even though the Jesuits were in most cases the second set of Europeans whom the Natives had encountered (trappers and traders usually being the first), most of the people whom they heard tell stories, sing songs, or deliver orations had learned their verbal art skills before a European presence had become significant in their lives. Moreover, the Jesuits witnessed verbal performances in relatively natural contexts. Their very presence, of course, added an element of artificiality to those contexts, but the

Jesuits did not rely upon such devices of later ethnographers as formal interviews to gather their material. Consequently, we should be able to assume that much of what they reported was observed in situations more like those in which George Catlin and Rufus Sage heard verbal expressions than the formal ethnographic encounters of Franz Boas. The Jesuit material is also so extensive (more than two hundred documents in the Thwaites edition, much of which is given over to accounts of the Indians) that its sheer quantity makes it a valuable resource. A comparable body of texts and commentary did not become available until the researches of ethnologists working for the BAE began to be published in the late nineteenth century.

But how genuinely valuable are the materials on American Indian verbal art? Can anything recorded by Christian missionaries untrained in either ethnographic research or literary analysis and laboring under conditions adverse to scrupulous record-keeping be really useful for examining traditional verbal art on its own terms? Answering these questions requires more than just sweeping praise for the relatively respectful attitude of the Jesuits ("brave and indomitable explorers of the Indian mind" [Astrov 1992: 48], for example) or automatic dismissal. It is necessary to consider the Jesuits' received ideas, their purposes in writing, and the probable effects of both these factors on how they presented verbal art.

The intellectual milieu out of which the Jesuits emerged, both that specific to their religious vocation and the general array of ideas that characterized the European worldview of the early seventeenth century, provided important constructs for treating the Natives of North America. As far back as the glimmerings of an anthropological consciousness can be found in European tradition, one encounters "a series of ethnographic commonplaces" that were applied to the cultures of exotic peoples. Greeks like Herodotos, who wrote about the Scythians and other "barbarians," and Romans like Tacitus, who dealt with the customs of the "uncivilized" Germans, almost invariably emphasized such features as the absence of temples or images in their worship and their lack of interest in precious metals (Dickason 1984: 63–84; Hodgen 1964: 17–48; Pagden 1982: 15–26; Rowe 1965: 6). The "myth of the barbarian," which developed from these and other commonplaces, was both positive and negative: non-Europeans might represent the ideal in society and culture, or they might be subhumans who practiced anthropophagy and other customs that revolted Europeans. The positive view, to which many of the Jesuit missionaries to New France seemed to have subscribed, often connected geographically remote societies with a way of life previously abandoned in Europe, a golden age of uncorrupted virtue. The contemporary barbarian represented what the Europeans' ancestors were like in a more pristine age. "[E]xempt from our heavy burden of ancient culture," the barbarian—so the primitivistic argument ran—was "untainted and good, as we are supposed to have been until the dawn of our history" (Baudet 1965: 10). When initial reports of the American Natives reached Europe, many commentators automatically applied these concepts of conventional primitivism to them. Perhaps Montaigne in the mid-sixteenth century deserves as much credit as anyone for clearly articulating that American Indians embodied the primitivistic qualities of an unadulterated state of nature and were, in fact, "Noble Savages" (cf. Brandon 1986; Fairchild 1961; Hodgen 1964; Jaenen 1976: 34).

The Jesuits who missionized in New France brought much of the primitivism of the European intellectual tradition to bear on the peoples whom they encountered in the Canadian forests. A very early Jesuit account, which emphasizes the diversity of Native cultures, stresses the lack of "civilized" institutions among peoples who possess "neither laws nor arts." Though the missionary (probably Pierre Biard) who wrote these words undercut the Indians' noble image by characterizing them as a "race [that] consists of men who are hardly above the beasts" (*JR* 2:201), their perceived lack of institutional life reveals clearly the influence of primitivism on his description. Other Jesuits, though, forthrightly identified the nobility of the Natives of New France. In a letter written to his brother in 1639, François du Peron claimed, "The nature of the Savage is patient, liberal, hospitable" (*JR* 15:155). Moreover, he continued, though deceitful and childish, "[t]hey nearly all show more intelligence in their business, speeches, courtesies, intercourse, tricks, and subtleties, than do the shrewdest citizens and merchants in France" (*JR* 15:157). If they did not employ a specific tribal or national designation, the word that the Jesuits consistently used for the Native North Americans was *sauvage* (the word *indien* appears nowhere in the Jesuit documents and did not become a primary French usage until the nineteenth century), a term that might suggest something different from the connotations of its English translation. Derived ultimately from Latin *silva*, "forest," it fundamentally meant one who lives apart from civilized society (cf. Berkhofer 1978: 13; Dickason 1984: 63–64; Jaenen 1976: 153; Jennings 1975: 73–78; Lafitau 1974–1977: 1:lxx). One of the major concerns of the Jesuit missionaries, in fact, was to protect the Natives from most civilizing influences, which they believed would have a deleterious effect on their essential virtue (Moore 1982: 36–37, 190–196).

Two factors, though, operated against the Jesuits' belief in the basic nobility of the *sauvages*. On one hand, they noted clear evidences of what they perceived as Native immorality. They could hardly ignore— especially if they themselves were being tortured—the brutal cruelty that some Natives practiced against their captives, even if that cruelty were no more extreme than that used by contemporary Europeans. Nor—and more crucial in their moral evaluations—could they escape from observing sexual practices and arrangements that they regarded as promiscuous and depraved. At the same time, they had to face the fact that the *sauvages* were non-Christians. The earlier documents in the collected works of the Jesuits (what one commentator has called "the monstrous Satanic world of the *Jesuit Relations*" [Jaenen 1982: 49]) sometimes present a graphic catalog of Native American atrocities against each other and against the Jesuits themselves.[5] While they could not explain away such behavior, the Jesuits first tried to account for it in terms reminiscent of their contemporaries, the Puritans of New England. Cruelty and promiscuity arose ultimately from the superstitious religious beliefs with which Satan had poisoned the minds of the Natives (cf. Pearce 1952; Pearce 1988: 19–31). Thus, Le Jeune could depict some Iroquois who had been taken prisoner by the Montagnais to whom he ministered as "poor slaves of Satan" (*JR* 5:47). Before long, though, their belief in the fundamental nobility of those living in a state of nature persuaded many Jesuit missionaries to attribute errors in behavior to "ignorance and easily corrected human fancy" (Healy 1958: 152). Later Jesuit writings, in fact, included fewer atrocity stories (probably due as much to the reporting habits of the missionaries, who may have exaggerated earlier, as to any change in Native American behavior).

The Jesuits also attributed the Natives' lack of Christianity to faulty reasoning, a failing that could be turned to the missionaries' advantage. Representing a general point of view among his colleagues, Paul Le Jeune noted in his *relation* for 1656–1657 that God could easily employ their non-Christianity for the sake of Christianizing them: "God makes use of their superstitious and false piety to derive his glory from them. He gives us the means of sanctifying their tendency to practice some Divine worship and to perform some ceremonies of Religion; we make them change the object of these, and address to the true God the invocations and words of adoration that they formerly employed in their sacri-

fices, when they offered the best of what they possessed to some unknown Divinity" (*JR* 43:285).[6] Moreover, many of the passages in the
Jesuits' writings that celebrate the nobility of the *sauvages* actually
refer to Christian converts, not those Natives still immersed in what
the missionaries regarded as barbaric superstitions.

The very nature of the missionary enterprise, of course, produced a
negative view of its targets. Presuming to be a missionary entails a
belief that one has superior "knowledge of the most important Truth in
the world, to which all other knowledge is subsidiary and inferior." The
missionary inevitably desires "most of all to reduce the heathens to
a proper submission to his [or her] God" (Jennings 1975: 57). But the
seventeenth- and eighteenth-century Jesuits had a higher regard for
those to whom they missionized than did many of their counterparts.
The general tradition of primitivism in European intellectual life found
particular support in some concepts more or less peculiar to the Jesuits:
Molinism, which emerged in codified form in the late sixteenth century and was thus an idea current during the missionary era in New
France; Figurism, the theory developed to explain the remarkable correspondences that Jesuit missionaries in China found between Eastern
religions and the Judaeo-Christian heritage (Healy 1958: 147–148, 156–
157); and Probabalism, which posited that morality varied with a society's circumstances and knowledge (Duignan 1958: 70).

In 1588, Spanish Jesuit Luis de Molina had posited a fourth state of
human nature to add to those already recognized by theologians. The
"state of pure nature" placed humans in a situation without either sin
or grace, but fully possessing the faculty of reason. Though originally
viewed as just a hypothetical condition of existence, the state of pure
nature helped the Jesuits to account for positive features in the way of
life of those peoples such as Native North Americans who had not yet
been exposed to the grace of God through Christianity. Though contam-
inated by original sin and consequently fallen, they possessed the fundamental faculty of reason, practiced virtue based on that faculty, and
were thus susceptible to the Christian message (Palmer 1961: 31–33).

Figurism, a Jesuit amplification of the traditional theory of "natural
revelation" and subsequent degeneration, also influenced the way the
missionaries in New France perceived the *sauvages*. This idea took
form during missionary activities in China. Jesuits there noted analogues between Eastern religions and the Hebrew and Christian tradition. They attributed these to a revelation of the true God, possibly
pre-Mosaic, to all peoples. Consequently, even in cultures seemingly
most removed from Christendom, including those indigenous to North

America, traces of genuine religion might be found (Rowbotham 1956). According to the Jesuits, the religions of the North American Natives had degenerated from the one true faith, vestiges of which were evident especially in *sauvage* beliefs in a creator god and in the immortality of the soul (Hodgen 1964: 265–269; Moore 1982: 153). In fact, one of the principal purposes of Joseph François Lafitau's *Moeurs des Sauvages Ameriquains comparées aux moeurs des premiers temps* (first published in 1724), the only theoretical overview of the Native cultures of New France written by a Jesuit, was to demonstrate that such correspondences with Christian teachings in *sauvage* religions proved an ethical and religious unity between western and eastern hemispheres attributable to a universal revelation in prehistory.

Probabalistic ethical views also affected how the Jesuits regarded the Natives of New France. Taking to heart the instructions of Pope Gregory that indigenous cultural forms that did not deter the progress of Christianity should be preserved and adapted for missionary purposes, they assumed a stance toward *sauvage* life that anticipated twentieth-century cultural relativism. Though shocked by some aspects of Native cultures, the missionaries adopted the Probabalistic position that the absence of "universally applicable ethical principles" caused morality to become "a matter of conscience related to the needs of everyday life and dependent upon the level of civilization attained by each man in his particular society" (Duignan 1958: 729; cf. Jaenen 1976: 51). Reinforcing the secular concept of the Noble Savage, then, were the Jesuits' own ideas regarding the innate reasonableness of the *sauvages*, the vestiges of divinely revealed insight that might still be encountered among them, and their moral acceptability.

In addition to the influence of this set of intellectual constructs, the generally positive image of Native Americans conveyed in the *relations* submitted by the Jesuits in New France also derives from the original purpose of these documents. The concept of the *relations* apparently began in the sixteenth century when Francis Xavier, Apostle of India and Japan, had missionaries to India file periodic reports which, after some editing and consolidation, were forwarded to Rome "to bear witness to the faith, to describe the spread of the gospel and the experiences and obstacles the missionaries encountered, and to edify readers generally, for the greater glory of God" (Kennedy 1950: 77). Preparing such documents became standard practice for missionaries. The Jesuits also employed the *relations* quite frankly as propaganda to encourage support (especially financial) for their missionary enterprise—as "optimistic reports of their evangelical labours" (Jaenen 1976: 32; cf. Berkhofer

1978: 74; Brandon 1986: 69). Appearing annually between 1632 and 1674 and occasionally thereafter, the *relations* that came out of the missions in New France were prepared by the superior, who sometimes wrote an original narrative, but usually submitted edited and unedited accounts from mission outposts. After approval and emendation by the provincial in France, the *relations* were published for general public consumption. While the Jesuits probably intended to record accurately what they experienced and observed, the nature of their purpose and audience must have colored some of their presentation. Consequently, one would expect the writers to stress the dedication of the missionaries and the adversities they faced. But at the same time, they had to demonstrate that their efforts were not pointless—that, in fact, the basic nature of the *sauvages* deemed them capable of responding to Christian teachings. The *relations* had to convince their readers of what the Jesuits themselves were certain: "that the Indians were endowed with reason and able to learn, and . . . would eagerly accept the Gospel and the education offered to them" (Bitterli 1989: 90). The fundamental intelligence of the *sauvages* and their perceived lack of developed institutions joined to produce a prime target for missionizing. As a commentator writing on the missionary experience in Virginia (but whose observation applies equally to New France) has noted, "The less the natives knew, the fewer their cultural encumbrances, the more readily they would be formed anew in the white man's image" (Sheehan 1980: 121). Upon the *sauvages* as depicted in the *relations* the Jesuits hoped to erect a North American church "to outshine the faith and practice of old Europe" (Moore 1982: 44). In fact, they apparently believed that the essential nobility of the North American Natives, when combined with proper Christian instruction, would serve as a reproach to European Christians, whose devotion to their religion often seemed superficial.[7]

Obviously, then, the Jesuits did not record verbal art in a vacuum. The effects of their attitudes and purposes on what they did and did not record differed according to the expressive genre involved. The value of the reports written by the Jesuits varies according to whether the writer is dealing with myth, song, or oration.

Regarding myth, the Jesuits were almost invariably negative in their comments. For example, Joseph Jouvency, who equated the Algonquian word *manitou* with "Satan," lamented the prevalence of mythology among the *sauvages:* "It is wearisome to recount the tales which they invent concerning the creation of the world. Soothsayers and worthless quacks fill with these the idle and greedy ears of the people in order that they may acquire an impious gain" (*JR* 1:287). Over a century later, in a letter written to his brother in 1723, Sebastien Rasles described the cosmogony of the Illinois, to whom he had ministered in the 1690s, as being "as senseless as it is ridiculous" (*JR* 67:153). Very few real textualizations of myth narration exist in the writings of the Jesuit missionaries. Instead, the sacred stories of the *sauvages* are summarized or simply commented upon—the only positive points being statements of some similarity with classical or (in support of Figurist theory) Hebrew mythology. For example, in his *relation* for 1633, Le Jeune reported on the creation myth of the Montagnais—a "tradition of that great universal deluge which happened in the time of Noë, but [which] they have burdened . . . with a great many irrelevant fables," as he characterized it in the following year's *relation* (*JR* 6:157). Le Jeune retold the principal "irrelevant accretion" as follows:

> He [the culture hero] sent a raven to find a small piece of the earth, with which to build up another world [after an inundation caused by the overflowing of a lake]. The raven was unable to find any, everything being covered with water. He made an otter dive down, but the depth of the water prevented it from going to the bottom. At last a muskrat descended, and brought back some earth. (*JR* 5:155)

Perhaps the earliest full report in North America of the widely known Earth Diver creation myth,[8] Le Jeune's account had the positive effect of revealing to potential financial backers that "the Savages have some idea of a God" (*JR* 5:157), but for the most part stories of this sort were characterized as the products of "gross ignorance" (*JR* 10:133), "stupid" (*JR* 10:149), and "very ridiculous" (*JR* 12:31).

Undoubtedly, several factors contributed to the Jesuits' dismissive attitude toward myths and their failure to textualize narrations of them, including the fact that they did not witness many authentic performances of stories that Natives surely knew would earn only opprobrium from the French missionaries. For example, Jacques Buteux reported to Le Jeune a circumstance when he heard "a thousand . . . foolish tales." Accompanied by Jean Nicolet, well-versed in Algonquian languages from a two-year residence among the *sauvages* beginning in 1620, Buteux engaged in a theological conversation with a Native who "acts the part of a Wiseacre" (*JR* 9:125). This person related some basic principles of his cosmogony as illustrated by myth and then submitted to being catechized by the missionary, who quizzed him through Nicolet. This gist of Buteux's questions explored the fundamentals of the creation account. He asked, for instance, where the creator god dwelt before fashioning the earth. On being told that the deity rested in a canoe that floated upon the primordial waters, the missionary noted that accepting this detail required the existence of trees from whose bark the canoe had been made and land on which they grew. The necessary land and trees, according to the Native informant, had existed before the flood. But who had created this prediluvian land? asked the missionary. The *sauvage* replied in frustrated despair, "I know nothing about it; you have more intelligence than I have, do not ask me anything more" (*JR* 9:127). Such an experience, apparently common enough since the Jesuits believed themselves bound to correct Native "misconceptions," would certainly have discouraged myth-tellers from performing when the Jesuits were present.

Moreover, even if the Jesuits had heard myths and other narratives in performance, the nature of this material would probably not have interested them enough to encourage scrupulous documentation. While such "fables" demonstrated the need for Christian enlightenment, they contributed little to the image of the Natives as the reasonable Noble Savages ripe for conversion that undergirded Jesuit preconceptions and that they needed to present in their *relations*.

Yet there is some valuable material on storytelling in the writings of the Jesuits. An example is Paul Ragueneau's description of this verbal art among the Hurons, included in the *relation* for 1645–1646:

> The elders of the country were assembled this winter for the election of a very celebrated Captain. They are accustomed, on such occasions, to relate the stories which they have learned regarding their ancestors, even those most remote,—so that the young people, who are present and hear them, may preserve the memory thereof, and relate them in their turn, when they shall have become old. They do this in order thus to transmit to posterity the history and the annals of the country,—striving, by this means, to supply the lack of . . . books, which they have not. They offer, to the person from whom they desire to hear something, a little bundle of straws a foot long, which serve them as counters for calculating the numbers, and for aiding the memory of those present,—distributing in various lots these same straws, according to the diversity of the things which they relate. (*JR* 30:61)

Such descriptions of storytelling situations, though, are rare.

The Jesuits also directed only limited attention to songs. The French missionaries' attitude toward the musical abilities of the Natives varied according to what was being sung. On one hand, they were highly critical of musical performances that occurred as part of Native ceremonials. Paul Le Jeune, for example, wrote about the singing at a Huron feast, "I believe that if the demons and the damned were to sing in hell, it would be about after this fashion; I never heard anything more lugubrious and more frightful" (*JR* 14:61). Barthelemy Vimont described the singing of a Huron "*magicien*" as "like a damned soul" (*JR* 26:177). Pierre Roubaud characterized Abnaki singing as resembling "the cries and howling of wolves" (*JR* 70:97). But when, after being converted, the *sauvages* sang Christian hymns, their natural musical abilities emerged. "[A]ll the savages have much aptitude and inclination for singing the hymns of the Church," noted Jean Enjalran in a letter written in 1676 (*JR* 60:145). François Nau, writing in 1735, portrayed Native hymn singing in similar fashion: "Neither cordeliers nor nuns ever sang as do our Iroquois men and women. Their voices are both mellow and sonorous, and Their ear so correct that they do not miss a half-tone" (*JR* 68:275). As people in a state of pure nature possessing reason, then, the *sauvages* had the ability to sing effectively as long as what they sang was Christianly proper. What better evidence of both the potential for Christianity among these Noble Savages and the importance of ensuring that they had the opportunity to realize their potential?

The Jesuits did not textualize many songs (either words or music) probably because they assumed it would serve no particular purpose to record additional evidences of how reason had become corrupted among the *sauvages* and because of the practical problems of documenting the often difficult and obscure language of the songs and the equally difficult rhythms and intervals of the music. Among the few songs whose words are recorded in the *Jesuit Relations*, two are untranslated fragments from the Algonquian language of the Montagnais (*JR* 6:185; *JR* 12:9–11), one is a series of songs by Christian Iroquois that may have been sung originally in French (*JR* 42:115–117), one is the "death song" of a Christian Iroquois presented in the original and with a translation (*JR* 57:173), and one is the Native-language record (words and music) for a song for the Calumet Dance among the Illinois (*JR* 59:137).

The Iroquois death song illustrates as effectively as any of these examples how and why the Jesuits presented sung material. Reported by Jean de Lamberville, who missionized at Onondaga, in the *relation* for 1672–1673, the words in the original Iroquois are presented as follows: "*Egiheia onne . . . garonhiagué agatsiennonnia; nictouenha Jesousgué ouagué, Jesous tagitenra*" (*JR* 57:173). Lamberville also offered a translation into French: "*Enfin ie meurs Je vas au ciel voir Jesus. [V]oila qui est bien, Jesus ayez pitié de moy"* (*JR* 57:172) [Finally I am dying. I am going to heaven to see Jesus. That is good. Jesus, have pity on me]. The Jesuit reported this song not for its verbal artistic merit, but to show the constancy of Christian converts among the *sauvages,* even when they confronted the cruelest persecution. The dying woman, "very old" and "blind for a Long time," had been attacked by a drunken man who "bruised Her entire face, Broke Her jaw, pierced Her cheeks, inflicted several wounds in Her head and shoulders, and Left Her for dead on The spot." Lamberville reported that after he had dressed her wounds and heard her final confession, she sang the song "five or six times" before dying (*JR* 57:171–173).

Native American oratory received much different treatment from the Jesuits. Their generally positive depictions of Native oratorical skills and their numerous recordings of the words of speeches foreshadow the importance that this genre of American Indian verbal art would assume for later Euroamerican commentators. Though Paul Le Jeune's report of the Ottawa *capitaine's* speech to Champlain was at second hand, the *relations* and related writings by the Jesuits contain a multitude of first-hand descriptions of oratorical performances and of attempts to textualize them. The bulk of the material far outweighs all the other data on verbal art combined. A major reason for this, of course, is that the public nature of oratory made it easily accessible to the missionaries. Traditional situations for oratory in Native American cultures had been the assembly and council, so the Indians naturally employed oratorical skills when interacting publicly with the Jesuits and other representatives of European civilization. During their initial contacts, the Jesuits could fully comprehend the Natives' speeches only through interpreters. Even without understanding what a speaker might be saying, though, French missionaries such as Pierre Millet were impressed by the performances: "[T]he oldest or the most eloquent person of the family delivers a harangue,—either standing erect, or, more frequently, walking about. At times, he speaks in lugubrious tones, drawling out his words; at others, in a sharp tone calculated to produce emotion; sometimes in a joyful voice, intermingled with songs" (*JR* 58:185).

The admiration for the orators' skills only increased when the Jesuits considered what they were saying. It became "axiomatic" to note Indian eloquence (Dickason 1984: 257). The Jesuits cited the Natives' facility with language—which was more clearly revealed in oratory than in any other context—as proof of their possession of the faculty of reason. For example, Francesco Bressani, an Italian who participated in the Jesuit mission in New France, tellingly wrote in 1653 that the languages of the *sauvages* "are very different . . . from ours, but most beautiful and regular, which makes us see that God alone is the Author thereof,—it being impossible that so excellent a System, which surpasses that of all European languages that we know, is the product of minds rude and unversed in every science" (*JR* 39:119). A half century later, Sebastien Rasles praised an Illinois speaker whose address he had heard in the 1690s: "I confess to you that I admire his flow of language, the justness and force of the arguments that he presented, the eloquent turn he gave to them, and the choice and nicety of the expressions with which he adorned his speech" (*JR* 67:163).

The use of figurative tropes by Native speechmakers particularly impressed the Jesuits,[9] since it forcefully revealed the influence of reason and also suggested the need for the civilizing influences of Christianity. References to the *sauvages'* use of "allegories and metaphors" (*JR* 43:169), "comparisons, time-words, and proverbs" (*JR* 10:123), "figurative expressions and Personifications" (*JR* 12:59), and "various circumlocutions, and other rhetorical methods" (*JR* 10:257) abound in the Jesuits' writings. As Le Jeune warned, "Metaphor is largely in use among these Peoples [Hurons, in particular]; unless you accustom yourself to it, you will understand nothing in their councils, where they speak almost entirely in metaphors" (*JR* 10:219). Only speakers whose intellect was rooted in reason could choose figures as appositely as did the Native orators. At the same time, the need for such figures indicated the "poverty" of the Native languages and concomitantly of Native thought. Like many other commentators on *sauvage* language before and since, Jesuits frequently noted the lack of abstraction in Native oratory: "[R]ude and untutored as they are, all their conceptions are limited to sensible and material things; there is nothing abstract, internal, spiritual, or distinct" (*JR* 2:11). The Native languages were unaccustomed to the high concepts of Christianity, which existed only in vestigial remnants even though (according to Figurism) they had been revealed to the Natives' ancestors eons previously.

It accorded with the Jesuits' preconceptions of humanity in the state of pure nature and their purposes in writing about their experiences to emphasize Native oratorical skills. They did this in three ways: through lavish praise of speechmaking abilities of Native spokespersons, through relatively full descriptions of performance dynamics, and through attempts to record the verbal component of speeches. First, Jesuit writers might offer broad generalizations in praise of Native oratorical art. The *sauvages* of Canada were "the greatest speech-makers in the world," according to Pierre Biard (*JR* 2:45). Moreover, their speeches "would excite the admiration of the most experienced in the arena of eloquence," commented Josephy Jouvency (*JR* 1:279). Pierre Roubaud "more than once" heard orations "which would not have been disavowed by our finest minds in France" (*JR* 70:99). Reflecting one of the basic tenets of Noble Savagery, Paul Le Jeune believed that this verbal art emerged from uncorrupted nature, not culture: "[S]ome seem to be born orators" (*JR* 10:259).

The Jesuits grounded these generalizations by describing how orators delivered their speeches, taking into account paralinguistic and situational factors as well as what the *sauvages* might say—though some like Paul Ragueneau anticipated the frustration of later textmakers at being unable to communicate in writing "the charm" imparted to an orator's performance "by the tone of his voice and the expression of his countenance" (*JR* 36:221). Yet many went so far as to describe audience response to speeches, as Jean de Brebeuf did in a generalized account of the "order" observed by Hurons in their councils that appeared in the *relation* for 1636: "Each one ends his advice in these terms, *Condayauendi Ierhayde cha nonhwicwahachen*: that is to say, 'That is my thought on the subject under Discussion:' then the whole Assembly responds with a very strong respiration drawn from the pit of the stomach, *Haau*. I have noticed that when any one has spoken to their liking, this *Haau* is given forth with much more effort" (*JR* 10:259). Lafitau presents a fairly full generic description of Iroquois oratory:

> The Iroquois, like the Lacedaemonians wish a quick and concise discourse. Their style is, however, full of figures of speech and quite metaphorical; it is varied according to the different nature of the business. On certain occasions, it gets away from ordinary language and resembles our courtly style; on others, it is sustained by a keener action than that of our actors on the stage. They have, withal, a capacity for mimicry; they speak with gestures as much as with the voice and act out things so naturally as to make them seem to take place under their audience's eyes. (1974–1977: 1:298)

More commonly than for oral narratives or for the words of songs, the Jesuits offered what purport to be verbatim translations of what orators said in their speeches. Writings by the missionaries contain many translated orations, most of which illustrate the innate reason of the *sauvages*. In fact, Francesco Bressani complained that European readers "have believed that their speeches and addresses, which we reported in our relations[,] were fictitious." But he strongly asserted that, in fact, "most of these, when translated . . . into another language, are much less powerful than in their own" (*JR* 38:263). For example, in the *relation* for 1636 Paul Le Jeune presented the French translation of a brief speech given by an Algonkin upon presenting to the French commandant at Québec a young Iroquois woman who had been taken captive:

Ecoutez, François, ie vous vais tancer, car que pourroit faire autre chose vn gros animal comme moy, qui prend la hardiesse de parler deuant des Capitaines? Si i'estois Capitaine i'aurois droit de parler; ie ne suis qu'vn chien, si faut-il que ie parle, & que ie vous sasse vne querelle d'amitié. Nos Peres & nos vieux Capitaines se sont entr'aimez, ils sont morts maintenant, nous nous entr'aimons & François & Sauuages; nous nous entr'aimons, ouy nous nous entr'aimons: c'est pourquoy il eust esté biē à propos de voir quelques-vns de vos ieunes gens parmy nous a la guerre; mais cela nous ayant manqué, nous auons fait ce que nous auons pu. Voicy vne ieune prisonniere que nous vous presentons pour mettre en la place de l'vn des trois François qui ont esté tuez il y a quelque temps bien prés d'icy: ie voy encor le sang tout rouge qui accuse la cruauté de nos ennemis & des vostres: ce present en cachera vne partie, c'est peu de chose, mais c'est tout ce que nous auons, le reste ayant esté tué: si nous eussions esté secourus, nous eussions fait dauantage, mais on nous a quitté de tous costez (*JR* 9:266). [Listen, Frenchmen, I am going to scold you, for what else could a great animal like me do—one who is bold enough to speak in the presence of captains? If I were captain, I would have the right to speak. I am only a dog, yet I must speak about a friendly disagreement with you. Our fathers and our old captains loved each other. They are dead now. We—both Frenchmen and Natives—love each other. Indeed, we love each other. Therefore, it would have been very fitting if some of your young men had joined us in battle. But since that did not happen, we have done as well as we could. Here is a young female prisoner, whom we present to you to take the place of one of the three Frenchmen who were killed near here some time ago. I still see the deep red blood that accuses the cruelty of our common enemy. This offering will erase part of it. It is a little thing, but it is all we have, since the rest were killed. If we had received some help, we would have done more, but we were deserted on all sides.]

Of course, we have no way of knowing how reliable such translations are, since Native-language versions were not preserved. And despite Bressani's protestations, we may suspect that material was presented in such a way as to demonstrate the points about *la pensée sauvage* that the Jesuits needed to make in their publications—that is, the essential "Identity" of verbal expression despite a superficial encrustation of "Difference." Moreover, the Jesuits' use of terminology from the Western rhetorical tradition such as "peroration" to describe the Natives' speeches suggests that their experience with this verbal art form in Europe may have affected how they depicted what they heard the orators say.

To show how the Jesuits might place an oration in its performance situation—the ideal of ethnographic textualization—we can turn to the account of treaty negotiations conducted by representatives of the Iroquois with Charles-Jacques Montmagny, Champlain's successor as governor of New France, and representatives of several other Native groups. The *relation* for 1644–1645, written by Barthelemy Vimont, contains a richly detailed account of the oratorical performance of Kiotsaeton, spokesperson for the Iroquois. On 12 July 1644, he spoke to Montmagny and others, including Vimont, who had assembled in the courtyard of the garrison at Three Rivers, upriver from the community of Québec. In preparation for his performance, the Iroquois had stretched a cord between two poles, from which they intended for Kiotsaeton to hang "seventeen collars of porcelain beads" (i.e., wampum belts) representing the points that the speaker planned to raise.[10] Taking one of the belts in hand, Kiotsaeton began his speech:

> *Onontio* [the name used for Montmagny] *preste l'oreille, ie suis la bouche de tout mon pays, tu escoute tous les Iroquois entendant ma parole, mon coeur n'a rien de mauuais, ie n'ay que de bonnes chansons en bouche, nous auons des tas de chansons de guerre en nostre pays, nous les auons toutes iettées par terre, nous n'auons plus que des chants de resjouissance* (*JR* 27:252). [Onontio, lend an ear. I am the mouth of my whole country. You listen to all the Iroquois in hearing my words. My heart has no evil. I have only good songs in my mouth. We have many war songs in our country. We have thrown them all to the ground. We now have only songs of rejoicing.]

Vimont carefully noted Kiotsaeton's performance following these remarks. The Iroquois orator "walked about that great space as if on the stage of a theatre; he made a thousand gestures; he looked up to Heaven; he gazed at the Sun; he rubbed his arms as if he wished to draw from them the strength that moved them in war" (*JR* 27:253). Then Kiotsaeton hung the belt from the cord.

The pattern of oratorical "harangue" usually followed by a dramatic enactment of what had just been said preceded similar disposition of the remaining sixteen belts. For example, following Kiotsaeton's description of his worries about the hardships that a French captive being returned by the Iroquois to his people through the wilderness might face, he acted out the wilderness journey in a manner that surpassed in ingenuity that of any *"tabarin"* (i.e., comic actor) in Paris:

> He took a stick, and placed it on his head like a bundle; then he carried it from one end of the square to the other, representing what that prisoner had done in the rapids and in the current of the water,—on arriving at which he had transported his baggage, piece by piece. He went backward and forward, showing the journeys, the windings, and the turnings of the prisoner. He ran against a stone; he receded more than he advanced in his canoe, because alone he could not maintain it against the current. He lost courage, and then regained his strength. In a word, I have never seen anything better done than this acting. (*JR* 27:255)

When Kiotsaeton spoke about the rivers being cleared of war canoes, he "made use of a thousand gestures, as if he had collected the waves and had caused a calm, from Quebec to the Iroquois country." And when he lamented the dangers that rapids and waterfalls posed for river travel, "with his hands and arms he smoothed and arrested the torrents" (*JR* 27:259). At one point, the Iroquois spokesperson addressed the importance of uniting all the peoples represented at the assembly and illustrated his point by linking one arm with one of the French and the other with an Algonkin, a traditional gesture used by Iroquois orators when speaking of intergroup and intratribal relationships (Druke 1987). Throughout his performance, he utilized what Vimont characterized as "appropriate gestures" (*JR* 27:261).

The Jesuit who observed Kiotsaeton's performance was more punctilious in recording the body language of the orator than the words of his speech. Of the oration's verbal component, Vimont "gathered only some disconnected fragments" through the intermediation of an interpreter "who spoke only in a desultory manner and did not follow the order observed by the Barbarian." However, he was able to note, "Every one admitted that this man was impassioned and eloquent" (*JR* 27:265).

The Jesuits were also attracted to Native speechmaking because of its potential to aid their mission. Once a *sauvage* who possessed indigenously acquired skills in oratory was converted to Christianity, his or her abilities could be harnessed in the Jesuit cause. Though they prided themselves on their linguistic abilities,[11] the Jesuits realized that Native lay preachers could sometimes communicate more effectively with their fellow *sauvages* (Moore 1982: 163–169).

In terms of the approach to the textualization of oral expression that informs this study, how do the Jesuits measure up? Do the texts they made come anywhere near being accurate, comprehensive representations of the performances and other kinds of expression that they encountered and recorded? If they fail to do so, can anything of value be retrieved from the Jesuit *relations* and associated documents?

The answers to the first two questions must be negative. The Jesuits did little in the way of full textualization of any Native verbal expression except for oratory. And the verbal components of their oration texts are often based upon interpreter's versions (most likely extremely loose) or even on secondhand reports of what was said. However, they did at least textualize some performances with a degree of thoroughness previously unmatched. They even recognized some of the problems inherent in the textualization process, such as the inability of the French alphabet to accommodate all of the sounds made by singers and speakers in *sauvage* tongues. But whatever value their material offers lies not so much in its representation of what was said or sung as in the Jesuits' depictions of the situations of expression. Like George Catlin and unlike Franz Boas, they did encounter verbal art, particularly oratory, as authentic performance and often carefully described how performers delivered their songs or speeches as well as the nature of the occasions when these performances occurred.

Meanwhile, the assumptions brought by the Jesuits to the Western Hemisphere, intellectual constructs that "tended to combine cultural relativism with religious absolutism" (Bidney 1954: 323), caused them to treat different genres of verbal art in different ways. They dismissed mythology, for example, but respectfully treated oratory as evidence of the innate reason possessed by the *sauvages*, thus foreshadowing the attention that commentators during the eighteenth and nineteenth centuries would continue to pay to oratory. Before accepting or rejecting the Jesuits' data on a particular example of verbal art, we should consider the implications its genre might have for them.

However, we would do well to use all the materials provided by the Jesuits more circumspectly than did, for example, Francis Parkman ("authentic and trustworthy historical documents" [1983: 343]) or Joseph D. McGuire ("there is no reason to question their accuracy" [1901: 257]). Certainly, the texts made even from oration performances are at best suggestive of content and style. Yet the Jesuit interest in verbal art and other aspects of the Native cultures of Canada was unmatched in

North America for over a century after their mission ended. Not until the Smithsonian Institution organized its Bureau of Ethnology in 1879 did a similar corpus of material on American Indian cultures, including verbal art, begin to appear in textualizations. However, the intervening years were not completely blank; some efforts at studying Native American verbal art were made. Moreover, contemporary with the French colonial period in Canada, British colonists farther south were taking occasional notice of the expressive culture of the Natives whom they were displacing.

CHAPTER FOUR

"A SORT OF LOOSE POETRY"

Henry Timberlake's Cherokee War Song

The Canadian Jesuit precedent in studies of Native American verbal art was not followed closely from the British colonies in America and their successor nation for two centuries. While the missionaries published texts, descriptions, and summaries of Native American verbal expression as early as the seventeenth century in their ethnographically oriented *relations*, the lack of a similar publishing program among New England Puritans or among "discoverers, explorers, and settlers" (Franklin 1979) in the middle and southern colonies resulted in a much scantier record even for the translated texts of orations. Projects like that of Increase Mather to gather evidence of the working of Providence in New England had ethnographic potential, but when the resulting materials treated Indians at all, they did so in terms that demonized them. For Puritans in Massachusetts Bay, Indians represented the "Satanic principle" that figured into their theory of cosmic history (Nash 1974: 76–80; Pearce 1952; Pearce 1988: 19–31; Hodgen 1964: 379). Few Puritan depictions of Native American cultures, especially their religious dimensions, were free from what Francis Jennings has called "devil language"—the tendency to identify Indians with the dark forces at work in the cosmos (1975: 47). Occasionally, missionaries like John Eliot found it useful to learn and document Indian languages. Eliot also published some sermons by "dying Indians" that may have reflected the survival of a Native speech-making esthetic in Christian garb (Murray 1991: 34–35). But texts of oral narration and singing are missing from the Puritan records.

Similar conditions obtained in the middle and southern colonies,

though accounts by explorers and soldiers often include occasional oration texts and summaries of myths and other oral narratives. And in his
account of the Jamestown colony (written in 1612 but not published
until 1849), William Strachey had written out the following "scorneful"
song sung "in manner of tryumph" by Powhatan's people after having
killed and captured several Englishmen:

> 1. Matanerew shashashewaw erawango pechecoma
> Whe Tassantassa inoshashawyehockan pocosack.
> Whe whe, ya haha nehe wittowa, wittowa.

> 2. Matanerew shashashewaw erawango pechecoma
> Capt. Newport inoshashaw neir mhoc natian matassan
> Whe whe, etc.

> 3. Matanerew shashashewaw erawango pechecoma
> Thom. Newport inoshashaw neir inhoc natian moncock:
> Whe, whe, etc.

> 4. Matanerew shashashewaw erawango pechecoma
> Pochin Simon moshashaw ningon natian monahack,
> Whe, whe, etc. (1849: 79–80)

Though he provided no translation for the song, Strachey did offer some
interpretive commentary:

> Which maye signifie how they killed us for all our poccasacks, that is
> our guns, and for all that Captain Newport brought them copper, and
> could hurt Thomas Newport (a boy whose name in deede was Thomas
> Savadge, who Captain Newport leaving with Powhatan to learne the lan-
> guage, at that tyme he presented the said Powhatan with a copper
> crowne, and other gifts from his Majestie, said he was his sonne) for all
> his monachock, that is his bright sword, and how they could take Symon
> (for they seldome said our surname) prisoner for all his tamahanke, that
> is his hatchet, adding, as for a burden unto their song, what lamentation
> our people made when they kild him, namely, saying how they would
> cry whe, whe, etc., which they mockt us for, and cryed againe to us yah,
> ha, ha, Tewittawa, Tewittawa; for yt is true they never bemoane them-
> selves nor cry out, gyving up so much as a groane for any death, how
> cruell soever and full of torment. (1849: 80)

In addition to the historical curiosity that the priority of Strachey's material affords, it holds some interest in anticipating some of the concerns of contemporary textmakers: Strachey's care to preserve poetic form, his reproduction of the vocables that conclude each stanza (though he may very well misinterpret them in his commentary), and his recognition of the situation-specific significance of the material. A fully Englished version of a Native American "poem," though, had to wait until 1765, and then it came from an unlikely source.[1]

Henry Timberlake refers to himself as "a raw Virginian" (1765: 119). "[U]nsophisticated" and "naive" are the terms that one modern commentator has used to describe him (Evans 1976: 49, 51). Stranded in London in late spring of 1765 after escorting his second delegation of Cherokees from America to the English metropolis, Timberlake was desperately in need of funds. Much of his own capital, he claimed, had been expended in support of his Indian charges. In fact, his entire military career, which began in 1756 as a member of the Virginia Militia commanded by George Washington, had been marked by his use of his own resources for the sake of carrying out his patriotic responsibilities. Wrongly accused of having profited from the first group of Cherokees with whom he had visited London in 1762, Timberlake decided to justify himself to the British public. Exchanging his customary "sword for a pen," he tried by writing his memoirs to make the case that he had been wronged by both his accusers and those who refused to reimburse him for his legitimate expenses. "[C]onstrained by the clamours made against the unnecessary and extravagant expences into which the reception of the Indians had drawn the government" and "compelled by the necessity of vindicating myself," Timberlake set out to detail the "principal dangers I have passed through, and the expences I have been at" (1765: vi–vii). Yet despite the work's tone, which is both pathetic and mercenary, *The Memoirs of Lieut. Henry Timberlake* represents an important milestone for students of Native American verbal art.

In 1761, Timberlake had served in the Second Virginia Regiment's campaign to aid in suppressing the bloody Cherokee Rebellion against the British in the Carolinas that had begun the previous year (Corkran 1962: 191–254). Led first by Colonel William Byrd III and then by Colonel Adam Stephen, the Virginians had seen no military action, but their presence in southwestern Virginia some two hundred miles from the arena of conflict constituted a potential threat for the Overhills Cherokees, those who inhabited what is now eastern Tennessee. In November 1761, while Attakullaculla (The Little Carpenter), principal negotiator for the Cherokees, was pursuing peace at Charleston, Stephen's Virginians attempted to hasten an end to hostilities by advancing down the Holston River upon the Overhills communities. They reached a point about 140 miles from the Cherokee settlements, where they paused to construct Fort Robinson. The Cherokees responded with a delegation led by Connetarke (Standing Turkey), Fire Chief of the Cherokees since the death of his father, "Old Hop," in 1759, who concluded a treaty with Stephen that from the Virginians' and the Cherokees' perspectives effectively ended the war (Corkran 1962: 265–266). Because their previous dealings with the British had created an atmosphere of distrust, the Indians requested Stephen "to send an officer back with them to their country, as that would effectually convince the nation of the good intentions and sincerity of the English towards them" (Timberlake 1765: 39). Lieutenant Timberlake volunteered his services and was joined by Sergeant Thomas Sumpter, interpreter John McCormack (apparently himself a Cherokee), and a servant for a visit to the Overhills communities.

The trip began on 28 November 1761, when Timberlake and his companions set out by canoe downriver from Fort Robinson. Though Connetarke had advised against traveling by water at this time of the year, the lieutenant wanted to investigate the route in case hostilities between the British and the Cherokees should erupt in the future. But the Indian's advice had been sound. Low water and intense cold made the journey excessively difficult. Loss of their guns due to mishaps and the threat of Shawnee hunting parties, who, though currently at peace with the British, would not appreciate a journey designed to promote a treaty between the Virginians and their traditional Cherokee enemies, added to the travelers' hardships. Twenty-two days down the Holston and then up the Tennessee finally brought the party to Cherokee hospitality near the site of Fort Loudoun, which had been destroyed by the Indians during the war.

Though the account of his arduous journey certainly underlined the sacrifices Timberlake had made for the sake of patriotic duty, his book's most interesting section from today's viewpoint presents ethnographic data drawn from three months' worth of observing the Cherokees at first hand. In his preface, Timberlake had noted that while plenty of other accounts of Cherokee life were available, he had encountered none that presented its data "to my perfect satisfaction," since usually they came from accounts of traders who were "ignorant and incapable of making just observations" (1765: vii). During his stay among the

Cherokees, Timberlake enjoyed the hospitality of Ostenaco, whom he refers to as "the commander in chief" (1765: 30; cf. Evans 1976).

Sponsored by this influential figure, who urged his countrymen to comply with the treaty particulars, Timberlake was able to visit several other Cherokee towns, where he was appropriately feted. He made himself useful to his hosts by writing letters for them to be sent to the Carolina government in Charleston, where peace negotiations were still in progress. During his stay among the Cherokees, Timberlake was able to observe enough of their culture to provide basic ethnographic information on a range of subjects, including agriculture, fishing, bodily ornamentation, dress, weaponry, basic personality structure, care for the elderly and poor, language, music, architecture, canoe construction, arrowmaking, commerce, religious beliefs and ceremonialism, childbirth practices, burial customs, government, social structure, naming traditions, games, and dances (1765: 42–80).

Toward the end of February, Timberlake became uneasy because of rumors spreading among the Cherokees that Shawnees, acting under the instigation of British troops, had killed several of their number near Fort Robinson. Remembering the recent massacre of those who had surrendered Fort Loudoun, Timberlake feared for his own safety and began to petition Ostenaco to escort him back to the English settlements. After several delays, the party set out on 10 March 1762.

About 150 Cherokees under the leadership of Ostenaco accompanied Timberlake by way of Fort Robinson, which had been abandoned, all the way to Williamsburg. Ostensibly because he wanted to meet King George III, whose portrait he had seen at the colonial capital, and certainly because he wanted to replicate the experiences of Attakullaculla, who had visited London in 1731 with Alexander Cuming, Ostenaco requested a trip to England with Timberlake as escort. Accordingly, three Cherokees—Ostenaco, Tchanohawithten (The Pigeon), and Connetarke—with Timberlake and William Storey as interpreter, set sail aboard the *Epreuve* from Hampton, Virginia, on 15 May 1762. The party, minus Storey, who had died en route, landed at Plymouth on 16 June and arrived in London two days later. They did not receive an audience with the king until 8 July. In the meantime and for a month or so following their meeting with the monarch, the Cherokees took in the city's sights and themselves became objects of curiosity, a fact that figured prominently in press reports (Foreman 1943: 72–77). Timberlake himself was accused of "accepting money to permit people to see his wards" (Foreman 1943: 76), a charge that he strongly rejected in his

memoirs, laying most of the blame on a Mr. "Caccanthropos," who had
been the party's landlord. The Cherokees returned to America aboard
the *Epreuve* from Portsmouth about 25 August, leaving Timberlake
stranded in London with virtually no money.

Despite his financial embarrassment, which prevented his returning
to America until the following spring, Timberlake married sometime in
late 1762 or early 1763. When the newlyweds did finally return to Virginia, Timberlake found no solution to his money problems. Petitions
to the Virginia House of Burgesses for his expenses were unsatisfactory.
Then, in 1764 a party of five Cherokees requested to go to London to
protest British violations of treaty guarantees. Upon being refused by
the colonial government, they enlisted Timberlake, who was apparently planning to return to England anyway in the role of tobacco factor,
as their guide. Three of the Cherokees made the trip, arriving in mid-
October and returning the following March. Though their visit was
much more low-key than that of Ostenaco's delegation, Timberlake
nevertheless incurred considerable expense on their behalf, a situation
that stimulated the publication of his memoirs, in which he details the
financial wrongs that had been perpetrated against him.

Timberlake's was not the first ethnographic description of the Natives of the Southeast, including the Cherokees (Randolph 1973: 108–
141).[2] What is apparently the earliest extant document on the social and
religious life of these Indians was written in 1725 by Alexander Long,
who had lived and traded with the Cherokees for more than a decade
(Corkran 1969). Other Euroamericans who provided ethnographic data
on the Cherokees that predated Timberlake's memoirs include George
Chicken, who served as Commissioner of Indian Affairs for South Carolina in the 1720s (Chicken 1928); explorer Alexander Cuming, who
visited the Cherokee towns in 1730 and accompanied a delegation of
Cherokees to England (Cuming 1928); trader Ludovick Grant, whose
recollections from the 1720s were recorded in the Charleston probate
records thirty years later (Grant 1909); and Presbyterian missionary
William Richardson, who worked among the Cherokees in 1757, 1758,
and 1759 (1931).

However, for our purposes Timberlake's memoir stands out from
these and other earlier ethnographic descriptions because of its attention to verbal art, represented in translations, summaries, and performance descriptions. For example, he reported a couple of "harangues"
delivered by Ostenaco, one urging the Cherokees' compliance with the
British (1765: 33–34) and another responding to unfounded rumors of
Cherokee deaths at the hands of Shawnees who had allegedly received

British encouragement (1765: 85). Presenting such translations of oratory represented no particular innovation, since they had become commonplace in British accounts of their interactions with Native Americans. In fact, speeches by Cherokee orators appear in the writings of some of Timberlake's ethnographic predecessors—for example, Cuming (1928: 142–143), Grant (1909: 62–63), and Long (Corkran 1969: 14–16). Timberlake did distinguish his treatment of Ostenaco's first oration, though, by providing glosses on a couple of points that might be obscure to English readers: the now-clichéd practice of burying a hatchet to signify the end of hostilities and an apparent conflict between the Cherokee system of punishing malefactors and that specified in the treaty (1765: 33).

In addition to these quoted (in translation only) speeches, Timberlake's memoirs include a paraphrase of a legend about a gem that grew on the head of a "monstrous serpent," which was now in the possession of a "conjurer," who, Timberlake supposed, "hatched the account of its discovery." He justified including what he considered a spurious tale by noting, "I have however given it to the reader, as a specimen of an Indian story, many of which are much more surprising" (1765: 48–49). While accounts of narrative traditions, even in paraphrase or summary, are much more scarce in pre-nineteenth century treatments of Native American cultures than orations, even his inclusion of this now widely known legend (e.g., Alexander 1916: 300–301; H. Thompson 1939: 298)[3] does not really distinguish Timberlake's work from what others had already done. Alexander Long, for instance, retold several myths and legends in his description of Cherokee culture (Corkran 1969: 26–30, 40–42).

The really significant feature of Timberlake's memoirs from the point of view of verbal art studies is his presentation of "A Translation of the WAR-SONG, *Caw waw noo dee, &c.,*" which he offered "without the original in Cherokee, on account of the expletive syllables [vocables], merely introduced for the music, and not the sense, just like the tolderols of many old English songs" (1765: 56). What follows are two eighteen-line stanzas in heroic couplets, the gist of which announces the warriors' intention to defeat their enemies in the latter's country and to exact retribution should they attempt to retaliate:

> Where'er the earth's enlighten'd by the sun,
> Moon shines by night, grass grows, or waters run,
> Be't known that we are going, like men, afar,
> In hostile fields to wage destructive war;

Like men we go, to meet our country's foes,
Who, woman-like, shall fly our dreaded blows;
Yes, as a woman, who beholds a snake,
In gaudy horror, glisten thro' the brake,
Starts trembling back, and stares with wild surprize,
Or pale thro' fear, unconscious, panting, flies.
Just so these foes, more tim'rous than the hind,
Shall leave their arms and only cloaths behind;
Pinch'd by each blast, by ev'ry thicket torn,
Run back to their own nation, now its scorn:
Or in the winter, when the barren wood
Denies their gnawing entrails nature's food,
Let them sit down, from friends and country far,
And wish with tears, they ne'er had come to war.

We'll leave our clubs, dew'd with their country show'rs,
And, if they dare to bring them back to our's,
Their painted scalps shall be a step to fame,
And grace our own and glorious country's name.
Or if we warriors spare the yielding foe,
Torments at home the wretch must undergo.
But when we go, who knows which shall return,
When growing dangers rise with each new morn?
Farewel, ye little ones, ye tender wives,
For you alone we would conserve our lives!
But cease to mourn, 'tis unavailing pain,
If not fore-doom'd, we soon shall meet again.
But, O ye friends! in case your comrades fall,
Think that on you our deaths for vengeance call;
With uprais'd tommahawkes pursue our blood,
And stain with hostile streams, the conscious wood,
That pointing enemies may never tell
The boasted place where we, their victims fell.

(1765: 56–58)

Its heroic couplets, epic simile, and consciously "literary" language have caused modern readers of Timberlake's translation to question how well it actually represents Cherokee song. John R. Swanton, for example, laments that the lieutenant "unfortunately, thought it necessary to introduce English rhythms" into his translation (1946: 692).

Brian Swann evokes "pity" that Timberlake had produced something "that might have come from one of Dryden's dramas" rather than from the lips of a Cherokee warrior (1993: 147). Arnold Krupat notes that Timberlake's lines are "bound to strike the contemporary reader as inevitably very distant from what any eighteenth-century Cherokee warriors might have actually sung" (1992a: 176). But despite their validity, such dismissals of this translation ignore what light it can shed on Cherokee verbal art. A more thorough investigation of the translation itself, its place in the agenda for Timberlake's book, and the intellectual milieu that affected it may suggest its value in the history of the study of Native American verbal art.

In content, the poem does seem to reflect accurately the military practices of the Cherokees and other southeastern Indians during the eighteenth century.[4] Timberlake provides footnoted explanations of several of those practices, some of which are corroborated by other observers. For example, Timberlake glosses the lines "Just so these foes, more tim'rous than the hind, / Shall leave their arms and only cloaths behind" by noting, "As the Indians fight naked, the vanquished are constrained to endure the rigours of the weather in their flight, and live upon roots and fruit, as they throw down their arms to accelerate their flight thro' the woods" (1765: 56–57n). A more recent writer on southeastern Indian warfare also notes that warriors generally dressed "only in a breechcloth and moccasins" during battle (Hudson 1976: 247).

The line that begins the second stanza, "We'll leave our clubs . . . ," merits the explanation from Timberlake that "It is the custom of the Indians, to leave a club, something of the form of a cricket-bat, but with their warlike exploits engraved on it, in their enemy's country, and the enemy accepts the defiance, by bringing this back to their country" (1765: 57n). Others have identified the war club as the "main symbol of war" in the Southeast (Hudson 1976: 245). John Lawson, who had written about the Carolina Indians in 1708, recorded the custom of leaving "hieroglyphic" signs during a military expedition so that the enemy would know who was responsible for the incursion (cited in Swanton 1946: 689). In a survey of Native American cultures of the region, Charles Hudson characterizes the custom of raiding parties to leave "a red war club at the scene of a killing so their enemy would know who had perpetrated the raid" (1976: 247).

A few lines farther on, the war song addresses the plight of captives who must suffer "[t]orments at home." Timberlake comments upon Cherokee treatment of war captives at some length:

The prisoners of war are generally tortured by the women, at the party's return, to revenge the death of those that have perished by the wretch's countrymen. This savage custom has been so much mitigated of late, that the prisoners were only compelled to marry, and then generally allowed all the privileges of the natives. This lenity, however, has been a detriment to the nation; for many of these returning to their countrymen, have made them acquainted with the country-passes, weakness, and haunts of the Cherokees; besides that it gave the enemy greater courage to fight against them. (1765: 57–58n)

Probably because it confirmed some Euroamerican preconceptions about the inhuman brutality of the North American Natives, the torture of captives by Cherokees and other southeastern Indians received considerable attention, especially from writers predating Timberlake (Hudson 1976: 255–257; Williams 1930: 416–430). For instance, writing specifically about the Cherokees in the 1730s, Mark Catesby reflected the views of a number of his contemporaries: "Their savage nature appears in nothing more than their barbarity to their captives, whom they murder gradually with the most exquisite tortures they can invent. At these diabolical ceremonies attend both sexes, old and young, all of them with great glee and merriment assisting to torture the unhappy wretch, till his death finishes their diversion" (quoted in Swanton 1946: 691). That Timberlake suggests these practices had abated among the Cherokees probably reflects changes in Euroamerican perceptions as much as in Native American practices.

Finally, Timberlake explains the last few lines by noting, "Their custom is generally to engrave their victory on some neighbouring tree, or set up some token of it near the field of battle; to this their enemies are supposed to point, as boasting their victory over them, and the slaughter that they made" (1765: 58n). Again, other ethnographic descriptions confirm Timberlake's account. Particularly when an enemy contingent was totally wiped out, war parties would leave some indicator of their victory—perhaps a war club with identifying symbols, marks carved into a tree, or pictographs painted upon rocks. Each was done so that "there could be no doubt as to who the killers were, taunting the other side to retaliate" (Hudson 1976: 251).

In terms of broad content, then, the poem that Timberlake presents as a translation of a Cherokee war song does seem "authentic"; at least in its details of the ethnography of warfare it finds confirmation in the writings of those who had themselves observed southeastern Indians during the colonial period and of recent synthesizers of these primary sources. It is more difficult, though, to assess some of its other features—for example, its value as a translation. No matter what our suspicions, we have no precise way of judging how closely the poem matches the vocabulary and syntax of the original Cherokee. Timberlake did not publish an original-language version. In fact, for the English source from which he worked he undoubtedly relied upon an interpretation by John McCormack, who had accompanied him from Fort Robinson and whom one author has characterized as "a renegade" (Corkran 1962: 191), or perhaps another interpreter. Interpreters played a vital role in Euroamerican interactions with Native Americans. Such figures were largely responsible for what we know about the content of Native American verbal expression during the eighteenth century. Generally, exact word-for-word translation seems to have been the exception, even the precision needed for treaty negotiations allowing the interpreter to render what he heard in paraphrase (Davis 1978: 221–230). Timberlake may very well have gotten only a general idea of the content of the war song from his interpreter, who unless he was extremely sensitive to artistic nuances in both Cherokee and English would be unlikely to capture much of the indigenous poetry.

Timberlake chose to render what the interpreter had relayed to him in a verse form, perhaps somewhat hackneyed but still the most popular poetic style in the late eighteenth century. The Drydenesque heroic couplets certainly make the war song accessible to English readers, the audience to whom Timberlake wanted his memoirs to appeal, but they undoubtedly depart markedly from Cherokee oral poetics of the same period. Timberlake probably had to submit the interpreter's English to considerable torture before fitting it into rhymed lines of iambic pentameter. The "heroic" nature of the poem may also have inspired Timberlake to incorporate the epic simile that compares the defeated enemy to a frightened woman reacting to a snake "[i]n gaudy horror." To think of Timberlake's final product as a "translation" may, in fact, be using that term too loosely, for it more nearly resembles the "versions" (e.g., Swann 1993) and "workings" (e.g., Rothenberg 1972; 1986; see chapter 2) of Native American originals by some twentieth-century poets. Like many poetic translators of Native American verbal art much closer to our era and with the benefit of modern ethnopoetic insight, Timberlake certainly assumed that the original—at least as it came to him through interpretation—needed some improvement before being passed off as literature to a sophisticated English readership. "Both the ideas and verse are very loose in the original," he commented (1765: 59). That he chose the principle of "Identity" to "present Cherokee song as recognizably literary, accessible to readers of, say, Dryden" (Krupat 1992b: 6) seems natural, given that his memoir was designed to present the Indians in as favorable a light as possible so that he might recover some of the money he had spent on their behalf.

Alan Dundes's identification of "text, texture, and context"—all of which figure into the "text," as that term is used here—as important components of verbal expression (1964b) allows a preliminary assessment of Timberlake's war song. In terms of "text" (by which Dundes means specifically the linguistic component of the expression), he may be deemed somewhat successful insofar as the ethnographic data presented in the song find confirmation in the writings of others. However, the translation of the war song must receive a failing mark in respect to "texture," the stylistic features of *how* it was rendered. Turning to "context," the particulars of by whom, when, where, and why it was performed (that is, its situation of expression), provides another measure of its value as textualized Native American verbal art.

Timberlake does not clearly identify who sang the song, but two possible candidates emerge from his narrative. One is Ostenaco himself, the Cherokee for whom Timberlake apparently had the most regard and whose good character receives some defense in the lieutenant's memoirs. The case for making Ostenaco the singer of the war song rests, first, on Timberlake's close association with the Second Warrior, which would have placed him and his interpreter in situations where they were likely to hear anything Ostenaco might sing or recite, and, second, on some specific instances of Ostenaco's singing reported by Timberlake. One of these occurred during the trip back to Virginia from the Cherokee towns. As the party approached the town of Chota, Ostenaco "sung the war-song," which, however, included "a prayer for our safety thro' the intended journey," a feature not present in the translated poem. In a performance note to this event, Timberlake indicates that the Second Warrior "bellowed out loud enough to be heard at a mile's distance" (1765: 98). A second instance of Ostenaco's singing takes place upon the arrival of the *Epreuve* at Plymouth. Here the Cherokee sang a "dirge" in thanks for the party's safe arrival after their Atlantic crossing. Again Timberlake offers a description of the performance: "The loudness and uncouthness of his singing, and the oddity of his person, drew a vast crowd of boats, filled with spectators, from all the ships in the harbour" (1765: 115).

Since we know a good deal about Ostenaco's life and, through Timberlake's memoir, at least something about his singing performance, it would be nice to assign the war song translated by the lieutenant to

him. However, the case for being its performer is stronger for Willinawaw, headman of the town of Toquo and a cousin of Attakullaculla.
Though an "extreme nativist" (Corkran 1962: 29), he had become an
early advocate of peace during the Cherokee Rebellion. In 1760, he had
accompanied his cousin, widely known for his diplomatic skills, on a
peace mission to Colonel Byrd in Virginia and the following March
undertook such a mission on his own as Attakullaculla's replacement.
Willinawaw may have been a member of the delegation led by Connetarke that made peace with Colonel Stephen in November of 1761
and had been instrumental in bringing Timberlake to the Overhills
communities (Corkran 1962: 264).

Regarding the singing of war songs, Timberlake wrote that the "chief"
of the military party "strives . . . to inspire" his warriors "with a sort of
enthusiasm, by the war-song, as the ancient bards did once in Britain"
(1765: 70). As Fred Gearing has noted, Cherokee war leaders apparently
had "no legitimate compulsion" to urge their men to fight (1962: 49–50)
and, consequently, may have had to rely on devices of persuasion such
as songs to raise and maintain military forces, a manifestation of the
Cherokee ethos that valued persuasion over compulsion in most matters of life (Gearing 1962: 38). This suggests the situation during which
the translated song was performed and thus strengthens the case for
Willinawaw as its author. During Timberlake's stay at Tomotly with
Ostenaco, the headman of Toquo had led a war party against the Shawnees, the only military action that Timberlake reports as having occurred during his visit and consequently the only opportunity he would
have had for hearing a war song performed under the circumstances
described by him and confirmed by Gearing. Moreover, he notes that
when Willinawaw's war party returned, they "marched around it [the
town-house] three times, singing the war-song, and at intervals giving
the *Death Hallow*" (1765: 92). At either the beginning or the conclusion
of this expedition, Willinawaw may have sung the song that Timberlake
translated.

The singing of war songs indeed figured into both the onset and conclusion of Cherokee military operations (Hudson 1976: 244). According
to Arthur Barlowe, Indians "sing songs as they march to wardes the
battell, in steede of drummes, and trumpets" (quoted in Davis 1978:
150). James Adair wrote that the leader of war parties among southeastern Indians (especially Cherokees) would lead their soldiers forth
singing "the solemn and awful song . . . which they never sing except at
that occasion." The rest of the party punctuated the song by "now and
then sounding the war whoo-whoop" (Williams 1930: 409). According

to manuscript data from the 1830s just before the removal of most of the Cherokees to Indian Territory, a declaration of war occurred when the "chief voted for war and, if the others [in council] assented, he went out in the yard, rattled his gourd, and raised the war whoop, singing a loud song of mourning for himself and his warriors" (Gilbert 1943: 351). Similarly—in a description reminiscent of Timberlake's depiction of the return of Willinawaw's war party—as a band of warriors returned from battle to their home community, "two men followed by the women of the village came forward to meet them singing a song in honor of the warlike deeds and valor of the warriors. The women caught up the refrain and praised the returning soldiers" (Gilbert 1943: 354). James Mooney, who collected several syllabary manuscripts of Cherokee sacred formulas and prayers in the late nineteenth century, suggested that Ostenaco's singing on setting out for Williamsburg and arriving in London—and perhaps Timberlake's translated war song, no matter by whom it was sung—were essentially prayers of protection, "sung or recited especially before setting out on a journey, or when about to meet a group of people" (Mooney and Olbrechts 1932: 149). Mooney also presented Cherokee words and English translation of a formula "What Those Who Have Been to War Did to Help Themselves," which had been written out for the ethnologist by A'wani'ta, a noted herb doctor. The "doctor" recited the formula on four consecutive nights for as many as eight soldiers who were about to go to war (Mooney 1891: 388–389). More than likely, the translated war song achieved some degree of efficacy through formulaic repetition that Timberlake did not reproduce.[5]

Though Timberlake—like most textualizers and translators of Native American poetry—did not attempt to reproduce the music to which the war song was sung, he did comment in general terms on Cherokee and other tribal musical performances. Instead of automatically dismissing such performances as nonmusical noise as did most of his contemporaries, Timberlake evinced some appreciation for the singing of the Cherokees. For example, he characterized the musical performances at the Green Corn Dance as "far from unpleasing" (1765: 65). He also noted that both words and music seemed to be composed "off hand, according to the occasion." Some tunes, he remarked, "especially those taken from the northern Indians, are extremely pretty, and very like the Scotch" (1765: 65). With Timberlake's comments we can compare the description of Cherokee singing at the installation of the "King of Estatowhee," as described by J. G. W. DeBrahm, who had been involved in constructing forts among the Cherokees prior to the rebellion. He contemptuously characterized the singers as "howlers," but admitted to the performance's rhythmic qualities: "altho' savage as the Music and their Dance appears, yet there is the nicest Regularity kept up" (De-Vorsey 1971: 112).

A consideration of factors contributing to Timberlake's pioneering translation must take into account the context out of which his efforts emerged, particularly the motivations that Timberlake may have had for the unprecedented inclusion of this translation among his ethnographic data. Simply put, his motivations probably derived from his desire to present the Cherokees in as positive a light as possible so that his own handling of them while in England would deserve an equally positive treatment, which in turn would merit his being recompensed for the expenses he had incurred. Like the Jesuits, writing ethnographic descriptions of potential converts in New France to solicit funds from evangelically minded donors, it was in Timberlake's best economic interest to depict the Cherokees as positively as possible. Fortunately for Timberlake, opinions regarding Indians, especially in the middle and southern colonies, had developed in ways that supported his personal motivations.

At least among the lettered inhabitants of the English colonies from Virginia southwards, opinion regarding Native Americans had swung toward the favorable end of the scale by the middle of the eighteenth century. From the beginnings of their encounters with the Americas, English explorers, traders, and colonists had brought a "split" image of American Indians with them (Sheehan 1980: 1–8). One side of that image, as Gary B. Nash has noted, portrayed Indians as "savage, hostile, beastlike" creatures who appeared to be "closer to the animal kingdom than to the kingdom of men" (1972: 199). The natives of the "New World," so this image suggested, were "bestial, cannibalistic, sexually abandoned, and, in general, moved entirely by passion rather than reason" (1972: 201). On the other hand, Indians, though certainly "backward," might be regarded more positively as "receptive" beings (a view shared with the Jesuit missionaries) with whom "amicable and profitable relations might be established" (1972: 205). When trade was the major goal of British-Indian contact, as it was in the late sixteenth and early seventeenth centuries, emphasis was placed on the Indians' "good" qualities; they were people who "could be wooed and won to the advantages" of commerce (1972: 206). But when competition for land emerged as British entrepreneurs tried to establish permanent colonies in America, it became efficacious for the British to view Native Americans as savage beasts with no human claims to territory (1972: 210). The savagery and ferocity of the Indians became especially evident in the massacre of 1622, which confirmed "that all Indians were inherently treacherous, cunning, and infinitely hostile" (1972: 218). This view endured until early in the following century.

But as Indians began to offer less overt resistance to British settlement, particularly in the way of attacks on established communities, and as they moved westward beyond the Appalachian frontier, intellectuals in the southern colonies began to revise their view of Native American cultures. Looked upon dispassionately, Indians and their way of life were seen to have such positive qualities as bravery, loyalty, hospitality, generosity, and cleanliness (Nash 1972: 225–228). Even when Indians came into open conflict with British colonists as they did during the Cherokee Rebellion, apologists attributed the hostilities more to the villainies of French and Spanish agitators than to the Indians themselves. By the 1760s, then, the prevailing view of the intellectual elite in the British colonies—among whom Timberlake should be numbered—recognized that Native Americans exhibited many admirable personal and cultural traits (cf. Davis 1978: 117–122).

Timberlake's ethnography emphasizes these traits. Although he does not sound just one note throughout the section of his memoirs that characterizes Cherokee culture, what emerges is a largely positive view of these Indians, one that certainly stresses the humanity they share with the British, especially those Londoners whom Timberlake believed were unjustly besmirching the images of Ostenaco and his companions. His treatment of Cherokee oratorical ability illustrates the generally positive image that Timberlake conveyed. "They have many of them a good uncultivated genius," he wrote, "are fond of speaking well, as that paves the way to power in their councils; and I doubt not but the reader will find some beauties in the harangues I have given him, which I assure him are entirely genuine" (1765: 54–55). Timberlake described the Cherokee language itself as "not unpleasant, but mostly aspirated, and the accents so many and various, you would imagine them singing in their common discourse" (1765: 54–55). In deference perhaps to his English readers—and in keeping with the "poverty-of-language" convention—he admitted not being able to "say much for the copiousness of their language" since "the ideas of the Cherokees are so few" (1765: 55).

The relatively sophisticated verses that comprised the translation of the Cherokee war song demonstrated the verbal agility and innate abilities of these Indians. Though lamentable from a present-day ethnopoetic perspective, Timberlake's choosing to dress it up in heroic couplets, an epic simile, and formal poetic diction may very well reflect his essential respect for it and for the Cherokees. He selected a verse form reserved for standard English poetic expression and thus signaled that he regarded at least the sentiments enunciated in the war song worthy of that expression. As Arnold Krupat has written of Timberlake's effort, its effect is to demonstrate to the reader that the works of Cherokee oral performers "could be taken as sophisticatedly artful—no less so than Western literary art" (1992b: 6). The singer of the war song—if not specifically Ostenaco, at least someone in a position of leadership much like his—should receive high regard and not be dismissed as the rowdy, uncouth savage that Timberlake's critics were apparently depicting. The oral poet who could produce verses such as these deserved respect— as should, incidentally, the Virginia lieutenant who escorted him (or someone like him) at his own expense all the way to London to meet the king.

Timberlake's efforts were undoubtedly enhanced by a predisposition for the British reading public to see evidence of artistry in oral expression. In 1760 James Macpherson had published the first volume of poetic material that he claimed to have lasted in Scots oral tradition for centuries since their original composition by the poet Ossian.[6] Other volumes appeared in 1762 and 1763, and 1765, the year Timberlake's memoirs came out, saw the publication of the collected poems of Ossian. As one commentator on Macpherson's Ossian poems remarked, they met "with immense and universal popularity." Soon translated into German, Italian, Spanish, French, Dutch, Danish, Swedish, Polish, Russian, and Greek, they elevated their translator to considerable prominence: "No English author before him, not Shakespeare, Milton, Addison or Pope, had found such hosts of foreign admirers; no one after him except Byron, hardly even Sir Walter Scott and Dickens, has had a greater fame" (Smart 1905: 11). The published works of Ossian stimulated an interest in apparently primitive poetry—an "Ossianic rage" (Friedman 1961: 174). As Alan Dundes has written, "The possibility of eliciting oral poetry from the Scottish Highlands meant that epic poetry could come not just from the ancients, but also from modern untutored peasants. The glorification of the noble savage sprang from the same source" (1985: 8). In fact, Thomas Percy may have taken the idea of looking for old ballads from Macpherson's publications. When the former published his *Reliques of Ancient English Poetry* in 1765 (again the significant year for Timberlake), he ushered in a ballad revival that further elevated the poetry of the unlettered (Friedman 1961: 199). Such poetry might also come from the Noble Savages of North America. Percy himself recognized the potential artistry of Native American oratory, a specimen of which he had acquired from Samuel Henley of the College of William and Mary. Calling it a "masterpiece of its kind," Percy noted that the oration was "exceedingly admired by all who see it." Its "eloquence of *sentiment*" addressed "the soul,—infinitely more forcible than the eloquence of language" (quoted in Davis 1978: 231). The German romantic philosopher J. G. Herder had also imagined that Ossianic materials might come from across the Atlantic:

> Read through the poems of Ossian. In all their themes they resemble those of another people that yet lives, sings, and does deed upon the earth, in whose history, without prepossession or illusion, I have more than once recognised that of Ossian and his forefathers. It is the Five Nations of North America [i. e., the League of the Iroquois]. Dirge and war-song, lay of battle and of burial, the praise of their ancestors,—everything is common to the bards of Ossian and the North American savages. . . . Travellers who knew the Scots, and who had long dwelt with the American Indians, acknowledged the manifest likeness in the songs of both nations. (quoted in Smart 1905: 7)

While Herder's statement appeared long after Timberlake's translation came out, the lieutenant—a lettered man who spent considerable time in London in the 1760s—was undoubtedly aware of the impact that Macpherson's Ossian poems had made. He may very well have made the transition from the Scots Gaelic bard of antiquity to contemporary Cherokee war leaders and recognized the potential for creating a favorable image of his Indians by hitching them to Ossian's bandwagon. Even in the unlikely event he was ignorant of Ossian, other indications of British receptivity to American Indian "poetry" abounded.

For example, the British public had already developed some interest in "quasi-Indian songs." During the 1760s at least two besides that of Timberlake became available in London: "The Other Thing, A Song, or the American Rabbit. Said to be lately presented to the Q. by a Chief of the Catawbas" (ca. 1760); and "Death Song of the Cherokee Indians. An original air, brought from America, by a gentleman, long conversant with Indian Tribes, particularly with the Cherokees. The words adapted to the air by a lady" (1762) (Davis 1978: 151).[7]

Timberlake may also have been aware of the controversy that surrounded Macpherson's Ossianic publications. The first published challenge to the authenticity of the material reputed to have been composed by the Scottish bard came in 1762, and from then until Macpherson's death in 1796, considerable attention was paid to whether Macpherson had actually translated his poems from oral tradition, had amplified them from a slim base in such tradition, or had manufactured them out of whole cloth (Smart 1905: 129–162). That controversy, which was particularly emphatic during the mid-1760s, may very well have come to Timberlake's attention and may have been a factor in his decision to render the war song in heroic couplets rather than in an approximation of the archaic style used by Macpherson—one that "connotes translation" (Murphy 1986: 576). Macpherson's Ossianic style has been characterized as a "rhetorical trick designed to express literality, faithfulness." Casting himself as "humble translator," Macpherson resorted to a style that reinforced that role (Murphy 1986: 576). Timberlake, on the other hand, heads off the sort of criticism that Macpherson faced by frankly admitting that he had omitted material from the "loose" original. His singer of war songs emerges as a poet, but Timberlake does not claim that he is translating with anything near fidelity.

Moreover, Timberlake's views regarding Native American poetic ability may have paralleled his notions of the Indians' technological potential. "They have of late many tools among them," he noted, "and, with a little instruction, would soon become proficient in the use of them, being great imitators of anything they see done" (1765: 61). Just as the Cherokees needed some European assistance before they could become fully effective users of implements, Timberlake may have sensed the need for some poetic assistance before an example of one of their songs could become fully effective literature. Anticipating the practice of the translators and textualizers from early in the nineteenth century whose work is treated in chapters 5 and 6, he found the basis for literary expression among the Indians themselves, but in order for that basis to become the sort of literature that would win a good opinion for the Cherokees, especially Ostenaco and the other visitors to Britain, it required some embellishment. Indirectly, then, Timberlake serves as a "founding instance of what would become . . . paradigmatic" (Krupat 1992a: 177) for translators of Native American verbal art even into the late twentieth century: a practice based on the recognition of the need to "improve" texts so that they would become both palatable and accessible for European and Euroamerican readers.

But Timberlake's influence in America was only indirect, if it existed at all. His memoirs were not reprinted on this side of the Atlantic until the twentieth century—and then only in relatively obscure editions. His book did exert some influence in England and on the continent in the years immediately following its 1765 publication. A German translation appeared in 1767, and a rendering into French came out in 1796.

The poet Robert Southey is reported to have used materials from Timberlake's Cherokee ethnography for his epic poem *Madoc*, originally published in 1805 (Williams 1927: 16). But those may be the only real effects of the work until its rediscovery by ethnographers like John Swanton early in this century and then by students of Native American verbal art more recently.

Timberlake ends the volume on a poignant note: "[W]hen I can satisfy my creditors, I must retire to the Cherokee, or some other hospitable country, where unobserved I and my wife may breathe upon the little that yet remains" (1765: 160). Maybe Mrs. Timberlake did enjoy some peace and prosperity among the Natives of North America. Henry Timberlake, though, died in London on 30 September 1765, perhaps even before his volume of memoirs saw print.

CHAPTER FIVE

"TOKENS OF LITERARY FACULTY"

*Texts and Contexts in
the Early Nineteenth Century*

Henry Wadsworth Longfellow had good reason to be concerned with how Native American verbal art was translated and presented to Euroamerican readers. His epic poem *The Song of Hiawatha*, issued in 1855—one of his most commercially successful works—drew extensively on the Ojibwa oral narratives that had appeared in *Algic Researches*, a collection published by Henry Rowe Schoolcraft in 1839. Unlike most twentieth-century commentators on Schoolcraft's work (which will receive specific attention in chapter 6), and even of some contemporary critics, Longfellow apparently assumed the material in *Algic Researches* to be very reliable. Shortly after its publication, he sent a copy of his poem to Schoolcraft as "an acknowledgment of my obligations to you; for without your books I could not have written mine." His letter accompanying the poem urged Schoolcraft to notice how "very faithfully" he had adhered to "the old myths" (Longfellow 1966–1982: 3:509).

Longfellow had been interested in Native American verbal art for at least a decade before the publication of *Hiawatha*. In 1843 he sent Ferdinand Freiligrath, who was later to translate Longfellow's epic into German, a copy of "a wild ballad, with the war-whoop in it," which had been translated from the original Choctaw by "a gentleman from Mississippi." One stanza of the three comprising the "Song of the Ancient Choctaws" suffices to give its flavor (Longfellow 1966–1982: 2:516):

> I slew the chief of the Muskokee,
> And burned his squaw at a blasted tree,

> By the hind-legs I tied up his cur.
> He had no time to fondle her.
> > Hoo! hoo! hoo! the Muskokee!
> > Wah! wah! wah! the blasted tree!

From this we get a sense of what Longfellow, the nineteenth century's most ambitious adapter of Native American verbal art into his own creative efforts, conceived American Indian poetry to be. More importantly for present concerns, the lines provided by the still unidentified "gentleman from Mississippi" represent the typical product of the textualization and translation of Native American verbal art in the early nineteenth century.

The loss of interest in Indian songs, stories, and orations after the seventeenth-century Jesuit *relations* began to reverse itself in the late eighteenth century—a development reflected not only by Henry Timberlake's translation of a Cherokee war song in 1765. Influenced by the interest in indigenous American languages among European philologists, the emergence of an Euroamerican intellectual class that included such figures as Thomas Jefferson, the continued expansion of the new nation westward into Indian lands, and the need by the federal and state governments for an Indian policy founded on reliable data about Native Americans (see Bieder 1986), students of American Indian cultures found an increasingly receptive audience for their books and essays, in which verbal art—represented by performance descriptions and (usually) translations of the words, particularly of oratory—appeared more and more often. Even the most casual observers of frontier America in the early nineteenth century might refer at least in passing to Native American verbal art.

As one might expect from the precedent set by Timberlake's war song, most translations of that verbal art fall far below the modern ethnographic criteria that increasingly stress the importance of accurately and comprehensively representing the entirety of the expressive event (Dundes 1964b). But as in the case of Timberlake or of the Jesuit writings, to ignore these early nineteenth-century translations may result not only in a failure to appreciate nineteenth-century attitudes toward Native American cultures, but even more importantly for this study's concerns, the loss of the insights into American Indian verbal art that can be salvaged from them. Consequently, this chapter aims at reconstructing some of the ideas that shaped how textmakers in the early nineteenth century went about their work. These shaping ideas— seldom articulated in straightforward statements of method—emerge in opinions about literature and about Native American cultures, especially languages, on the part of translators, critics, and even casual observers of Indian North America. They represent components of the textmakers' intellectual and esthetic milieu.

The principles that shaped textualization during the early nineteenth century developed primarily from beliefs about the probable effects of the impact of Euroamerican civilization on Indian cultures. Prevailing opinion, as developed from the complex image of the savage—"the primal myth in European culture" (Sheehan 1980: 1)—which, in varying refractions, had colored the attitudes of the Jesuit missionaries in New France, the New England Puritans, and the settlers in the middle and southern colonies, held that Native Americans as representatives of "savagism" stood in direct and inescapable opposition to civilization (Pearce 1988). For good or (more often) for ill, Native cultures appeared to be the obverse of Euroamerican ones and were destined to be totally obliterated as civilization fulfilled its westering destiny (Dippie 1982). The songs, stories, and orations of the Indians had so little artistic merit that they deserved the same fate as the cultures in general. Since they could be consigned to oblivion with no esthetic loss, translating them served at most the purposes of those who sought to understand Native Americans for the sake of efficiently subjugating them.[1] Representing this point of view was Lewis Cass, who as governor of Michigan Territory had begun a systematic study of that region's Native cultures in order to place their governance on a sounder footing than that provided by the reports of eastern armchair ethnologists (Brown 1953). In an essay in the *North American Review* in 1826, Cass, who became one of his era's most knowledgeable students of American Indians, found little to recommend itself in their mental culture, especially language, the principal key to a society's collective intellect according to contemporary philologists (Bieder 1986: 16–54, 155–160). Of the speech of the Wyandots, for example, he wrote, "Of all the languages spoken by man, since the confusion of tongues at the tower of Babel, it least deserves this character [of being harmonious and musical]. It is harsh, guttural, and undistinguishable; filled with intonations, that seem to start from the speaker with great pain and effort" (Cass 1826: 74).

As has often been the case when Europeans and Euroamericans have confronted representatives of "Otherness,"[2] Cass perceived the supposed debility of Native American languages as symptomatic of profounder problems for these "savages," the weakness and narrowness of their intellects. Following the "poverty-of-language" argument, he drew the conclusion: "The range of thought of our Indian neighbors is extremely limited. Of abstract ideas they are almost wholly destitute. They have no sciences, and their religious notions are confused and circumscribed. They have but little property, less law, and no public offences. They soon forget the past, improvidently disregard the future, and waste their thoughts, when they do think, upon the present" (1826: 79). While Cass himself had translated a couple of war songs from the Algonquian language of the Miami (1822: 1), he apparently agreed in principle with his protege C. C. Trowbridge, who replied to an item about Native American poetry on a questionnaire that Cass was distributing in the early 1820s that "at most it is nonsense. They have no poetry or rhyme in any shape" (quoted in Weslager 1978: 184). For Cass, Trowbridge, and indeed the majority of Euroamericans who shared their views, attempts to translate Native American verbal art into printed English were futile and useless except for immediate political advantage.

A more positive attitude maintained a precarious coexistence with the idea that the Indians and their way of life merely hindered the progress of civilization. Inspired more directly by the historical philosophy of such Enlightenment figures as Adam Ferguson than by the similar ideas of the Jesuit missionaries in New France, some Euroamericans believed that Native Americans were not necessarily in direct antithesis to civilization, but possessed—often, to be sure, in small portions— the spiritual and intellectual raw material to become civilized themselves. The idea that the Indian was a "European *manqué*" (Pearce 1988: 4) had asserted itself in the English colonies quite early—principally among the clergy, as it had in New France, and perhaps even in the Valley of Mexico, where its manifestation has been called the "Sepulveda Syndrome" from the Spanish theologian who cited European superiority as a model for the development of the "uncivilized" Natives of the Americas (Wynter 1976: 84; cf. Pagden 1982). For example, Alexander Whitaker's 1613 account of the Natives of Virginia in an appeal for funds to the Virginia Company in London noted in the Indians living near his church in Henrico "unnurtured grounds of reason" (1613: 27). As evidence of their potential for becoming civilized, he cited their archery skills, devotion to a (false) religious faith, concept of property, system of morality and law, and "rude kinde of Common-wealth" (1613: 25–27). Always in conflict with the more negative side of the split image that consistently figured in British conceptualizations of Native Americans, the position represented by Whitaker had helped to shape Henry Timberlake's Cherokee ethnography. Though less popular by the time the new American nation began to develop its Indian policies, it continued to provide a philosophical foundation for the efforts of those missionaries and others who glimpsed occasional intimations of civilizable potential among Native Americans. They saw Indians existing on the "horizon" of culture, as conceived by the developing anthropological consciousness of the early nineteenth century, yet capable of becoming fully "cultural" beings (McGrane 1989: 14, 108).

Indians possessed the raw materials of civilization and awaited only the molding influence of the Euroamerican: although this belief seems a natural parallel to the "virgin land" image (Smith 1950), which represented the "New World" as a fecund wilderness that needed only civilized cultivation to become an Edenic garden, supporters of the theory of Indian potential could cite in its favor some particulars of Native American cultures. Most prominent was the one that Cass cited as evidence of Native Americans' unredeemable savagism: language and verbal expression. The "natural eloquence" of the Indians—a trait recognized, of course, in North America as early as the seventeenth century by the Jesuit missionaries and with a long history of documentation in Euroamerican sources—had become an article of faith for some in the early nineteenth century. For instance, a firsthand account such as that of Moravian missionary John Heckewelder, first published in 1819, could heap praises on the unstudied oratorical style of Lenape public speakers: "The eloquence of the Indians is natural and simple; they speak what their feelings dictate without art and without rule; their speeches are forcible and impressive, their arguments few and pointed, and when they mean to persuade as well as convince, they take the shortest way to reach the heart" (1876: 132). A generation later, in 1849, Mary Henderson Eastman, an Army wife who had lived among the Dakota in Minnesota, offered similar testimony about the orator Shahco-pee: "We could but admire his native eloquence. Here, with all that is wild in nature surrounding him, did the untaught orator address his people. His lips gave rapid utterance to thoughts which did honor to his feelings" (1849: 115).

An unsigned piece in the periodical *Ariel* entitled "Indian Eloquence" echoed the sentiments of Heckewelder and Eastman from a secondhand perspective. With no apparent effort, the reviewer contended, the Native American " 'speaks as he doth ruminate,' in the sympathy of his heart." The language of Indians, the reviewer continued, "is the more beautiful, from its very simplicity and brevity. . . . Himself the child of Nature, he speaks her eloquent language. He has no far-fetched and pointless expressions—no poor and insufficient similes—but without circumlocution . . . he images forth his eloquence in every sentence"

("Indian Eloquence" 1828: 142). Such simplicity, though appealing to ears tuned by romanticism and jaded with the pomposities of Euroamerican rhetoric, represented only the beginnings of truly literary expression. Native American oratory, the special admiration of sympathetic Euroamericans, reflected "the infancy of language," according to a contemporary unsigned review of Heckewelder's book (Review of *An Account* 1819: 72), and stood ready to be guided to maturity by a sensitive, civilized intelligence. Hoxie Neale Fairchild was probably correct to suspect "that the rhetoric of the redman was more influential than his barbaric chants in establishing his poetic reputation" (1961: 492).

If Native Americans as persons possessed the fundamentals requisite for becoming civilized, and if their languages evinced the natural eloquence that lay at the base of civilized expression, their verbal art also exhibited literary potential. One of the earliest citations of this potential appeared in the first volume of the *North American Review* in 1815. In an essay in which he blamed the lack of a truly American literature on the sad circumstance of America's having no distinctive national language, Walter Channing suggested that "the oral literature of its aborigines" had to suffice as America's literary heritage, an opinion foreshadowing views that colored enthusiasm for Native American verbal art a century later. Channing portrayed Indian speech as "the very language for poetry" and argued that its "objects are the very elements for poetry" (1815: 313), and went on to rhapsodize, "[I]t is as bold as his [the Indian's] own unshackled conceptions, and as rapid as his own step. It is now as rich as the soil on which he was nurtured, and ornamented with every blossom that blows in his path. It is now elevated and soaring, for his image is the eagle, and now precipitous and hoarse as the cataract among whose mists he is descanting." American Indian verbal art, Channing asserted, provides "genuine originality." All who encounter it are delighted with "what appears its haughty independence" (1815: 314).

Channing was writing about Native American natural eloquence only a few decades after Alexander von Humboldt had characterized American Indian arts as "still at that stage" where they were of only "historic interest." Von Humboldt warned his readers, " 'Let us not be surprised . . . by the grossness of style and the incorrectness of the contours of the art of the peoples of America.' " But he anticipated a future "in which European would be able to assist the Amerindian in his slow and painful struggle toward" civilized life, including art (quoted in Pagden 1993: 8). As an advocate of the Indian-as-European-*manqué* view, Channing (and presumably von Humboldt before him) perceived Native

American verbal art as inchoate literature, rich in raw material that needed only the disciplinary guidance of the civilized literary artist to take its rightful place among the world's literatures. In the words of William Gilmore Simms, who wrote a generation later than Channing, the Indian "was not without very decided beginnings of a literature. This may have been rude enough . . . but it is sufficient that he had made a beginning" (1962: 137). That beginning—the inchoate features of Native American verbal art—was manifested variously to observers in the early nineteenth century. They mentioned most frequently the wealth of imagination, the employment of figurative tropes, rhythm, and parallelism.

Simms, who, like Longfellow, was heavily influenced by School-craft's translations of Ojibwa narratives in his own treatments of Indian themes in fiction, built a case for the richness of the Native American imagination in a review, published originally in 1845, of two of his mentor's books. He called attention to the "vast pneumatology" of the Indians "which found spirits, divine and evil,—as numerous as those of the Greeks or Germans—in their groves, their mountains, their great oceans, their eternal forests, and in all the changes and aspects of their visible world" (1962: 132). Simms believed that closer investigation of Native American supernaturalism would reveal a complexity of design that only bold and active imaginations could create. Pantheons of spiritual beings in various Native American cultures, particularly among Schoolcraft's Ojibwa, "attest all the preliminary conditions of an intellect" with literary tendencies (1962: 144). Native Americans' imagining the existence of beings beyond their sensory perception constituted, according to Simms, "the literary susceptibilities of a people" (1962: 132).

The figures of speech—especially metaphors—employed by Indian orators and other verbal artists caught the attention of many early nineteenth-century observers. Even Lewis Cass singled out the use of metaphor in a Miami lyric: " 'A clear sky' is a metaphorical expression, and conveys to an Indian the same ideas which are conveyed to us by the words good fortune" (1822: 1). But for the Michigan governor, such usage was a symptom of the Indians' poverty of language, which, as has so often been noted by Euroamerican commentators on the natural eloquence of "savages," required the use of concrete images where more civilized speakers had apt abstractions at their disposal. For others, though, figures of speech in Native American oral expression suggested literary potential. Among Cass's contemporaries, missionary John Heckewelder devoted the most systematic attention to tropes in Native American verbal art. Chapter 12 of his ethnographic study of the

Delaware treats "Metaphorical Expressions." Not finding them particularly appealing himself, Heckewelder regarded the Lenape fondness for metaphors as "to their discourse what feathers and beads are to their persons, a gaudy but tasteless ornament." However, he admitted that many literary traditions "[e]ven in enlightened Europe" viewed the use of metaphor highly and "the immortal Shakespeare, himself, did not disdain" to use this figure (1876: 137). Heckewelder then listed forty-nine examples of metaphors used by Indians (presumably Lenape) beginning with "*The sky is overcast with dark blustering clouds*" (meaning that some sort of trouble lies ahead) (1876: 137) and ending with "*To bury deep in the earth*" (meaning to dismiss something totally from one's memory) (1876: 140). For most commentators the copious supply of figures of speech, most of them involving comparisons between abstract concepts and natural phenomena, which came readily to Native American lips, testified to the literary possibilities of Native American intellects.

Although metaphor was the most frequently cited figurative device among early nineteenth-century commentators on Native American verbal expression, others were occasionally mentioned. For example, an anonymous essayist, writing on "Indian Eloquence" in *The Knickerbocker* in 1836, cited an example of irony. The Onondaga leader Grangula, in reply to a blustering Frenchman who was trying to persuade him not to trade with the British, responded to his interlocutor's empty threats by facetiously claiming that the Onondaga menfolk had had to restrain their women and children from attacking the very heart of the French garrison in Québec (quoted in Clements 1986: 6).

Rhythm and parallelism also received some attention from the Euroamericans who found intimations of literary potential in the stories, songs, and speeches of Native Americans. Heckewelder noticed that when Delaware warriors assembled to recount their battlefield exploits, they narrated in "a kind of half-singing or *recitative*" with a drumbeat regulating the rhythm of their presentations (1876: 210). Occasionally, literary critics tried to plug the rhythms used by Indian verbal artists into Euroamerican concepts of patterned repetition, as did the anonymous writer who, in an 1840 *Southern Literary Messenger* article, asserted that "the trochee predominates" in all Native American song texts, because "[t]he polysyllabic character of the language is adverse to short lively meters" ("North American Indians" 1840: 192). More often observers were content with vaguer descriptive terms—for example, the "expressive cadences" used by Rufus Sage, whom we met in chapter 2, to describe a Brulé oration (1846: 57)—when they emphasized the rhythm in Native American verbal art. Even more vague was Heckewelder's characterization of Delaware songs as "not without some kind of measure" (1876: 210). For most writers on the subject, American Indian verbal art demonstrated clear traces of rhythm, which suggested literary tendencies, but ones that only rarely had achieved sufficient sophistication to merit the metrical taxonomy used by civilized poets and their reviewers.

In a similar manner, hints of parallelism suggested Native American literary potential. In a letter to Ferdinand Freiligrath, Longfellow justified his stylistic appropriation of this device from the Finnish *Kalevala* for *The Song of Hiawatha*: "*parallelism* belongs to Indian poetry as well as to Finnish, and not only belongs to it, but in like manner is the 'rule and law of it'" (Longfellow 1966–1982: 3:517). Oft-cited comparisons between Native American oral poetry and the Hebrew psalms focused on parallelism as the literary feature most obviously shared by the two (e.g., "North American Indians" 1840: 192).

Yet these traits of Native American verbal art lacked what was needed to be truly literary in the Euroamerican sense, the only sense recognized by the textmakers of the early nineteenth century. Accordingly, in supposed fairness to the Indians and their groping efforts toward literary artistry, translators did what was necessary to convert the products of Native American oral expression into full-fledged literature.[3] That meant adding rhyme to song texts as well as regularizing their meters, extending metaphors and other figures more fully, fleshing out features of narration—especially scenic description and rounded characterization—that were absent or presented cursorily by Indian storytellers, deleting unsuitable materials such as vocables ("meaningless nonsense syllables") from songs and scatological elements from tales, and emphasizing features of narratives that conveyed straightforward or allegorical moral messages. In short, many translators who were sympathetic to Native American cultures saw their responsibility as one of molding "pre-literature" into true literature. Their attitude toward Indian verbal art paralleled that of the Reverend Samuel Parker toward Indian singing. In the mid-1830s Parker undertook a journey at the behest of the American Board of Commissioners for Foreign Missions that led him across the Great Plains and Rocky Mountains all the way to the Oregon coast. Parker was impressed with most of the Indians he met along the way. He characterized the intellectual power of the Oglalas, for instance, as "above the ordinary stamp" (1838: 63) and of the Pawnees as "very good, but [in] need [of] cultivation" (1838: 53). Remarking upon the singing of Plateau groups such as the Flatheads and Nez Perce, he mentioned their "flexible and sweet-toned voices." Parker was delighted to encounter in the western wilderness "the sounds of melody and harmony, even in the most simplified strains." Yet the singers, he added, "are conscious of the inferiority of their tunes to ours, and wished to be instructed in this department of knowledge" (1838: 241). Most Native oral performers might not be so reasonable as these Plateau singers who recognized the truncated development of their art, but certainly those Euroamericans who admired their literary potential were. Moreover, some precedent existed for "improving" the verbal art of "primitives" so that it might assume civilized literary status. Richard Steele, for example, had written of the process of translating songs from Lapland: "I was agreeably surprised to find a spirit of tenderness and poetry in a region which I never suspected for delicacy. . . . I have ventured to bind it in stricter measures, as being more proper for our tongue, though perhaps wilder graces may suit the genius of the Laponian language" (quoted in Fairchild 1961: 471). And more immediately pertinent to the specifics of the current topic, William Gilmore Simms's opinion that Native American verbal art "needed but little help from civilization to grow into a vast and noble literature" (1962: 144) and could be "wrought into symmetry and shape with the usual effects of time and civilization" (1962: 132) represented a viewpoint shared by many appreciative critics of American Indian cultures during the first half of the nineteenth century.

In her preface to Mary Henderson Eastman's *Dahcotah; or, Life and Legends of the Sioux Around Fort Snelling*, a Mrs. C. M. Kirkland fully articulated this set of ideas by calling attention to the literary powers of Native Americans as well as to their need for Euroamerican guidance:

> The Indians themselves are full of poetry. Their legends embody poetic fancy of the highest and most adventurous flight; their religious ceremonies refer to things unseen with a directness which shows how bold and vivid are their conceptions of the imaginative. The war-song—the death-song—the song of victory—the cradle-chant—the lament for the slain—these are the overflowings of the essential poetry of their untaught souls. Their eloquence is proverbially soaring and figurative. . . . They, indeed, live poetry; it should be ours to write it out for them. (quoted in Eastman 1849: x)

The idea that responsible textmakers, eager to represent Indian narratives, songs, and orations as literature, should do whatever was necessary to enhance their texts' literary features resulted in the publication of material whose Native qualities might be obscured beneath a heavy veil of Euroamerican accretions. Consider, for example, a Brulé tale reported by Rufus Sage (1846: 90–91) from the oral narration of an "old man" (Tahtunga-egoniska; see chapter 2) who told it in response to some heavy betting on a game of hand.[4] After an introduction in which he boasts of the rarity of his martial failures, the storyteller proceeds with his tale:

> We were proceeding against the Crows, and, like experienced warriors, had sent our spy in advance to look for the enemy. Hurrying on, in momentary expectation of a conflict, the stout hearts of our braves were appalled by his return without robe or arms, and scalpless—and with a face suffused in blood.
>
> This was his story: The enemy, aware of our approach, were awaiting us in great numbers. Encountering their scouts, he had been robbed and scalped, and left for dead. In this situation he lay till darkness shut down upon the mountain and the night-breeze gave him strength to meet us and advise our speedy return.

The party returns to camp in humiliation to face mockery for their lack of success. After "[t]hree moons sped," they go back to the field. Once again, the scalpless warrior acts as spy, but this time comes back triumphantly bearing two scalps. The party follows his lead, successfully engages the enemy, and finds among the dead "one whose scalp was wanting." The spy explains:

> "Behind yon hill," said he, "a fountain chants melody fit for warriors' ears,—let's to it, that we may drink."
>
> Following his direction, he led to a silvery spring overhung by crags and shaded by cottonwoods.

Here had occurred the event that accounted for the earlier humiliation of the spy, the two scalps he now possessed, and the scalpless dead Crow. The spy continued:

> "Three times has the night-queen turned her full face to smile upon the prowess of Lacota arms, since at this very spot I met an enemy. We rushed towards each other for the attack. 'Twas then he cried:
>
> " 'Are we not both braves? Why should we fight? When our people meet in the fray, then may we join arms,—till then, a truce.'

"To this I replied,

" 'Says Crowman peace?—then, be there peace.'

"Thus said, we shook hands and sat down by the fountain.

"Willing to amuse the foe, I gathered a pebble and proposed a game of hand. The challenge was accepted, and we played,—first, arrow against arrow, then bow against bow, robe against robe, and scalp against scalp.

"I was unsuccessful and lost all,—arrow, bow, robe, and scalp. I gave up all, but with the extorted promise that we should here meet again for another trial of skill.

"True to the word, we did meet again. We played, and this time, the Good Spirit showed me kindness.

"Winning back arrows, bow and robe, I staked them all against the lost scalp. The game was a close one; but again the Good Spirit favored me, and I won.

" 'Crowman,' said I, 'scalp against scalp.'

"The banter was accepted, and the play continued. He lost, and I, with my winnings, arose to leave.

" 'Warrior,' exclaimed the luckless player, 'meet me in the fight, that we may try the game of arms.'

" 'Thy words please me,' I answered. 'Will the Crowman name the place?'

" 'A valley lies beyond this hill,—there my people await their enemies, and there let me hope to see you with them.'

"To that place I led you. We fought and conquered. My opponent at play was among the slain. Need I tell you who took his scalp?"

Several elements in this story probably derive more from Sage than from the oral narrator. For instance, the scenic description (the "silvery spring overhung by crags and shaded by cottonwoods") must reflect the romantic literary esthetic of Sage's time. The careful pacing of the narrative with each phase of its progress fully explained and related to earlier phases suggests the hand of the textmaker, as does the attention to detail in the dialogue, especially the story-within-the-story. Throughout the piece, the language strikes twentieth-century ears as too formal for a story of this sort—a personal anecdote devoid of apparent ritual associations. And one must wonder to what extent the English words Sage has employed in his translation represent what the narrator actually said. For example, Sage uses the English terms "conflict," then "fray," and then "fight." Are these translations of the same Lakota word? If Sage's three words, in fact, reveal real variations in the narrator's diction, do they catch the different shadings of the original Lakota vocabulary? The mixture of somewhat formal, "literary" English usages (for instance, "a face suffused in blood") with stereotypical "Indianisms" ("Three moons sped")—a mixture reminiscent of the language of Black Hawk's autobiography—also raises questions about the tonal level of the text. Yet Sage did not see himself as being unfaithful to his originals. Regarding another translation of a Brulé story, he wrote, "In penning the above I was guided solely by the leading incidents as related in my hearing" (1846: 95). In truth, though, he was also guided by his sense of the literary—of what was necessary to make a good tale in a written European language.

Another example of how nineteenth-century Euroamericans handled the Native American verbal art they translated and published comes from a series of travel letters written by Charles Fenno Hoffman. The twenty-third in the series, sent from Prairie du Chien on the Upper Mississippi on 12 February 1834, concludes with an "Indian serenade." Unlike Sage, Hoffman included a Native-language version "in a sort of Lingua-Franca, or mongrel tongue, much used on the frontier, made up of words taken alike from the Ottawa and Ojiboai or Chippewa, and possibly other languages" (1835: 2:15) and a literal translation. However, the latter seeming "very bald," Hoffman tried to "better" it with his own rendering:

> Fairest of Flowers, by fountain or lake,
> Listen, my Fawn-eyed-one, wake, oh! awake.
> Pride of the prairies, one look from thy bower
> Will gladden my spirit, like dew-drop the flower.
>
> Thy glances to music my soul can attune,
> As sweet as the murmur of young leaves in June:
> Then breathe but a whisper, from lips that disclose
> A balm like the morning, or autumn's last rose.
>
> My pulses leap toward thee, like fountains when first
> Through their ice-chains in April toward Heaven they burst.
> Then, fairest of flowers, by forest or lake,
> Listen, my Fawn-eyed-one, wake, oh, awake!
>
> Like the star-paven water when clouds o'er it lower,
> If thou frownest, belov'd, is my soul in that hour;
> But when Heaven and Thou, love, your smiles will unfold,
> If their current be ruffled, its ripples are gold.

Awake, love! all Nature is smiling, yet I—
I cannot smile, dearest, when Thou art not by.
Look from thy bower, then—here on the lake,
Pulse-of-my-beating-heart—Wake, oh! Awake!

(1835: 2:18)

Whether Hoffman's translation represents an improvement over the Native original is questionable, but the "Indian Serenade" has become definitely more "literary" in the Euroamerican sense. Now it rhymes, has a regular meter, and develops its comparisons between the beloved and nature in an orderly fashion. Were it not for the Native-language version, which might allow a restoration of the original poetics in a translation,[5] Hoffman's treatment would be less valuable than Timberlake's treatment of a Cherokee war song seventy years previously, because it lacks the ethnographic setting provided by the lieutenant.

Though still subject to the "improving" processes that characterized translations of all American Indian verbal art at the time, orations, which proliferated in print in the wake of such famous speeches as that of Logan, celebrated by Thomas Jefferson, may have fared slightly better in the hands of early nineteenth-century translators than narratives and poetry did. Virtually every publication on Native American life from the period had at least one example of "Indian eloquence," and many travelers along the frontier who had no special interest in Indian cultures still found space for a speech or two in the published accounts of their adventures. For instance, John Bradbury, who toured the "Interior of America" for a couple of years beginning in 1809, appended an oration that Big Elk, an Omaha, delivered "over the grave of the Black Buffalo," a Teton leader, to the 1819 edition of his travel journal. The first few lines of Big Elk's speech addressed the inevitability of death and of concomitant grief in universal terms: "Do not grieve—misfortunes will happen to the wisest and best men. Death will come, and always comes out of season: it is the command of the Great Spirit, and all nations and people must obey. What is passed, and cannot be prevented, should not be grieved for" (Bradbury 1819: 228). The remainder of Big Elk's short address, apparently intended for the Euroamerican military officers who were present, dealt with his own death, which he predicted would be inglorious, and the disposition of his body—"my flesh to be devoured by the wolves, and my bones rattled on the plain by the wild beasts" (Bradbury 1819: 229).

Although, like the original of Sage's Brulé story, the original Omaha version of this oration is lacking (and although evidence exists of the latitude with which Euroamericans handled speeches by Indians in the nineteenth century [e.g., Kaiser 1987]), fewer reasons for doubting the reliability of the translation immediately suggest themselves. Though it articulates the image of the "vanishing American" that shaped Euroamerican thinking about the future of the Indians (Dippie 1982), such an image probably colored the view of many Native Americans. And while the diction obviously suggests the vocabulary of early nineteenth-century Euroamericans, no obvious stylistic accretions from literary romanticism stand out.

One of the ironies of textmaking during the early nineteenth century was that translators who regarded American Indian verbal art as the product of unredeemable savagery—and perhaps the unknown person who rendered Big Elk's speech into English was among them—probably produced more reliable materials than their more sympathetic contemporaries. Though fragmentary, Lewis Cass's handling of a Miami lyric may be nearer to what was actually performed than the translations by Sage and Hoffman reproduced above: "I will go and get my friends—I will go and get my friends—I am anxious to see my enemies. A clear sky is my friend, and it is him I am seeking" (1822: 1). Not only does this seem close, especially in its brevity and use of repetition, to songs in Ojibwa (like Miami, an Algonquian language) that Henry Rowe Schoolcraft (1848: 411–412) and later Frances Densmore (1910; 1913) published, but Cass and others who shared his view had no reason to embellish their materials. They regarded them as merely exhibits in the case against the savages of the American frontier and were consequently quite willing to preserve elements in them that did not meet Euroamerican literary expectations.

Yet except for orations, the examples of verbal art translated by proponents of the negative view are few. Such translation was more likely to be done by someone attuned to the civilizable potential of Native Americans. Our records of American Indian verbal art from the early nineteenth century are thus marked by a massive encrustation of Euroamerican embellishment with features judged essential to literature by the vaguely romantic esthetics of the early nineteenth-century textmakers and their contemporaries. Therefore, we can probably assume that such features of Native American song translations as rhyme and rhythms that fit neatly into the Euroamerican metrical system represent translators' outright additions. The same can be said of most attempts at characterization and scenic description that appear in narratives, especially when romanticized Euroamerican traits such as an abstract appreciation of natural beauty and a willingness to die for love are attributed to American Indians. Embellishments also included enhancing features that were already present in the Native American originals. For example, figures of speech were extended, and moral messages were enhanced. Stylistically, then, most translations from the early nineteenth century probably offer little that is truly Native American.

However, they do have some value. Though most early nineteenth-century translations of Native American verbal art are clearly inadequate for characterizing *how* the material was rendered in oral expression, they can provide insights into *what* was being expressed. I think we can trust, for example, Kirkland's list of song types among the Dakota reported upon by Mary Henderson Eastman as affording insights into what kinds of songs were being sung. We can also trust the general content of the Brulé narratives that Rufus Sage included in his account of his travels. Most of them, in fact, have more recent analogs, recorded in situations where their accuracy can be verified. For example, Nicholas Black Elk related a close parallel to the hand game story treated above to John Neihardt in 1944 (DeMallie 1984: 341–345). Twentieth-century versions and related texts for other narratives in Sage's book—even the Lover's Leap story treated in chapter 2—also exist (Around Him 1983: 23; Deloria 1932: 261–262, 266–268).[6]

Yet the most value to be derived from examining the work of early nineteenth-century translators may come from outside the linguistic texts themselves in the realm of context and performance. Many translators of and commentators on Native American verbal expression presented relatively thorough depictions of the conditions under which they heard stories, songs, and speeches, as well as of the ways the storytellers, singers, and orators delivered their material. Like similar materials from the writings of the Jesuit missionaries in New France, these records of natural situations afford insights often unavailable from later textmakers, who may have recorded and translated the words they heard more scientifically, but who frequently did so in highly artificial situations devoid of natural performance variables.

Examples abound in the writings of almost every figure whose opinion has been sampled above, even Lewis Cass. For example, the Michigan governor described in some detail how a Miami warrior would characteristically narrate his martial exploits during a war dance:

> He speaks with great emphasis and violent gesticulation—describes the number of the enemy whom he has killed; the mode in which he accomplished it, and the dangers he encountered. He relates the most minute circumstances, and shows the manner in which he crept silently upon his enemy, and took aim at his heart. He exhibits his scars, and relates the occasions upon which he received them. (Cass 1822: 2)

John Heckewelder portrayed a similar situation, but focused on the pattern of performance among several participants during a Lenape storytelling session:

> The oldest warrior recites first, then they go on in rotation and in order of seniority, the drum beating all the time, as it were to give to the relation the greater appearance of reality. After each has made a short recital in his turn, they begin again in the same order, and so continue going the rounds, in a kind of alternate chanting, until every one has concluded. (1876: 210)

Sage conveyed the style of the Brulé orator Marto-cogershne:

> He commenced in a low, distinct tone of voice. His robe, d[r]awn loosely around him, was held to its place by the left hand, exposing his right arm and shoulder. As he proceeded he became more animated, and seemed to enter into the full spirit of his discourse. The modulations of his voice, its deep intonations and expressive cadences, coupled with a corresponding appropriateness of every look and gesture, presented one of the most perfect specimens of delivery I ever witnessed. (1846: 57)

Even the most casual observer of Indians might provide valuable descriptions of the performance of verbal art. For example, Edwin James, who accompanied Stephen H. Long's expedition to the Rocky Mountains in 1819 and 1820, wrote of storytelling among the Omaha: "The narrator proceeds with a degree of gravity of feature suitable to the nature of the events of his story, and notes a variety of little circumstances in detail, which contribute much to give the whole an air of truth to his auditors, who listen with an undivided attention, uttering occasionally an interjection, as the feelings are excited" (1823: 329–330). Such performance descriptions provide insights into the nature of Native American verbal art that even the most accurately translated linguistic text cannot.

The idea that translators should transform Native American oral expressions into Euroamerican literature probably achieved its fullest explicit realization in the work of Schoolcraft, whose major publications spanned the period from 1839 until 1856 and whose work will be treated in chapter 6. But the attitudes toward American Indian verbal art that shaped this approach persisted after his work. For example, the phrase "tokens of literary faculty" quoted in this chapter's main title comes from the early 1880s, when John Reade used it in an address entitled

"The Literary Faculty of the Native Races of America," delivered to the Royal Society of Canada (1884: 25). Reade asserted that the Indians' literary faculty existed as a "*germ* in the legend of the tribe, the story-telling of the wigwam, and the speech-making of the council" (1884: 26, my emphasis). While many of Reade's contemporaries (some of whom are treated in chapter 7) had begun working from a different set of text-making principles—ones that foregrounded the scientific rather than artistic values of Native American verbal art—the idea that this art can and should assume the form of Euroamerican literature has not suffered a total eclipse. For example, during the second decade of the twentieth century translators and literary critics like Mary Austin saw parallels between the words of Native American songs and imagist poetry and reworked those songs accordingly (Castro 1983: 5–45). Even some ethnopoetically oriented translators have received criticism for imposing their own postmodern poetics on their translations rather than drawing upon the Native esthetic (Bright 1984: 83; see also chapter 2). Even if that critique is unfair to specific textmakers working from the perspective of ethnopoetics, it reminds us of a danger that any translator faces— a danger exacerbated when the material to be translated comes from a culture the translator perceives as undeveloped and emerges through a medium the translator considers inappropriate for literary expression. Albert Bates Lord's characterization of the textualization of epic poetry certainly applies to what happens to Native American verbal art: "[P]ublished texts do not reproduce what the singer said, but what the editor thought that the singer should have said, or intended to say" (1991: 36).[7]

The early nineteenth-century textmakers could not avoid this danger. The rhyming, regularly metered Choctaw war song that Longfellow sent to his friend Freiligrath illustrates in the extreme what usually happened to Native American verbal art in the hands of a Euroamerican translator.[8] Hence, the insights into American Indian verbal art gained from examining translated material from the early 1800s seem slight when compared with what we wished we knew and with what commentators, using material that is often no better, have sometimes claimed they did know. The period's major figure, Henry Rowe Schoolcraft, has also been the one whose translations have been most often used in ways for which they are not equipped. A close look at some of the ways in which Schoolcraft textualized the Ojibwa verbal art that he encountered in Michigan Territory during the 1820s and 1830s is the subject of the next chapter.

CHAPTER SIX

"ALL WE COULD EXPECT FROM UNTUTORED SAVAGES"

Schoolcraft as Textmaker

Best known today for providing Longfellow with the material from which the poet fashioned *The Song of Hiawatha,* his attempt at an American Indian epic, Henry Rowe Schoolcraft (1793–1864) was at various times during his life a businessman, chemist, geologist, explorer (he "discovered" the source of the Mississippi River), poet, lobbyist, and Indian agent.[1] Yet his most enduring accomplishment has been the translation and publication of Native American verbal art. One historian of folklore studies has characterized Schoolcraft as the "first scholar of American Indian culture to collect and analyze a large body of Indian folklore" (Zumwalt 1976: 44). Another commentator, though concentrating on Schoolcraft's fourteen-year career as an explorer, argues that he "for all practical purposes, discovered the existence of Indian mythological tales in the [Old] Northwest." His publication of these tales and associated research on Native Americans "contributed directly to the study of Indian cultures and the beginnings of American ethnology" (Bremer 1982: 51). Even with the predecessors that have been examined in the previous three chapters of this study, Schoolcraft should still be identified as the first Euroamerican actively and systematically to create a corpus of linguistic texts from Native American oral expressions. His immediate influence was felt by a number of American intellectuals of his own and the next generation, including not only Longfellow, but also Francis Parkman, William Gilmore Simms, and Henry David Thoreau (Marsden 1976: 169–175).

Schoolcraft apparently encountered American Indians within a holistic tribal setting for the first time in 1820 when, as a geologist accompanying Lewis Cass's unsuccessful expedition to locate the source of the Mississippi River, he had to interact with some of the Ojibwa inhabitants of what is now Minnesota. Richard G. Bremer has succinctly characterized Schoolcraft's reaction: "He clearly did not like what he saw. . . . he showed a marked distaste for the Indians themselves, whom he dismissed as begging savages and drunkards" (1982: 48–49). Schoolcraft himself writes explicitly of his response to the Ojibwa in the narrative journal of the Cass expedition that he published in 1821. For example, his entry for 29 June 1820 reveals his attitude toward the Native Americans he was seeing for the first time and focuses particularly on their ceremonial performances: "It [Ojibwa dancing and music] is perhaps all we could expect from untutored savages, but there is nothing about it which has ever struck me as either interesting or amusing, and after having seen these performances once or twice, they become particularly tedious" (1953: 128). The comments, which reveal what one commentator has called his "deep-rooted dislike of Indian music" (Stevenson 1973: 416), do little to anticipate Schoolcraft's subsequent interest in translating materials performed in similar situations.

Several factors may have contributed to Schoolcraft's change of mind about the Ojibwa and their culture. The first occurred in 1822 when Secretary of War John C. Calhoun—urged by Lewis Cass—appointed Schoolcraft as Indian agent at Sault Ste. Marie, where his charges would be the very Ojibwa who had appeared so distasteful to him when he first saw them. While it may seem inconsistent, given his published opinion of the Indians, for Schoolcraft to accept such a charge, financial exigency and hopes ultimately for an appointment as superintendent of a Missouri lead mine convinced him to take what he assumed would be a temporary position. When he arrived at this outpost of Euroamerican civilization in the remote Northwest, Schoolcraft met the family of John Johnston, an Irish fur trader who had immigrated in 1793. Johnston, who presided over a thriving establishment at the Sault, had married the daughter of Waubojeeg, a famous Ojibwa leader, and consequently exercised a good deal of influence among the Indians. The Johnstons' eight children reflected their bicultural heritage, and the family, with whom Schoolcraft boarded, awakened his appreciation for some features of Ojibwa culture. In 1823 he married the Johnstons' oldest daughter, Jane, but was also impressed with her mother.[2] Writing in his journal on 28 July 1822, he described the daughter of Waubojeeg: "Mrs. Johnston is a woman of excellent judgment and good sense; she is referred to on abstruse points of the Indian ceremonies and usages, so that I have in fact stumbled, as it were, on the only family in North West America who could, in Indian lore, have acted as my 'guide, philosopher, and friend'" (1851a: 107–108). Schoolcraft's relationship with the Johnstons was a fortunate one for the development of the ethnological study of American Indians, especially their verbal art. It was undoubtedly the most significant factor in changing his initial antipathy for the Ojibwa.

Schoolcraft's particular interest in "Indian ceremonies and usages" grew under the stimulus of his mentor Lewis Cass, who had been collecting data on various Native American groups by distributing questionnaires to persons having knowledge of or access to those groups (Brown 1953: 287–290). Cass asked Schoolcraft to complete one of these questionnaires. Though the questionnaire consisted of some 350 questions on twenty-one topics with more than four pages devoted to language alone, the newly appointed Indian agent exploited his position to obtain the required information.

Schoolcraft also became interested in the Ojibwa language, a concern influenced perhaps by his relationship with the Johnstons and by the fashionable interest in Indian languages among contemporary American intellectuals (Andresen 1990: 45–46; Bieder 1986: 16–54, 155–160). Some years later Schoolcraft was to write of the centrality of language to his studies. In a review of an archeological treatise published in *North American Review*, he noted that if the Indians "shall be found to have left no other monument to perpetuate their history, they offer, at least, a language [especially that of Algonquian-speakers], philosophical in its structure, rich in its powers of combination and syllabic transposition, and sonorous in the majestic flow of its polysyllables" (1837: 58). As linguistic data could supply lacunae left in the archeological record, it was also the principal source of "literary data from a people who are wholly destitute of books." The study of Native American languages "enables us . . . to speak with by-gone generations, by supplying facts for analogy and comparison." In fact, Schoolcraft opines in his archeological review, "by far the most enduring 'monuments' which our native tribes possess, are to be sought in the sounds and syntax of their languages" (1837: 34–35). Like many of his contemporaries who evinced even an avocational interest in studying American Indian cultures, Schoolcraft foregrounded linguistic research. A modern historian of nineteenth-century American ethnology has summarized the perspective that supported this foregrounding:

Unlike the relics of the mounds or the artifacts of living tribes, language was not originally a "thing of man's device" but the "spontaneous production of human instinct" modified by the mental and physical peculiarities of specific peoples and environments. Divinely inspired but humanly altered, language straddled the realms of the universal and the particular. Herein lay its great promise. Eventually, it seemed, knowledge of linguistic principles would permit philologists to distinguish between similarities due to mental structure and those due to historical connection. (Hinsley 1981: 47)

Schoolcraft's linguistic interests (as well as his developing concerns with Ojibwa culture in general) would also help him, he hoped, to avoid social blunders with his charges that would hinder his work at the agency (Bremer 1987: 92).

Schoolcraft's journal for 28 July 1822 records how he used his position in the agency to obtain ethnological and linguistic materials: "My method is to interrogate all persons visiting the office, white and red, who promise to be useful subjects of information during the day, and to test my inquiries in the evening by reference to the Johnstons, who, being educated, and speaking at once both the English and Ojibwa correctly, offer a higher and more reliable standard than usual" (1851a: 107). The association with the Johnstons joined other factors in awakening Schoolcraft's interest in the culture he had found so "particularly tedious" in 1820. His attitudes were further transformed by his developing religiosity, which climaxed in 1831 when he made a public profession of his Christian faith.

Schoolcraft's religious preoccupations had been evident throughout most of the 1820s and manifested themselves in his abhorrence of alcohol, his strict sabbatarianism, and what one commentator has called his "somewhat priggish village-bourgeois outlook" (Bremer 1982: 46). It also affected the way he viewed his Indian charges. More and more, he recognized "civilized" humanity's responsibility to Native Americans as well as the fundamental kinship of all peoples. For example, in his account of his explorations of the central Mississippi Valley published in 1825, he responded to a Native American woman's killing herself and her children instead of allowing their capture with a sensitivity—albeit of the patronizing variety—that recalled the attitudes of the Jesuits in New France: "We should charitably consider these barbarities as the effects of wrong education, and false ideas of independence and heroism, while we ought to regard their virtues as the unerring evidences

timations of how faithfully his translations represented Native American storytelling and style. On one hand, an unsigned evaluation of *Algic Researches* that appeared in the *North American Review* in 1839 assumed that Schoolcraft had not polished the material at all. If he had done so, the reviewer argued, "[t]he standard which we now have for measuring Indian intellect, and judging of Indian imagination and powers of invention, of Indian mythological notions and superstitions . . . would have been falsified and erroneous" (Review of *Algic Researches* 1839: 360). Writing in the same periodical in 1847, an anonymous reviewer opined in an evaluation of Schoolcraft's report on the Iroquois done at the behest of the legislature of New York that a "tradition" published therein was "doubtless given as it was received. It has all the marks of Indian crudeness and extravagance about it, and may therefore be regarded as genuine" (Review of *Report on the Census* 1847: 312). The same reviewer had noted earlier in the piece that the Iroquois materials in Schoolcraft's report had "doubtless lost their original texture, have lost nearly all that gave them, in their day of freshness, their beauty, their force, and their distinctiveness of character," but apparently attributed the material's devolution to the vagaries of oral tradition and the deleterious effects of encounter with Euroamerican civilization rather than Schoolcraft's textmaking practices (1847: 309).

On the other hand, a Dr. E. Diffenbach complained of the narratives in *Algic Researches* that Schoolcraft "had too much modernized their dress." If Schoolcraft could "reduce that dress" and present the material "however abrupt and unconnected, as they fell from the mouth of the narrator," he might be able to "remove all doubt that he had taken poetic liberties" with them (quoted in Bremer 1987: 251). Though influenced by Schoolcraft in his own work on American Indian history, Francis Parkman believed that *Algic Researches* represented a missed opportunity. Attributing the translations to Jane Johnston Schoolcraft, "an educated Ojibwa half-breed," Parkman believed their value to be "much impaired by the want of literal rendering, and the introduction of decorations which savor more of a popular monthly magazine than of an Indian wigwam" (1983: 400–401).

Because almost invariably condemnatory, modern opinion regarding Schoolcraft's work has not been so mixed. For instance, while recognizing that Schoolcraft's efforts serve "as a landmark in the history of the recording of American Indian tales," Stith Thompson questioned the worth of the translations he produced: "Unfortunately, the scientific value of his work is marred by the manner in which he has reshaped the stories to suit his own literary taste. Several of his tales, indeed, are distorted almost beyond recognition" (1929: xv). Recently, Arnold Krupat has written of Schoolcraft's handling of an Ojibwa song, "The translation is as typical of its period's deliquescent Romanticism as Timberlake's couplets are of the high Drydenesque" (1989: 103). Even more sympathetic critics of Schoolcraft have realized that he "did not merely translate, he interpreted" (Bierhorst 1969: 3). Why did Schoolcraft diverge in his practice from his professed regard for the accuracy of his material, particularly when that accuracy was essential if the narratives were to reflect ways in which Indians thought? A historian of folklore studies has suggested that Schoolcraft had an eye on the marketplace when he failed to reproduce the narratives exactly as he had heard them—a suggestion that finds support in his customary impecunious circumstances and his continued concern with self-promotion (Zumwalt 1976: 51).[4] Perhaps more to Schoolcraft's credit, it has also been suggested that his "improvements" represented an attempt to "stress the fundamental humanity" of the Indians (Bremer 1987: 252) and—by offering literary materials that fell toward the "Identity" pole of the continuum—perhaps even to influence federal policy in favor of Indians (Bremer 1987: 353). Moreover, Schoolcraft probably received most of the verbal art which he published in English translations made by his wife and her Ojibwa relatives, especially her brother George Johnston (Bremer 1987: 249). Yet the contradiction between Schoolcraft's practice and principle is probably more evident to twentieth-century readers than it would have been to him. He regarded Ojibwa oral narratives as literature, and his notions of what literature should be—his poetic esthetic—shaped how he conceptualized the linguistic texts that he made from the storytelling of Ojibwa narrators. The way in which Schoolcraft presented the narratives resulted in what for him was an *accurate* version of materials that were basically *literary*. Not to have made changes in them would have betrayed their esthetic quality and made them less literary. To see Schoolcraft's poetic esthetic more clearly, it is useful to examine how he treated Native American songs and oratory, which he collected along with the narratives.

In an essay entitled "Indian Music, Songs, and Poetry," which first appeared in *Oneóta*, issued serially by Schoolcraft in 1844,[5] he noted the difficulty of translating such material. While admitting that the "structure and flexibility" of the Ojibwa language was "highly favourable to this kind of wild improvisation" that characterized Native American songs, he lamented, "[I]t is difficult to translate, and next to impossible to preserve its spirit" (1848: 223). Regarding vocabulary, he averred, "[T]o find the equivalent single words in translation, appears often as hopeless as the quadrature of the circle" (1848: 224). Schoolcraft's solution to these problems seems to have been to reshape the Indians' verbal art into linguistic texts that as far as possible met his own criteria for literature—standards that were, in fact, those generally held by his contemporaries, some of whose work was treated in chapter 5. His self-imposed task was to create a recognizable *literature* out of an *illiterature*, but in doing so he was unable "to extricate himself from the literary graces" of the mid-nineteenth century (Hays 1964: 10). Though strongly worded, Elémire Zolla's evaluation of Schoolcraft's translation practice is probably not far from the mark: "[A]ctually he was copying the mincing, affected grace of Romantic verse. . . . Schoolcraft could not escape the attraction that fashionable poetic forms exerted on him. . . . Whatever purely oral and roughly sketched elements the originals may have had, he was sure to polish" (1973: 149–150).

Schoolcraft had discovered Ojibwa song and oratory before he encountered storytelling, which he probably encountered first in 1823. His response to his initial experience with Native American singing has been noted above, but a few years' intense contact with the Ojibwa, particularly his wife's relatives, mitigated his opinion to the extent that he was grudgingly ready to assign the term "poetry" to some of what he heard—"if it be not too violent an application of the term," as he hedged (1825: 427). Moreover, he came to admit that some of the Indians' public speeches, "although unmeasured, partake of the spirit of poetry" (1825: 432). Writing in his journal for 29 September 1826, he elaborated on the "poetic" elements of Native American oratory: "The great simplicity, and occasional strength, of an Indian's thoughts, have sometimes led to the use of figures and epithets of beauty. He is surrounded by all the elements of poetry and eloquence—tempests, woods, waters, skies. . . . His very position—a race falling before civilization, and obliged to give up the bow and arrow for the plough—is poetic and artistic" (1851a: 256). From this the fundamentals of Schoolcraft's poetic esthetic begin to emerge: the necessity of figures, the use of nature—particularly in its wildest manifestations—as the basis for those figures, an element of mystery, and at least a hint of melancholy.

Additional components of his poetics may be seen in material written much later in his career. For example, the questionnaire that he distributed to garner information to include in his congressional study of the American Indians included the following questions about "Indian songs": "Is there any rhyme in them? Are the words collocated so as to observe the laws of quantity? In other words, are they measured, or are the accents in them found to recur in fixed and regular intervals?

(1851b: 555). Some of the points raised by these queries also appear in his discussion of Algonquian-speaking orators in the sixth volume of the congressional study: "Their public speakers cultivate a particular branch of oratory; but they appear to have an accurate ear for the rythm [sic] of a sentence, and a delight in rounding off a period: the language affords great facilities for this purpose, by its long and stately words, and multiform inflections" (1857: 661). Thus, a concern with the way in which language sounds—especially the devices of rhyme and meter conventional in most poetry in English in the mid-nineteenth century— becomes a part of Schoolcraft's poetic esthetic.

The most complete statement of this poetic esthetic appears in "Indian Music, Songs, and Poetry." Early in the piece, he quotes "a modern American writer" (not identified) as claiming that the Indian's poetic capabilities are virtually instinctive: " 'He has animating remembrances—a poetry of language, which exacts rich and apposite metaphorical allusions, even for ordinary conversation—a mind which, like his body, has never been trammelled and mechanized by the formalities of society, and passions which, from the very outward restraint imposed upon them, burn more fiercely within' " (1848: 221). Yet Schoolcraft himself is not so positive about the products of this romantic Noble Savage's natural inclinations toward the poetic. For instance, he notes "the idiomatic and imaginative peculiarities of this species of wild composition—so very different from every notion of English versification." The poetry of Indians, he continues, has "no unity of theme, or plot, unless it be that the subject, war for instance, is kept in the singer's mind." Moreover, "both the narration and description, when introduced, is [sic] very imperfect, broken, or disjointed" (1848: 223). Indian oral poets cannot develop and organize their thoughts: "Prominent ideas flash out, and are dropped" (1848: 223). And they fail to fulfill their gift for figures of speech because references to the natural world around them "are mere allusions, or broken description, like touches on the canvass, without being united to produce a perfect object. The strokes may be those of a master, and the colouring exquisite; but without the art to draw, or the skill to connect, it will remain but a shapeless mass" (1848: 224). Essentially, Schoolcraft's poetic esthetic—in addition to emphasizing figures referring to wild nature and sound patterns familiar in English verse—required the sustained development of the figures and the themes they conveyed that were stressed by contemporary enthusiasts for Native Americana.

Schoolcraft believed that Ojibwa war songs demonstrated both the raw, natural poetic capacity of Indians and their inability to discipline that capacity into developed literature. Writing in the second volume of his congressional study, he indicated that the Ojibwa warrior, who performed his songs to arouse the militaristic spirit in his listeners,

> has no stores of measured rhymes to fall back on. All he can do is to utter brief and often highly symbolic expressions of courage, of defiance, of indomitable rage. . . . Under such circumstances, a few short and broken sentences are enough to keep alive the theme in his mind; and he is not, probably, conscious of the fact, that there is not enough said, in the theme of his song, to give much coherence to it. Such a song is, indeed, under the best auspices, a mere wild rhapsody of martial thought, poured out, from time to time, in detached sentences, which are, so to say, cemented into lines by a flexible chorus and known tunes. (1852: 60)

When he presented the translation of such a song in *Oneóta*, Schoolcraft included the note, "It will be perceived there is a unity in the *theme*. . . . This unity I have favoured by throwing out such stanzas as mar it, and afterwards arranging them together" (1848: 411, emphasis in original).

Since Schoolcraft viewed songs *"as facts or materials,* in the mental condition of the tribes" (1848: 229, emphasis in original) and as a "chapter in the history of the human heart, in the savage phasis" (1848: 397), we can now return to his treatment of narratives, which, of course, had the same significance for him. As he consciously or unconsciously imposed his poetic esthetic on the songs he presented to his readers, even knowing that he was presenting them primarily as sources of ethnological and psychological data rather than as art, so he did with narratives. He preserved as far as possible the figures of speech and references to wild nature—we can assume it was unnecessary to add these literary essentials to what the Native American narrators had said—as well as the tendency of the stories to become "allegory," a term he often applied to the tales he collected (e.g., 1851a: 109; 1851b: 316; 1853: 314). But he created for the tales a structured, orderly development, reflecting his own view of what their status as literature required. He also produced patterns of sound in his translations that conformed more to English-language prosody than to their expressions in the Native language. If the songs and stories from Native American verbal art were indeed literature, they should evince the qualities of literature—even if some of those qualities had to be added by the textmaker.

In addition to stylistic changes that his poetic esthetic demanded, Schoolcraft effected some substantive emendations in the verbal art he presented. Perhaps the most frequently cited of these changes was his elimination of what he considered to be indecent (Hays 1964: 19; Mc-Neil 1980: 143). Of course, some of what he heard had already passed through the self-censorship of the storytellers, who may have had enough previous experience with Euroamerican audiences of religious inclination to realize what was acceptable (Bremer 1987: 250). School-craft perceived the omission of "grossness" (1855: 246) and "vulgarities" (1856: viii) as a positive feature of the translations he published. He also deleted "the repetition of tedious verbal details," redundancies that in oral expression "serve no purpose . . . but to while away the time, while they hinder the denouement of events of the story" (1855: 246). Yet while he was willing to omit substance from the narratives "to avoid tediousness of narration, triviality of circumstance, tautologies, [and] gross incongruities," he asserted that he was guilty "of adding no incident and drawing no conclusion, which the verbal narration did not imperatively require or sanction" (1856: viii–ix).

When Schoolcraft's translations have been criticized by twentieth-century commentators, the convention has been to dismiss them as "sentimental" (e.g., Marsden 1976: 162; Thompson 1929: xv)—a charge so vague as to be of little use. What should be emphasized is that Schoolcraft—like the other textmakers examined in earlier chapters—brought to the study of Native Americans and their verbal art the pre-conceptions of his era, particularly the notion that the Indian was the "Vanishing American." Extensively studied by historians (e.g., Dippie 1982), this idea—which has been pretty much a constant in Native American-Euroamerican relations—arose from "the impression of the Indian as rapidly passing away before the onslaught of civilization" (Berkhofer 1978: 88). Schoolcraft's acceptance of this notion influenced what he found to be the recurrent theme in much Native American verbal art, probably shaped what his translations came to highlight, and perhaps provided the basis for the charges of "sentimentalism" leveled against him. For he perceived the Indian as afflicted with a deep malaise, characterized by a melancholy as profound as any suffered by a romantic poet. He wrote,

> Wherever Indian sentiment is expressed, there is a tendency to the pensive—the reminiscent. . . . He is a man of reminiscences, rather than anticipations. Intellectualization has seldom enough influence to prevail over the present, and still more rarely over the future. The consequence is, that whenever the Indian relaxes his sternness and insensibility to ex-

ternal objects, and softens into feeling and sentiment, the mind is surrounded by fears of evil, and despondency. To lament, and not to hope, is its characteristic feature. (1853: 327)

Schoolcraft discovered in Native American verbal art an abundance of the literary potential that some of his contemporaries were noticing. His task as textmaker was to ensure the realization of that potential. He believed that the "hunter state" in which the American Indian lived resulted from a process of devolution. In volume two of his congressional report, he wrote, "[T]he hunter state is a declension from the industrial, and . . . barbarism assumes its character, not only as the antagonistical point to civilization, but as a falling from it, and a direct consequence as [sic] the neglect of its higher and sublime principles" (1852: 44). American Indians still possessed the raw materials of their once-higher existence, but those materials required refining by civilized humanity. Likewise, Native American oral expressions, especially the most artistically rich performances, possessed the raw materials of literature, but needed the guiding pen of the textmaker to fulfill their potential.

Unsurprisingly, Schoolcraft did not attempt to reproduce paralinguistic and kinesic elements of verbal artistry in his texts—something that has been attempted systematically only recently. However, he was aware that Native American storytellers, singers, and orators relied upon more than just what they said to be effective in their presentations. For example, he characterized the pacing used by Mongazid, a noted Ojibwa orator:

He excels in that rapid, continuous flow of utterance, in which it seems to be the object of the speaker to go on, without a pause, as long and as vehemently as possible. In listening to this kind of outpouring of words, it seems as if a thousand syllables and words were amalgamated into one, and as if to pause in the middle, or at any intermediate point, would be to break the harmony, or to mar the sense. (1828: 105)

Schoolcraft more fully characterized the oral style employed by Native American orators in the introductory notes to his poem *Alhalla, or The Lord of Talladega,* which appeared in 1837:

Nothing is more characteristic of their harangues and public speeches, than the vehement, yet broken and continued stream of utterance,

which would be subject to the charge of monotony, were it not varied by
an extraordinary compass in the stress of voice, broken by the repetition
of high and low accent, and often terminated with an explanatory vigor,
which is sometimes startling. It is not the less in accordance with these
traits that nearly every initial syllable of the measure chosen is under accent. This at least may be affirmed, that it imparts a movement to the
narrative, which, at the same time that it obviates languor, favors that
repetitious rhythm, or pseudo-parallelism, which strongly marks their
highly complex lexicography. (1956: 302)

Schoolcraft reserved his most extensive and precise performance
notes for Ojibwa singing. For example, he commented that in general
Native American songs "are rather *recited,* or *chanted,* than sung"
(1848: 225, emphasis in original). More particularly, he described how
war songs were rendered in oral performance:

They are accompanied by the drum and rattle, and by the voice of one or
more choristers. They are repeated slowly, sententiously, and with a
measured cadence, to which the most exact time is kept. The warrior
stamps the ground as if he could shake the universe. . . . and while he
stamps the ground with well-feigned fury, he fancies himself to take
hold of the "circle of the sky" with his hands. Every few moments he
stops abruptly in his circular path, and utters the piercing war-cry. (1852:
59)

Though less vividly, Schoolcraft also described the ways in which Indian women performed the "Nursery and Cradle Songs of the Forest":
"[N]othing can be more delicate than the inflexions of these pretty
chants, and the Indian woman, like her white sister, gives a delicacy of
intonation to the roughest words of her language" (1848: 391).

Schoolcraft's most precise performance notes accompany the songs
he collected from Catherine Wabose, an Ojibwa woman whose life history he also recorded. He preceded the songs with some general comments about performance style, which incidentally relieved him of the
responsibility of recording the music of the songs:

It is a peculiarity observed in this and other instances of the kind, that
the words of these chants are never repeated by the natives without the
tune or air, which was full of intonation, and uttered in so hollow and
suspended, or inhaled a voice, that it could require a practised composer

to note it down. The chorus is not less peculiarly fixed, and some of its guttural tones are startling. (1851b: 397)

For some of Wabose's individual songs, he included specific comments on how they were performed: "Chorus of strongly accented and deeply uttered syllables" (1851b: 398); "Sharp and peculiar chorus, untranslatable" (1851b: 399); "Slow, hollow, peculiar chorus" (1851b: 399). Of course, these comments give only a vague and highly prejudicial account of performance style, but they do reveal Schoolcraft's recognition that how the linguistic texts were expressed orally merited some comment. Apparently, though, he did not deem the performance style of the narratives worth even the amount of commentary he offered for songs and oratory.

We are left, then, with materials that lack many of the most fundamental elements required by ethnographic textmakers in the late twentieth century. However, some of the original performance values may nonetheless be recovered. For example, both Dell Hymes (1981: 39–42) and John D. Nichols (1991) have devoted some attention to Schoolcraft's oft-reprinted linguistic text that he entitled "Chant to the Fire-Fly." Schoolcraft included the original-language version, a "literal" translation, and this "literary" translation (perhaps prepared by Charles Fenno Hoffman) when he published the poem in *Oneóta*:

> Fire-fly, fire-fly! bright little thing,
> Light me to bed, and my song I will sing.
> Give me your light, as you fly o'er my head,
> That I may merrily go to my bed.
> Give me your light o'er the grass as you creep,
> That I may joyfully go to my sleep.
> Come, little fire-fly, come, little beast—
> Come! and I'll make you tomorrow a feast.
> Come, little candle that flies as I sing,
> Bright little fairy-bug—night's little king;
> Come, and I'll dance as you guide me along,
> Come, and I'll pay you, my bug, with a song.
>
> (1848: 230)

Using the text in Ojibwa, Nichols could do a careful comparative analysis and produce a translation of his own that "follows the word repetitions in the Ojibwe text without adding others and attempts to mimic the syllabic structure of the Ojibwe text by using line lengths of six and four syllables":

> Firefly, flash light for me
> Before I sleep.
> Come here, come here!
> Firefly, firefly,
> A lantern, a lantern. (1991: 124)

Of course, Nichols cannot restore kinesic, paralinguistic, and contextual aspects of the performance that generated Schoolcraft's linguistic text, but he can reproduce some of the indigenous poetic esthetic—which contrasts markedly with Schoolcraft's own literary consciousness revealed in the literary translation, which one commentator has characterized as "simplistic, jog-trot, juvenile verse (reminiscent of 'Twinkle, Twinkle, Little Star')" (Zolla 1973: 150).

Unfortunately, Schoolcraft published few Native-language materials, so Hymes's and Nichols's leads cannot often be followed. We must accept that we can learn very little about stylistic features—linguistic or performance—from what Schoolcraft published. Nor can we really be sure that the translations represent the structures and patterns of the Native American originals. But perhaps we can learn something about the content of Ojibwa verbal art during the 1820s and 1830s from Schoolcraft's material. His narratives, songs, and orations let us identify some of the particular focal points that Indian performers believed important enough to stimulate artistic expression. We can also learn something about how that artistry shaped its content, for although Schoolcraft may have enhanced the importance of some figures and diminished the significance of others, he does provide us with some introduction to the nature of figurative language among Ojibwa performers almost two centuries ago. The student of American Indian verbal art who relies uncritically on Schoolcraft's work will be misled about that art, but understanding how he implemented ideas about American Indians and about literature that figured into his era's intellectual ambience provides a way to salvage something of value from what he produced.

"THE TRUE PRESENTIMENTS
OF THE INDIAN MIND"

Linguistic Texts as Data Sources

Though Henry Rowe Schoolcraft strove might-
ily to make his translations of Ojibwa oral narratives and other verbal art accessible as literature to a Euroamerican reading audience, he
shared his ostensible purpose in publishing the
material with the Jesuits in New France, Henry
Timberlake, his own mentor Lewis Cass—in
fact, with most who had summarized or tex-
tualized Native American oral expression. Orations, stories, poems,
and ritual discourse had documentary functions, they believed, and provided insight into the people who produced them. Such insight might
show the innate humanity and susceptibility to the Christian message
of the *sauvages,* make them more comprehensible to those who would
subdue them, trace their pre-contact histories, explore their languages
as *parole,* or afford a general overview of their mentality. The last provides the stated purpose for the fourth incarnation of Schoolcraft's rendering of the Ojibwa corn-origin myth, which appeared in 1859 in the
Southern Literary Messenger under the titles "Mental Character of the
Aborigines" (first section) and "Mental Traits of the Aborigines" (second section). Introducing the story itself, which appears in the most
ornately Euroamericanized of his renderings, Schoolcraft argues that
such oral narratives are "the true presentiments of the Indian mind, and
show more than any other species of inquiry, or research, their opinions
and beliefs on life, death and immortality" (1986: 56).

Indeed, much of the contemporary reaction to the Native American
verbal art published by Schoolcraft emphasized its documentary potential. One anonymous reviewer of Schoolcraft's study of the Iroquois for

the New York State legislature characterized the Ojibwa oral narratives published in *Algic Researches* as "the broadest and clearest mirror of the red man's intellect that has ever been set before the public eye" (Review of *Report on the Census* 1847: 296). Later the reviewer addressed at length the ethnological and historical significance of representations of verbal art:

> When we are looking for proofs of this intellectual power in the Indians, in what shape do we expect to find them? They have been a barbarous people from the beginning. With such a character, Indian intellect can be expected to display itself only in their traditions. Imagination is a faculty that develops itself in the infancy of a nation; it is strong almost in proportion as the nation is rude, and gradually loses its force step by step with the advance of civilization. . . . These traditions are the coins of the aborigines, often obscured and overlaid with extraneous matter; still, they are almost the only remains that bear the stamp of remote ages. (1847: 309–310)

The generation of serious students of Native American cultures who succeeded Schoolcraft and absorbed the principles of the new "science" of anthropology continued to foreground the documentary function of linguistic textualizations of Native American oral expression. Their approach to the process of textualization, which became formalized under the auspices of the Smithsonian Institution's Bureau of Ethnology and in Boasian academic anthropology, yielded a healthy commitment to accuracy in recording and transcribing the verbal component of the material they encountered. But it also resulted in their using methods of recording that removed the verbal art from its usual performance situations and consequently in their ignoring its artfulness, either because they viewed that artfulness as secondary to the material's value as a data source, because they believed it to be unrecordable and/or untranslatable, or because—as chapter 2 suggests—the circumstances of recording minimized opportunities for artistry.

Many students of Indian cultures anticipated this documentary emphasis. Using this perspective, we might examine the Jesuit relations, the accounts of discoverers, explorers, and settlers in the British colonies, captivity narratives, the literature of westward expansion, or the work of Schoolcraft himself. Though his immediate influence was undoubtedly minimal, one example of a forerunner of a "scientific" attitude toward linguistic texts who showed how oral tradition might serve to provide important data for historical research was William

Whipple Warren. Published in 1885 by the Minnesota Historical Society, Warren's *History of the Ojibways* was actually completed in 1852, a year before the author's death. The most thorough historical work written by an American Indian during the nineteenth century, Warren's history runs almost four hundred pages and draws upon a variety of sources.[1] The subtitle, *Based upon Traditions and Oral Statements*, though, identifies the principal source of his information. Warren, whose mother was Ojibwa,[2] shared the common belief that Native Americans were "fast disappearing before the onward resistless tread of the Anglo-Saxon" (1984: 23), an attitude that also inspired the "salvage anthropology" that relied upon the use of oral expressions to reconstruct what were perceived to be moribund cultures. Like the BAE researchers and Boasians, Warren believed he had the responsibility "to save their traditions from oblivion, and to collect every fact concerning them, which the advantages he [meaning himself] possesses have enabled him to procure" (1984: 25). Moreover, he recognized that oral tradition had an important advantage over written documents regarding the Ojibwas. Like Schoolcraft, he felt that oral tradition "would give a more complete insight into their real character, their mode of thought and expression, than any book which can be written concerning them" (1984: 27).

At the same time, Warren was aware of difficulties that the use of oral materials might pose for the writer who hoped to produce Euroamerican-style history from them. Traditional narratives may be "so obscure and unnatural that nothing approximating to certainty can be drawn from them." Often orally preserved history may be "vague" (1984: 55). In fact, he identified one source in particular as being so unreliable that he could not trust its historicity: "The incidents of this fight [between Ojibwas and Dakotas near the Minnesota River] were told to me by Waub-o-jeeg (White Fisher [apparently not the grandfather of Jane Johnston Schoolcraft]), a present living sub-chief of the Mississippi Ojibways, whose grandfather No-ka acted as one of the leaders of this party; but as his accounts are somewhat obscure, and much mixed with the unnatural, I refrain from giving the details" (1984: 235–236). Moreover, Warren believed, storytellers had been quite willing to mislead Euroamerican researchers such as Schoolcraft, who accepted tales made up especially for them as genuinely believed narratives about mythology and history (1984: 58). Often Indians' hesitation to reveal totally accurate information to Euroamericans might stem from concerns about self-image. That was particularly the case, Warren suggested, when data about non-Christian religion were sought (1984: 324). A careful

researcher, especially if he or she is an Indian, though, may be successful in overcoming these drawbacks to the use of oral materials.

Accuracy and clarity have supplanted artistry in Warren's determining what is valuable in Native American oral tradition. Consider, for
example, how he presents an oral narrative from Ojibwa storytelling
tradition. Throughout his history, Warren includes many translations
of stories and orations. One of these, which he calls the "Legend of the
Crane," demonstrates how and why he used such material. Warren's
stated purpose for including a translation of this "highly allegorical and
characteristic tradition" (1984: 86) was to show how members of the
Crane totemic group validated their claim to having been the first to
settle the southern shore of Lake Superior. Anticipating the exigencies
of ethnographic textualization, Warren first sets the scene for the storytelling. At a council between United States officials and Ojibwa leaders,
the identity of the "hereditary chief" of the site came up. To advance his
claims, the spokesperson for the Loon totemic group delivered "a most
eloquent harangue in praise of his own immediate ancestors, and claiming for the Loon family the first place and chieftainship among the
Ojibways" (1984: 87). This display was followed by Tug-waug-aun-ay,
representative of the Cranes and Warren's great-uncle, "a very modest
and retiring man," who offered a story instead of an oration:

> The Great Spirit once made a bird, and he sent it from the skies to make
> its abode on earth. The bird came, and when it reached half way down,
> among the clouds, it sent forth a loud and far sounding cry, which was
> heard by all who resided on the earth, and even by the spirits who make
> their abode within its bosom. When the bird reached within sight of the
> earth, it circled slowly above the Great Fresh Water Lakes, and again it
> uttered its echoing cry. Nearer and nearer it circled, looking for a resting
> place, till it lit on a hill overlooking Boweting (Sault Ste. Marie).

The bird chooses this site as its first resting place and summons Bear,
Catfish, Loon, Moose, and Marten, who form a community over which
the bird "whom the Great Spirit sent" presides. Soon the bird takes
flight again, settling on the southern shore of Lake Superior, where it
utters "its solitary cry."

> A voice came from the calm bosom of the lake, in answer; the bird
> pleased with the musical sound of the voice, again sent forth its cry, and
> the answering bird made its appearance in the wampum-breasted Ah-
> auh-wauh (Loon). The bird spoke to it in a gentle tone, "Is it thou that

gives answer to my cry?" The Loon answered, "It is I." The bird then said to him, "Thy voice is music—it is melody—it sounds sweet in my ear, from henceforth I appoint thee to answer my voice in Council."

The storyteller concluded that while the Loon has preeminence in council, the source of his authority is the Crane: "These are the words of my ancestors, who, from generation to generation, have repeated them into the ears of their children. I have done" (1984: 87–88).

Warren's interest in this story, whose linguistic component he presents in relatively straightforward fashion, lies not so much in its qualities as a work of verbal art, but in its historical significance. For while his commentary on it does note how the audience responded, his chief concern is to explain fully the "allegory," particularly the relative statuses of the Cranes and the Loons in Ojibwa society (1984: 88–89).

Warren seems to have regarded what he learned by listening to Ojibwa storytellers as, for the most part, accurate history even in the Euroamerican sense. He believed that despite their occasional vagueness the traditional narratives that he heard from Ojibwa elders were essential for learning anything about the group's pre-contact history. For instance, he noted that the story of Ojibwa migrations before settling in the upper Midwest absolutely required a knowledge of oral tradition: "[I]t is only through such vague and figurative traditions . . . that any degree of certainty can be arrived at, respecting their position and movements prior to the time when the tribe first lit their central fire" (1984: 81). Consequently, his manuscript is filled with narratives such as the Legend of the Crane quoted from his sources, often presented without qualifying comment, and usually with no descriptions of the expressive situations (e.g., 1984: 138–140, 147–148, 149–154, 157–162).

Of these numerous stories, the only one that seems consciously "literary" is a "simple, but affecting story" of conjugal devotion. Appended to but not integrated into a chapter on Ojibwa-Dakota warfare, the story is presented by Warren as a curiosity rather than a data source, and he renders it in a style reminiscent of Schoolcraft and other early nineteenth-century textmakers. The protagonist, a young Dakota warrior, is "eager to gain renown." He will not yield to his beloved wife's "soft persuasions" and "gentle caresses" that urge him to avoid the fighting of which her "dreams of ill-boding" have made her particularly apprehensive. When after the battle she discovers his body floating in a stream, she "pined away, and wept herself to death," dying "happy in the hope and belief of rejoining her young warrior husband, in the happy land of spirits" (1984: 232–234). The descriptive passages, the characterization, and the focus on individual human relationships give this story a flavor absent from the straightforward materials that function as historical data sources throughout Warren's book. Significantly, Warren sets the story off from the rest of the chapter with the capitalized subtitle "DAKOTA LEGEND" and makes no attempt to attribute any historical significance to it.

Oral tradition also provided the data by which Warren validated his contention that the Ojibwas had descended from the ten lost tribes of Israel. A widely accepted idea that had been given its fullest application to North American Natives in James Adair's *History of the American Indians* in 1775 (Williams 1930), by mid-nineteenth century the Hebrew-Indian theory was competing for support with other hypotheses regarding the ancestry of the Native North Americans, including derivations from Chaldeans, Welsh, Canaanites, or non-Semitic descendants of Noah.[3] The belief that Indians descended from wandering Hebrews, though, had the virtue of integrating the existence of Native Americans into the Old Testament version of history fairly easily. Moreover, it explained a problem that had vexed biblical scholars: the disappearance of ten of the twelve tribes of Israel from chronicles of Hebrew history after the return to the Promised Land from Egyptian captivity.

Warren does not assume that all Native Americans have Hebrew ancestors. The forebears of the Dakotas, for example, "might have formed a tribe or portion of the roving sons of Tartary, whom they resemble in many essential respects" (1984: 62). But he does devote an entire chapter of his history to "The Origin of the Ojibways," in which he develops a lengthy, though perhaps forced set of parallels showing that his mother's people (for whom he sometimes uses Schoolcraft's term "Algics") come from Hebrew stock. Those parallels include monotheistic belief in a high god, faith in dreams, worship through fasting and sacrifice, miscellaneous religious practices (exemplified by the Midé Society among the Ojibwas), and a social division into subgroups (tribes for the Hebrews, totemic clans for the Ojibwas). Especially important in establishing an ancestral identity is "the similitude which exists between the oral traditions and lodge stories of the Ojibways with the tales of the Hebrew patriarchs in the Old Testament" (1984: 70). He cites an example:

They tell one set of traditions which treat of the adventures of eight, ten, and sometimes twelve brothers. The youngest of these brothers is represented . . . as the wisest and most beloved of their father, and lying under the special guardianship of the Great Spirit. In one tradition under the name of Wa-jeeg-e-wa-kon-ay (Fisher skin coat) he delivers his brethren from divers difficulties entailed on them from their own folly and disobedience. In another tradition he is made to supply his brethren with corn. . . . The similarity between these and other traditions, with the Bible stories of Jacob and his twelve sons, cannot fail to attract the attention of any person who is acquainted with both versions. (1984: 70)

As a clinching argument, Warren recounts how upon his interpreting some "portions of Bible history" to Ojibwa elders, they "invariably" remarked, " 'The book must be true, for our ancestors have told us similar stories, generation after generation, since the earth was new.' " Warren believed any discrepancy between Ojibwa oral narratives and Old Testament history resulted from the inevitable effects of the former's word-of-mouth transmission (1984: 71).

Warren's interest in Ojibwa oral tradition focused on its value in reconstructing the historical development of a particular society. Though he was aware at least of the artistic potential of some Ojibwa verbal art forms, especially oratory (1984: 335), his principal concern was with the content of the material. Hence, as long as that was represented accurately, he did not need to worry about the stylistic features of oral expression.

Like the work of Warren and many others before and after him, the emergence of anthropology as a science during the 1860s and 1870s paralleled an almost exclusive interest in the documentary significance of Native American verbal artistry. William Elder praised Silas Rand's collection of Micmac oral narratives, for example, by stating, "From these we may learn much concerning the man, and the conditions of his life in the olden time" (1871: 4). Moreover, "Some knowledge of the ancient religious beliefs of the Micmacs may be gained from the legends and stories still told among them, and from the traditions which have been handed down from generation to generation" (1871: 9).

Increasingly, when linguistic textualizations of verbal art appeared in translation, the tendency was to eschew attempts to array them in Euroamerican literary splendor and instead to represent their indigenous qualities. Usually this meant preserving only the content for historical purposes. Then, as the anthropological enterprise came to be viewed less as an exercise in historical reconstruction either of a single society or of human development in general, oral tradition began to be regarded as a "mirror of culture," whose content reflected the present state of a society. Ultimately, texts constructed from the verbal component of oral expression have become the preeminent linguistic documents, and their reproduction on the printed page has required careful attention not only to content, but to every possible nuance of grammar, vocabulary, and pronunciation. But no matter what texts' scientific purpose might be, their esthetic qualities have usually suffered in the process of transmutation from oral expression to printed linguistic text. Moreover, representation of oral expression as an event has seldom figured into this textualization agenda.

Though appreciative of their artistic value, Daniel Garrison Brinton, the first American professor of anthropology (actually of ethnology and archeology at Philadelphia's Academy of Natural Sciences in 1884), believed that the most important quality of linguistic texts was their status as scientific documents. In a survey of the Native literature of the two Americas published in 1883, he wrote, "The monuments of a nation's literature are more correct mirrors of its mind than any merely material objects" (1883a: 59). Brinton was a physician by training, though ethnological and philological researches remained a constant part of his life, beginning with a stay in Florida during the winter of 1856–1857 that led to the publication of *Notes on the Floridian Peninsula* (1859), a monograph that included information on the contemporary Native Americans living there as well as the archeological remains in the state. Following Civil War service, Brinton settled in the Philadelphia suburb of West Chester and began to produce a series of books and articles that ranged over the scope of anthropology. His earliest interest was in the mythology of the Algonquian-speaking groups of the Northeast and Midwest. The direction taken by this interest influenced the approach to textualization and translation that Brinton later took.[4]

In 1868 Brinton published *The Myths of the New World* (second edition, 1876), hailed by Alexander F. Chamberlain as "the first really scientific attempt to analyze and correlate the rich mythology of the American Indians" (1899: 216). The analytical stance taken by Brinton in this book represents an Americanization of an approach to myth analysis worked out on Indo-European materials by the German-born Oxford don, Max Müller. Müller's approach emerged from his perception of the close interrelationships between myth and language among the prehistoric Aryans. According to Müller, the Aryan (or Indo-European) language was incapable of abstraction, a widely held notion about "primitive" languages that continues to inform thinking about oral cultures (e.g., Goody 1977: 37). Consequently, Aryans had to deal with some phenomena through concrete circumlocutions. Since the rising and setting of the sun were of vital concern to these primitive Aryans, much of their verbalization dealt with those events. Using their concrete linguistic resources, they might describe a phenomenon such as sunset with the figurative devices of personification and metaphor: "The sun god goes to bed beyond the western mountains." Thus, Müller argued, virtually every Aryan utterance generated a myth. As centuries passed and the Aryan language gave way to such descendants as Sanskrit, the original meanings of primitive concrete phrases were forgotten. By the time the Vedas, the Sanskrit religious books, were compiled, stories had developed to explain the obscure Aryan phrases. So a second layer of myth tried to explicate the first. The names of the Vedic gods and phrases about them produced mythic narratives that tried to account for those names and phrases. The scholar's task, as Müller defined it, was to determine the original meanings of gods' and heroes' names. Thus Dyaus, the chief god of the Vedas, was shown to be associated with the Aryan word for "sun, light, warmth," and Dyaus's conflicts, then, became solar allegories that represented the sun's struggles each day with the forces of darkness.[5]

Though no slavish follower of Müller, whose linguistic conclusions he sometimes criticized, Brinton found a similar process at work among Algonquian-speakers in North America. For example, he demonstrated how the Algonquian Trickster joined Dyaus (and such classical equivalents as Zeus and Jupiter [= Zeus Pater]) in the pantheon of solar deities and heroes. The root of Trickster's name is the Algonquian *wab*, which means, according to Brinton, "white" and by extension such related concepts as "light" and "warmth." Combined with an examination of ritual behavior, "antiquities," and other ethnological data, this linguistic evidence allowed Brinton to identify Trickster as the spirit of light and to equate him with the sun (1876: 173–180).

The implication for textualization of Brinton's philological approach to interpreting Native American mythology was its stress upon the necessity of understanding clearly the language in which the materials to be analyzed were originally articulated. The linguistic emphasis that had characterized American ethnology since its inception remained a central feature of Brinton's anthropology. He perceived the necessity of dealing with verbal art in its original language and of providing accurate representations in a format accessible to scholars. Consequently, Brinton anticipated BAE and Boasian ethnologists in producing textualizations and literal, word-for-word translations of the verbal components of oral expression with no attempt to suggest esthetic features, nonverbal dimensions, situation, or context. The result was raw scientific data that should ideally be presented in the original language accompanied by a translation that evinced as little extrinsic embellishment as possible. Though not interested in field ethnography in the modern sense, Brinton did consider his own researches to be based upon first-hand "fieldwork," which for him meant the use of primary documents—that is, manuscripts and archival materials (Darnell 1988: 21). That those materials should be rendered accurately was crucial to Brinton.

Like virtually every other anthropologist of the late nineteenth century, Brinton also accepted cultural evolutionism. Influenced by the scenarios worked out by Lewis Henry Morgan in the United States and Edward B. Tylor in Britain, he placed the Indian inhabitants of the Americas at earlier developmental stages than Euroamericans. But he also believed that Native Americans possessed the same mental capacities as their civilized counterparts. Evidence for the Indians' intellectual potential might be found in their verbal art—another reason Brinton was particularly concerned that textualizations of the linguistic aspect of that art be translated and presented as accurately as possible.

The intellectual potential of Native Americans as well as their cultures' place in the evolution of humanity toward civilization, according to Brinton, found expression in poetic expression, a faculty that he believed to be a human universal. Among American Indians this faculty was particularly evident in storytelling: "As a *raconteur* he [the Indian] is untiring. He has, in the highest degree, Goethe's *Lust zu fabuliren*. In no Oriental city, does the teller of strange tales find a more willing audience than in the Indian wigwam. The folk lore of every tribe which has been properly investigated has turned out to be most ample" (1883a: 10). The audience for Native American storytellers ensured that their performances manifested artistry, since they were "sticklers for nicety of expression; for clear and well turned periods; for vivid and accurate description; for flowing and sonorous sentences" (1883a: 11). Other evidences of the capacity of Indians for artistic verbal expression included the "copiousness of their vocabularies, their rare facility of expression, and their natural aptitude for the acquisition of other languages" (1883a: 12). In oratory Native Americans used language marked by such esthetic devices as "antithesis, repetition, elaborate figures, unusual metaphors, and more sonorous and lengthened expressions" (1883a: 44)—a list similar to, but more comprehensive than, the "tokens of literary potential" noticed by commentators with a more literary bent than Brinton.

For Brinton, the poetic faculty that he found among American Indians represented clear evidence for the psychic unity that undergirded cultural evolutionary theory. He believed that studying this faculty through rigorously presented linguistic texts and translations afforded an opportunity to explore the nature of a universal human mentality. Consequently, he "maintained consistently high standards for the preservation and publication of productions of aboriginal literature" (Darnell 1988: 80), which he found most highly developed from an evolutionary perspective in the written literatures of Central America.

Nevertheless, like the belletristic textmakers from earlier in the century, Brinton recognized that the verbal art of Native Americans had not developed to the level of Euroamerican literature. American Indian poetry lacked rhyme, alliteration, accent, and assonance. Since "their dialects do not admit of fixed vocalic quantity," Brinton wrote, Indian poetry cannot be said to be "measured." In fact, repetition "constitutes their [entire] poetic form," since the more sophisticated poetic resources of civilization are unavailable (1890: 285). In essence, he claimed, "We may look on their poetry as the biologist does on the rudimentary forms of organic life,—low in structure, if you please, but, after all, those which reveal to us most clearly the laws which underlie the highest forms" (1892: 329). But Brinton also stressed a kind of esthetic relativity by chiding those who might find the verbal art of the Eskimo, for example, to be "monotonous" with the reminder that "the Eskimo has his own notion of the music of verse, and it is a very advanced one" (1891: 63).

Brinton believed that the study of "aboriginal" poetry

> elevates our opinion of the nations whom we are accustomed to call by the terms savage and barbarous. We are taught that in much which we are inclined to claim as our special prerogatives, they too have an interest. In the most precious possession of the race, in its aspirations for the infinite and the forever true, they also have a share. They likewise partake, and in no mean degree, of that sweetest heritage of man, the glorious gift of song, "the vision and the faculty divine." (1890: 304)

Yet even though he is credited with writing the "first literary criticism of Native American poetry" (Castro 1983: 8),[6] Brinton realized that making that poetry and other kinds of Native American verbal art accessible to Euroamericans faced some serious obstacles. He held the work of most translators in low regard, remarking about oratorical texts that had been rendered into English that "for critical purposes, they are simply worthless" (1883a: 43). The major difficulty for translators, he believed in anticipation of many twentieth-century textmakers, lay in the material's situation of expression. For example,

> While all travelers agree that the tribes have songs and chants, war songs, peace songs, love songs, and others, few satisfactory specimens have been recorded. Those who have examined the subject most accurately have found that many so-called songs are mere repetitions of a few words, or even of simple interjections, over and over again, with an endless iteration, in a chanting voice. . . . Consequently, they show very poorly in translation, and are apt to convey an unjustly depreciatory notion of the nations which produce them. To estimate them aright, the meter and the music must be taken into consideration, and also their suitability to the minds to which they were addressed. (1883a: 47)

Furthermore, the "poetry of the ruder races," Brinton asserts, "is not composed to be read, or even recited, but to be sung; its aim is, not to awaken thought or convey information, but solely to excite emotion. It can have meaning only when heard, and only in the surroundings which gave it birth" (1883a: 47). Translation of oral expression became doubly difficult because "so much depends on the surroundings, on the spirit of the time and place" (1892: 330)—on the very features essential for ethnographic textualization.

Brinton had included several examples of oral material in his 1890 essay on "Native American Poetry": three Eskimo songs translated by Henry Rink, two Pawnee songs translated by John B. Dunbar, two Kiowa songs translated by Theodore Baker, and an Ojibwa song translated by Schoolcraft. But while textmakers such as these had usually responded to the problems of translating Native American verbal art by costuming it in decidedly Euroamerican dress, Brinton was apparently so daunted by the insurmountability of the task that when he began to undertake translations himself, he turned to the few available documents *written* by "aboriginal American authors." The results of his translation labors, though, are extremely important in the development of Native American textmaking. For he superintended and provided most of the material for what was the first systematic attempt to produce a corpus of Native American verbal art translated into English, maintaining throughout that corpus the linguistic standards that derived from his endorsement of the philological interpretation of mythology and of cultural evolutionism as scientific pursuits as well as his recognition of the documentary potential of oral expression.

In the 1880s and 1890s, periodicals such as the *Journal of American Folklore* were running advertisements for a group of volumes bearing the series title "Brinton's Library of Aboriginal American Literature." Consisting of eight volumes, the series was "intended for the publication of works *written* [my emphasis] in the Aboriginal tongues of America by native (Indian) authors, edited for the use of scholars," according to a notice appearing in the second volume of *Journal of American Folklore* in 1889. Brinton himself translated the material in six of the volumes: *The Maya Chronicles* (1883); *The Gueguence: A Comedy Ballet in the Nahuatl-Spanish Dialect of Nicaragua* (1883); *The Lenâpé and Their Legends* (1884); *The Annals of the Cakchiquels* (1885); *Ancient Nahuatl Poetry* (1890); and *Rig Veda Americanus* (1890). The other two volumes were contributed by Horatio Hale (*The Iroquois Book of Rites* [1883]) and Albert S. Gatschet (*A Migration Legend of the Creek Indians* [1884]). In his introduction to the Cakchiquels volume, Brinton stressed that his aim for the series was to "furnish materials for study, rather than to offer finished studies themselves" (1885: vi). Each volume includes a linguistic text in the relevant Native American language (always from a manuscript, not an oral source), a translation of that text, a thorough introduction to the text placing it in its cultural context, a discussion of philological matters, and a glossary.

Since Brinton's doubts about the ability of the translator to render oral expression adequately contributed to his focus on the translation of written materials, he necessarily concentrated on Central America, where the poetic faculty had developed more fully than among the nonliterate cultures to the north. But three volumes in the Library of Aboriginal American Literature present translations of material from North American Indians. Horatio Hale's *The Iroquois Book of Rites* translates two manuscripts that had been written after English missionaries in the eighteenth century had taught the Iroquois to write their own language. According to Hale, the leaders of the Iroquois Great Council recognized the advantages of preserving in writing "the forms of their most important public duty—that of creating new chiefs—and the traditions connected with their own body" (1883: 42). Consequently, they committed to writing the ceremonies, orations, and songs that constituted their proceedings when they met for the dual purpose of condolence for the death of one of their number and the induction of his replacement. One of the manuscripts Hale presented was from the Mohawk, written by Sakayengwaraton (J. S. Johnson) in 1832 during a cholera epidemic when one of the Council leaders was on his deathbed. Hale collated this with another Mohawk manuscript that had apparently been copied from still another manuscript in 1874. The two Mohawk manuscripts provide complementary materials, so that Hale could combine them into a fairly complete version of the Mohawk redaction of the condolence/induction ceremony. He also includes a

translation of an Onondaga manuscript that he obtained from interpreter Daniel La Fort in 1880 (1883: 42–44). Hale's translation seems to
focus on literal representation of content, though he does attempt to reproduce the artistry of some of the metrical sections of the manuscripts.

Albert S. Gatschet's *A Migration Legend of the Creek Indians* is
somewhat anomalous in Brinton's series. Most of the 250-page volume
provides an introduction to Creek culture and to the translated material, which itself takes only fourteen pages. A second volume was
promised to include more text, but that work never appeared as part of
Brinton's series.[7] The text that Gatschet translated had had a peculiar
history. In 1735 the Creek leader Tchikilli had delivered an oration in
the presence of James Oglethorpe, Governor of Georgia, and a number
of his own people. That oration contained an account of the historical
migrations of the Creeks. An interpreter wrote out a translation of Tchikilli's oration on a buffalo hide and presented it to the British, who took
it to London. The buffalo hide disappeared, but Gatschet had located a
German translation of the English translation of the Creek original.
That material, retranslated back into English and Creek, comprises the
ostensible focus of this volume (1884: 235–236). Perhaps the primary
value from the perspective of scientific ethnology and philology is that
the Creek translation was prepared by Judge G. W. Stidham, himself a
Creek, and thus reflects indigenous usage of the language.

Brinton's own North American contribution to the series was *The
Lenâpé and Their Legends*, a complete translation of the mysterious
and controversial document called the Walam Olum. Allegedly a poetic
chronicle of the Delaware (or Lenni Lenape) beginning with the cosmogonic myth and concluding with the arrival of Europeans in North
America, the Walam Olum originally consisted of a bundle of sticks on
which were painted pictographs, each representing one of the chronicle's 183 verses. Although the sticks themselves do not survive, a manuscript copy of the pictographs with accompanying linguistic text in
Delaware was written out in 1833 by Constantine S. Rafinesque, a bota-
nist and natural historian. Rafinesque claims to have obtained the pic-
tographic material from a "Dr. Ward" (perhaps John Russell Ward of
Carlisle, Kentucky) in Indiana in 1820 (Barlow and Powell 1986). Poetic
materials in Delaware came from two other sources, neither of whom
Rafinesque identified (though he cited one John Burns as translator of
some of the songs). Rafinesque published his translation of the poetry in
1836, but omitted the pictographs and the Delaware originals of the
verbal material. Thirteen years later, E. G. Squier (1849) retranslated the

material and published some of the pictographs and original Delaware poetry.

Yet because of Rafinesque's reputation for eccentricity and doubts about the ability of Native North Americans to maintain glyphic records of their history, serious concerns about the authenticity of the Walam Olum arose, and fears of a hoax like the one Macpherson had apparently perpetrated with the Ossian poems in the 1760s. One of Brinton's initial tasks involved determining whether the material did indeed represent Delaware verbal art.

He turned the original over to a Euroamerican-educated Delaware, the Reverend Albert Anthony, who gave the opinion that the material was a "genuine *oral* composition of a Delaware Indian" (Brinton 1884: 156). Anthony (and therefore Brinton) attributed occasional errors in grammar to the imperfect knowledge of the original language on the part of the person who transcribed the material from oral recitation. Brinton also suggested that the obscurity of much of the language in the Walam Olum testified to its authenticity, for if Rafinesque had perpetrated a fraud, then the Delaware vocabulary he used would be that found in dictionaries such as those compiled by David Zeisberger and John Heckewelder, Moravian missionaries who had studied the language. Instead, much of the Walam Olum's vocabulary, Brinton claimed, cannot be matched in previously published sources. Moreover, Brinton cited Rafinesque's mistranslation of some of the material as further proof that he had not based it on a previously published source. Finally, the inclusion in the Walam Olum of an account of a "golden age" period in Delaware mythological history that had not been published elsewhere lent weight to the document's validity (1884: 136n, 156–157; Darnell 1988: 27–28). Brinton's conclusion temporarily resolved one of the major debates in Native American studies during the nineteenth century:

> It is a genuine native production, which was repeated orally to some one indifferently conversant with the Delaware language, who wrote it down to the best of his ability. In its present form it can, as a whole, lay no claim either to antiquity, or to purity of linguistic form. Yet, as an authentic modern version, slightly colored by European teachings, of the ancient tribal traditions, it is well worth preservation, and will repay more study in the future. . . . The narrator was probably one of the native chiefs or priests, who had spent his life in the Ohio and Indiana towns of the Lenape, and who, though with some knowledge of Christian instruc-

tion, preferred the pagan rites, legends and myths of his ancestors. Probably certain lines were repeated in the archaic form in which they had been handed down for generations. (1884: 158–159)

In 1954, a research team working under the auspices of the Indiana Historical Society provided a general endorsement of Brinton's judgment about the Walam Olum's authenticity by considering its historicity, ethnographic and archeological background, relevance to Delaware physical anthropology, and manuscript history (Indiana Historical Society 1954). Though a more recent, but less rigorous, investigation has enthusiastically celebrated the Walam Olum's status as a genuine product of Native American historical and literary consciousness (McCutchen 1993), opinions that Rafinesque did indeed create a hoax continue to figure in discussions of the material (Darnell 1988: 27–28).

When examining the Delaware text, Brinton pays some attention to its literary style. He points out, "The rhythm is symbolic and accentual, with frequent effort to select homophones . . . and sometimes alliteration." While such effects "appear in the native American songs of many tribes," Brinton found the Walam Olum to be unique among available Algonquian materials in its use of rhyme and suggested that its use of this device might derive from the influence of "the music-loving Moravian missionaries [who] had made the Delaware familiar with numerous hymns in their own tongue, correctly framed and rhymed" (1884: 159–160). Despite his recognition of its artistry, though, Brinton's translation emphasizes correctness in matching the original's vocabulary with English equivalents. While the translation is metrical, he attempts no rhyme and deemphasizes other poetic devices.

Brinton's purpose in retranslating the Walam Olum—which he included with the complete Delaware text and all the pictographs (their first complete appearance in print)—was to put before the public an authoritative literal rendering for the purpose of philological and ethnological study. Rafinesque's translation was inadequate because of its mistakes and its failure to include the original Delaware version. Squier's translation, according to Brinton, was based on an inaccurate copying of the Rafinesque manuscript. In fact, some of the pictographs that Squier reproduced—and he did not include them all—were reversed in publication (Brinton 1884: 163).

Brinton's literal approach to translating the Walam Olum is evident throughout its 183 verses. Consider, for example, the second part of its first section, the cosmogonic myth, which treats ways in which a mar-plot disturbed the creative efforts of the "great Manito." The translation appears on right-hand pages facing the original-language version and drawings:

14. But an evil Manito made evil beings only, monsters,
15. He made the flies, the gnats.
16. All beings were then friendly.
17. Truly the manitos were active and kindly
18. To those very first men, and to those first mothers; fetched them wives,
19. And fetched them food, when first they desired it.
20. All had cheerful knowledge, all had leisure, all thought in gladness.
21. But very secretly an evil being, a mighty magician, came on earth,
22. And with him brought badness, quarreling, unhappiness,
23. Brought bad weather, brought sickness, brought death.
24. All this took place of old on the earth, beyond the great tide-water, at the first. (1884: 173–177)

Brinton performed what he saw to be a service to scholars in providing all of this raw material for their use. That purpose characterized his goal in all eight volumes of his series. As he wrote in the preface to *The Maya Chronicles*, he was guided by the "belief that the only solid foundation for the accurate study of American ethnology and linguistics must be in the productions of the native mind in their original form" (1883b: v). While he recognized the art of oral performance and, in fact, saw it as evidence of Native Americans' evolutionary potential, he apparently considered that art too elusive to be re-created in print. Moreover, his lack of interest in "fieldwork" in the modern sense meant that he had no firsthand contact with the oral expression of Native American verbal art.

About his renderings from Central American languages, Brinton admitted, "I have sacrificed every attempt at elegance in the English translation to an endeavor to preserve faithfully the style of the original, even to its needless repetitions and awkward sentences" (1883b: 192). But he argued that if he had translated it more "elegantly," the results "would not have represented the originals. For the sake of accuracy I have not hesitated to sacrifice the requirements of English composition" (1883b: 72). As a contemporary critic of Brinton's work has noted, his literalism and superficial treatment of literary matters in his commentaries reflects the "very secondary status" of esthetic evaluation of Native

American verbal art during the second half of the nineteenth century (Gingerich 1983: 114). As translator, Brinton created scholarly documents to be used by scholars as data sources.

   Though the lines of influence are not direct, other figures who foregrounded the documentary potential of Native American verbal art thought highly of Brinton's work. Franz Boas, for example, valued his Library of Aboriginal American Literature both for its "faithful rendering of the native tales" and its "scope" (1940: 451). While Boas differed profoundly from Brinton on many crucial issues involving the very essence of anthropology, he seconded Brinton's insistence on accurately presented linguistic texts as a foundation for anthropological study. Textualizations of oral expressions are identified primarily as sources for data most strongly in the work of Boas and his students, whose influence on anthropology, especially its linguistic aspect, continues to the present. Moreover, Boas's belief in the necessity of carefully recording texts for the purposes of linguistic and ethnographic data-gathering made him highly critical of most earlier presentations of Native American verbal art. Writing in 1914, Boas complained that until late in the previous century the only materials "available for scientific research" were publications by Henry Rink (from the Greenland Eskimos), E. Petitot (from Athabascan-speakers of northwestern Canada), J. O. Dorsey (from the Ponca), Stephen R. Riggs (from Lakota tradition), and Albert S. Gatschet (from the Klamath), thus tacitly dismissing several centuries' worth of textmaking. Because they attempted to render Native discourse faithfully, the work of the textmakers who earned Boas's commendation differed "fundamentally" from the "literary efforts" of Schoolcraft and others of his generation (1940: 451). That Brinton escaped Boas's censure and, in fact, earned some grudging praise despite their marked differences on most other ethnological issues reinforces the contention that the former did approach Native American verbal art and its textualization in a scientific spirit—as that spirit was defined in the late nineteenth century.

   On the ethnographic level, Boas repeatedly demonstrated his belief that verbal art, especially narrative, operates as a "mirror of culture" to reflect accurately the social system of a group of people. Clearly Boas did not originate the idea, which is akin to the "ethnic euhemerism" that David Bidney shows at work in the theories of eighteenth-century cultural philosopher Giambattista Vico and others (Bidney 1953: 306). Boas's more immediate source was probably Henry Rink, a Danish colonial official, who had collected oral narratives from the Greenland Eskimos. When he set out to write an ethnographic introduction for his collection, Rink drew upon the stories themselves for data on the language, social system, and other features of the culture. Rink argued that his methodology followed the lead of the Greenlanders themselves:

> [T]he traditions [i.e., oral narratives] are to be considered as including a system of religion and morals as well as of laws and rules for social life. Such knowledge as they convey is unconsciously imbibed by the native from his earliest childhood through listening to the story-tellers, exactly as a child learns to speak. And when the Greenlander nowadays is in doubt about any question regarding the superstitions or customs of his ancestors, he will try to find an answer by looking for some sample out of his tales, ancient or modern, the latter also containing elementary parts of ancient origin kept up in this manner by succeeding generations. The information used for our introductory remarks has also been chiefly derived from this source. (1875: 86–87)

Boas's discomfort with the allegorical theories of many of his contemporaries—the emphasis on solar and nature mythology that characterized at least the early opinions of Daniel Brinton, for example—also contributed to his belief that oral narratives reflected culture with considerable accuracy. In a 1916 essay, he wrote that instead of being based on "contemplations of nature," verbal art derived from everyday life:

> [T]he contents and form of mythology and folk-tales are determined by the conditions that determined early literary art. The formulas of myths and folk-tales . . . are almost exclusively events that reflect the occurrences of human life, particularly those that stir the emotions of the people. . . . [T]here is no reason why we should not be satisfied with explaining the origin of these tales as due to the play of imagination with the events of human life. (1940: 404–405)

Even when the incidents, objects, and themes in verbal art do not directly mirror cultural experience, they may represent "every-day wishes" (for example, revival of the dead or discovery of magical treasures), "exaggerations of our experiences" (for example, giants or dwarfs), or the "materialization of the objects of fear" (for example, monsters) (1940: 405). Since, Boas argued, cultural experiences provide the basis of content for verbal art, it stands to reason that art would mirror culture.

Trained in physics and psychology, Franz Boas began his ethnographic career in 1883, while studying the effects of geography on the culture of the Cumberland Sound Eskimos. He returned to his native Germany from the field and joined the staff of Berlin's ethnological museum. Here he remained until 1886, when he fully committed himself to anthropology through the first of many field trips to western Canada.[8] As he studied the Native cultures of the Northwest Coast, he came to realize the importance of recording verbal art. Boas published many collections of linguistic texts during his long career, material that often constituted the primary source from which he wrote his cultural descriptions.

One of Boas's early ethnographic interests was in the historical interrelationships among the varied cultures of the Northwest Coast. He believe that verbal art would reveal the nature of that relationship. In a letter to his parents written in 1886, he described mythology as "a useful tool for differentiating and judging the relationship of tribes" (Rohner 1969: 29). Because of differences in myths, he revealed in a letter written two months later, "I am coming more and more to the conclusion that originally there can have been very little intercourse between" two of the groups he was studying (Rohner 1969: 63).

Besides historical connection, myths and other oral narratives revealed much about the nature of tribal cultures—the essence of the mirror-of-culture idea. Explicit statements of this idea abound in Boas's published writings. In his 1914 essay "Mythology and Folk-tales of the North American Indians," he wrote that oral narratives "give a faithful picture of the mode of life and of the chief interests that have prevailed among the people during the last few generations" (1940: 477). In the same piece Boas claimed that "all the essential features" of Tsimshian life are "distinctly mirrored" in folktales (1940: 475). A decade later, in an essay on oral stylistics, he reiterated the point: "A detailed analysis of the traditional tales of a number of Indian tribes shows complete agreement of the conditions of life with those that may be abstracted from the tales. Beliefs and customs in life and in tales are in full accord" (1940: 497).

The richest products of Boas's use of verbal art as mirror of culture appeared in two important books: *Tsimshian Mythology*, which comprised much of the BAE Annual Report for 1909–1910, and *Kwakiutl Culture as Reflected in Mythology*, a memoir of the American Folklore Society published in 1935. The former volume, which runs over a thousand pages, presents sixty-seven narratives that Boas had translated from the collections of Henry W. Tate. (The volume includes no Native-language texts.) Using just this material, Boas develops an eighty-four-page chapter, "Description of the Tsimshian, Based on Their Mythology" (1916: 393–477). His introductory remarks to this chapter present the fundamentals of his mirror-of-culture methodology: "It is obvious that in the tales of a people those incidents of the everyday life that are of importance to them will appear either incidentally or as the basis of a plot. Most of the references to the mode of life of the people will be an accurate reflection of their habits" (1916: 393). Boas recognizes, though, that while the topics treated in a group's verbal art may not encompass the entire culture, a corpus of oral narrative "has the merit of bringing out those points which are of interest to the people themselves." In fact, verbal art constitutes "in a way an autobiography of the tribe" (1916: 393).

Boas then proceeds to thoroughly inventory Tsimshian culture as reflected in the narratives whose translations appear in the volume as well as twenty-eight Native-language texts he had published elsewhere (Boas 1902; 1912): towns, houses, household goods, manufactures, dress and ornaments; fishing, hunting, and gathering; foodways; travel and transportation; playing and gambling; quarrels and warfare; social organization; family life; chiefs, attendants, slaves, and councils; visitors and festivals; marriage and death; ethical concepts and emotional life; religious and magical practices; current beliefs; mythical concepts; and shamanism. The first paragraph of the section on dress and ornament, one of the briefest in the ethnography, offers a sense of how Boas drew from the verbal art:

> Only few parts of the dress and few ornaments are described. Blankets were worn. Rich people wore sea-otter and marten blankets (193, 266 [the references are to page numbers earlier in the volume]). In one place a blanket of weasel skins set with abalone shells is mentioned (N [= Boas 1902] 199). In ceremonies dancing-blankets woven of mountain-goat wool were used (265). Elk skins are mentioned very often as valuable property (266), but their use as garments is nowhere described. The woman's apron is described (140). (1916: 398)

The Kwakiutl volume presents an ethnographic description of the culture, based almost entirely upon its representations in the verbal art that Boas had published as linguistic texts elsewhere.

For Boas, the most important ethnographic information provided by verbal art involved language usage. John P. Harrington pointed out that for Boas, "human language was the most important phenomenon to study in social science because language is . . . . the very core of custom, religion, and all that distinguishes man" (1940: 97). Melville Jacobs, whose own work with Clackamas Chinook oral narratives transcended its Boasian influences by treating the literary qualities of Victoria Howard's stories, wrote that Boas was "not interested in obtaining a large sample, much less the whole of an oral literature. He was concerned with supplying linguistic materials that were sufficiently varied to document the study of the language. Indeed, Boas' first love was linguistic analysis" (1959: 119–120). Boas himself noted in his introduction to the first number of the *International Journal of American Linguistics,* one of the several forums in which he presented Native American linguistic texts that he edited, that vocabulary listings and grammatical notes, which comprised the extent of field linguistic research until the 1880s, were inadequate resources for the serious student of language. The need to understand language in the context of usage (*parole* rather than *langue*) required the availability of "large masses of texts" (1917: 1; see also Stocking 1992: 90–91). He recognized, however, that verbal art afforded a somewhat limited view of language, since usages associated with "daily occurrences, every-day conversations, descriptions of industries, customs, and the like" often did not occur in the myths and folktales he and his students collected (1917: 2).

For Franz Boas, then—as well as for his many students who contributed materials to *IJAL,* Publications of the American Ethnological Society, and the *Journal of American Folklore,* all of which Boas edited—textualizations of Native American verbal art were meant to function as sources of historical, general ethnographic, and linguistic data. The principal requirement for the presentation of texts, consequently, was accuracy. Embellishments such as Boas attributed to his predecessors in Native American studies (like those treated in chapters 5 and 6) had interfered with the texts' documentary purposes. Thus his criticisms of the literary emendations of earlier textmakers arose from his conception of why verbal art should be collected and why it should be textualized.

His own approach, which is still followed by many anthropologists, relied upon recording the original-language expression phoneme by phoneme. Even if the researcher did not understand what was said, he or she should capture the sound patterns of the language as scrupulously as possible—usually (at least before the development of mechanical recording devices)[9] by having the material dictated and re-dictated. The published textualization should begin with a representation in the original language, often accompanied by elaborate linguistic notes. A literal, perhaps interlinear translation converted the material into English. If Boas meant for his materials to receive general ethnographic instead of specifically linguistic usage, he might append a free translation that transformed the literal rendering into readable English.[10] Boas's linguistic texts include virtually nothing about the expressive situations, which he acknowledges cursorily in general introductions to some of his collections.

A representative Boasian presentation of the linguistic component of oral expression may be taken from the volume *Bella Bella Texts*, which Boas edited as the fifth volume of the Columbia University Contributions to Anthropology in 1928. Most of the material had been collected by dictation in 1897. Boas presents the narratives in the volume by juxtaposing the Bella Bella text with a more or less free English translation on facing pages. Virgules in the translation correspond to the ends of lines in the Bella Bella text. Parenthetical numbers introduce every fifth line, enabling the reader easily to match the two versions. Following is the first paragraph of Boas's translation of a myth that he has entitled "The Mink":

> Mink worked at his arrows. He was going / to play fighting with Blue Jay. / Now he shot. They shot back and forth with their arrows. / Mink shot and he just hit. Then tried (5) Blue Jay to shoot but missed. Then / Blue Jay became angry / because he missed the aim. He just became furious and he spoke abusingly, / "You bad one, you have no father!" Thus Mink was told by / Blue Jay. Then Mink cried. (10) He was crying "Hee'". He said while he was going, "Hee'". Thus he cried walking while / he was going to his mother. (1928: 3)

Boas did not intend for this translation to represent the artistry of the original Native-language text, much of which may have disappeared because of the recording situation. And he certainly intended to represent nothing of the artistry of the expressive event. In 1897 Boas found "only two sickly men . . . who were able to dictate" (1928: xi)—hardly a situation to promote fully realized artistry in an "authentic" performance. In 1923, he read the 1897 texts to his informants—he only mentions one, Willy Gladstone, by name—and they (or he) repeated them. At any rate, this translation should be considered only as a guide to the original-language text. Though Murray suggests (1991: 107) that the original-language texts appear in Boas's publications to act as the "'other'" of the English, Boas himself seems to have intended that the text in the Native language be regarded as the principal document. Though unreadable by virtually anyone, such material was for Boasians the raw material from which linguistic and other cultural data could be extracted. The English translation seems, in fact, to have been decidedly secondary (the "Other") for Boas.

The spareness of the translation from the Bella Bella original and its occasional awkwardness—both features of many of the free translations prepared by Boasians—contribute to the negative response that the ethnolinguistic approach to textmaking has elicited from literary-minded enthusiasts for Native Americana during the twentieth century. We saw samples of that response in chapter 2 (for example, Krupat's complaint that the literal accuracy "is purchased at a fairly considerable price in the loss of literariness" [1992: 13]), along with some defense of Boas. To that apologia, which emphasizes the nonperformance situations in which Boas usually encountered his raw material, may be added the role that he perceived English renderings as having. For Boas the translation was secondary—a key to the text in Tsimshian, Kwagul, or Bella Bella or a handy presentation only of content for mirror-of-culture uses. Like the translator of Black Hawk's autobiography, Boas probably saw no need to attempt a representation of artistic qualities that were irrelevant to the translation's function.

Yet it is true that those who read only the translations (which would include most who use Boas's material) may receive the impression that no artistry exists and that the intellects of the storytellers are prosaically dull. Boas's own "tone-deafness"—as a contemporary critic (Berman 1992: 126) has put it—may be taken by readers as the inadequacy of the storyteller. Moreover, the textualization approach employed by Boas and the mirror-of-culture idea on which it was founded assigned verbal art to a place outside of culture. As Greg Urban has put it, those who view verbal art as ethnolinguistic resource tend to perceive "discourse as a window through which culture can be glimpsed rather than as the locus of culture" (1991: 151). At least partially in reaction to this perspective, literary enthusiasts in the twentieth century have allowed linguistic text (and sometimes its paralinguistic and kinesic dimensions) to break free from context, which may disappear completely from the esthetic equation.

Of the three textmakers treated in this chapter—united in perceiving the linguistic text as documentary source—only Boas has made a lasting impression on the course of the study of Native American verbal art. However, Boas's work did not emerge *ex nihilo*. Nor did his influence inevitably produce the kind of texts that have been the despair of literary critics. On one hand, Ella Deloria's Lakota textualizations may be characterized as "Boasian in their lack of affect and nuance" (Rice 1992:

276). But on the other, Boas also had some indirect role in the literary enthusiasm of the early 1900s—the century's first "cycle of appreciation" of Indian verbal art (Evers 1983)—through his informal mentoring of Natalie Curtis, whose *The Indians' Book* awakened the interest of literati and artistes to the esthetic values of words, music, and things Indian.

CHAPTER EIGHT

NATALIE CURTIS IN HOPILAND

On 22 July 1903, Theodore Roosevelt wrote to Ethan Allan Hitchcock, his secretary of the interior, introducing Natalie Curtis, "a young lady who is particularly interested in the semi-civilized Indians of the Southwest." Roosevelt noted his thorough knowledge of Curtis's abilities and urged Secretary Hitchcock to follow up on suggestions that she had presented to the president regarding the policy of reservation schools that forbade or discouraged the practice of Native arts and substituted Euroamerican arts in their place. Roosevelt directed Hitchcock to discuss Curtis's ideas with Hamlin Garland and George Bird Grinnell and to submit a full report of the matter (Roosevelt 1951: 3:523).

Curtis's interest in encouraging instead of stifling Native American art arose from two immediate concerns. On one hand, she had noticed the incongruities resulting from current federal education programs for Indians. For example, the Hopi children who attended the government school at the foot of First Mesa were dressed in ill-fitting Euroamerican clothing instead of the traditional garb that centuries of adaptation to the harsh climate of northeastern Arizona had produced: "The native woven dress with its bright sash was replaced by a uniform gown of colorless check gingham. Upon the heads of the boys were crushed black felt hats, some three sizes too large. American suits of cheap ready-made clothing dangled upon even the little bodies of tots who could not have been more than three years old" (Curtis 1904b: 148). Even more startling to Curtis, though, was that while their elders were still creating songs from their traditional musical heritage, these children were climbing from the school to their homes atop the mesa singing "Marching Through Georgia" (1904b: 148).

Curtis was also concerned that government sanctions against performance of Indian music stymied her research on Native American music traditions. Not only did she feel intimidated by reservation officials, who seemed to be looking over her shoulder as she tried to persuade Indians to sing for her, but most potential Native collaborators in her project to make an enduring record of their songs refused to cooperate, fearing government reprisal. Her visit with Roosevelt, a family acquaintance, to complain was apparently successful, for within the next few years she gathered enough material for a number of periodical articles and two books on the subject—including *The Indians' Book* in 1907.

Natalie Curtis's background did not seem to have prepared her for the role in the study of Native American traditional music and in the textualization of verbal art that she would assume during the first two decades of the twentieth century. But personal circumstances and popular intellectual currents conspired to turn her away from total devotion to the career of concert pianist for which she had been formally educated and toward an interest in the vernacular expressive culture of peoples (first American Indians, later African Americans) whom she considered to be artistically disenfranchised.

Curtis was born 26 April 1875 in New York City. Her father, Edward Curtis, was a member of the faculty of the College of Surgeons and Physicians at Columbia University. An obituary of Natalie, which appeared in the 31 October 1921 issue of the *Santa Fe New Mexican*, noted that she had enjoyed "exceptional advantages" during her childhood. The family home on Washington Place in the city had received a variety of notables, and the Curtis family also spent time at Wave Crest in Far Rockaway, Long Island. Intent upon a career on the concert stage, Curtis studied piano and music theory with Arthur Friedheim at the National Conservatory of Music in New York City, Ferruccio Busoni in Berlin, Alfred Girardet in Bonn, and Julius Kniere in Bayreuth, where she became acquainted with the family of Richard Wagner. She returned to the United States "a pianist of unquestioned brilliant promise" (Grant 1921: 47).

Curtis was also interested in composing and before her twenty-fifth birthday had published two pieces for voice with piano accompaniment. In 1902 the Wa-Wan Press, music publishers specializing in compositions based on American—including Native American—themes, published what might have been Curtis's *magnum opus* had she not turned her attention to the collection and preservation of American Indian music. *Songs from a Child's Garden of Verses by Robert Louis*

Stevenson offers settings for seven of the Scottish writer's poems for children (Lawrence 1970: 1:157–175).

In short, Curtis seemed to be be bound for a competent, but conventional, career as performer, composer, and perhaps teacher when Native American music caught her attention. The personal circumstances that led her to American Indian studies remain somewhat obscure, but apparently she first heard the music of Southwestern groups, probably the Hopi, while visiting a brother who may have been living in Arizona for health reasons.[1] Frances R. Grant, who wrote Curtis's obituary for *Musical America,* asserted that the aspiring concert pianist spent a whole year with her ailing brother, performed the obligatory tourist duty of attending some Indian ceremonies, and "with her keen sympathies, recognized the beauties of an art the government was so ruthlessly trying to suppress" (1921: 47).

In fact, federal Indian policy of the time did aim at eradicating Indian cultures with the purpose of hastening assimilation, of converting Native Americans into civilized beings ready for the twentieth century, of carrying out the now infamous dictum of Colonel Richard Henry Pratt, director of Carlisle Indian School: "Kill the Indian, and save the man." Officials focused their attention on remolding Native Americans' system of values primarily by changing traditional attitudes toward the land and through the education of children. Traditional attitudes toward land had received direct challenges from the Omaha Allotment Act of 1882—championed by Alice Cunningham Fletcher, Curtis's principal forerunner in the collection of Native American music—and especially from the Dawes Severalty Act of 1887, both of which provided for the distribution of tribally controlled lands to individuals, with the goal of making yeoman farmers out of peoples whose traditional economies were often founded on the hunt. The civilized view of land as a commodity to be owned was supposed to replace the more spiritually based concept of land use held by many Native American peoples, thus undermining a fundamental feature of their cultural identity and making it easier for them to become civilized. While modern views recognize the ethnocentrism of this policy, in the 1880s it was heralded as very progressive and gained the support of many self-characterized "friends of the Indian" such as Fletcher (Lurie 1966; see also Mark 1988).

Meanwhile, education of Indian children—which interested Natalie Curtis more than concepts of land ownership—became more and more the province of federally endorsed agencies such as boarding schools on and off the reservation and reservation day schools, both of which stressed developing skills that would supposedly help young Indians fit into Euroamerican life. A modern historian of Indian education has summarized the standard procedure used for Hopi children attending the Keams Canyon Reservation School shortly after it was established in the 1880s: "The belief was that before Indians could begin to acquire the knowledge, skills, and attitudes of the white world, they must be stripped of all outward signs of their savage heritage. . . . They were forced to abandon traditional dress for . . . school uniforms. . . . After a change of dress, the new recruit was subjected to a haircut. . . . Finally, there was the need to change an Indian's name" (Adams 1979: 343).[2]

The assimilationist emphasis in education also discouraged Indian children from learning about their own cultures. Curtis had several horror stories to illustrate "the benighted policies" that amounted to "a ruthless campaign of destruction of all things pertaining to the indigenous culture of the red race" (1919a: 399): the Hopi children singing "Marching Through Georgia" ("a song they could not understand, [while] weighted in mind and body with the misfit garments of civilization" [1904b: 148] and the standard art lessons that involved imitating Euroamerican models ("painting pansies on plush pillows, embroidering strawberries, drawing roses in red chalk, and carefully shaded kittens playfully emerging from unbuttoned boots" [1913: 630]), for example. One of Curtis's Native American acquaintances summarized the federal philosophy of educating Indian children: " 'The white man thinks that no people in the world can be any good unless they talk his language, swear like him, pray like him, and wear his ugly and uncomfortable clothes' " (1919a: 399). The artist Angel De Cora, a Winnebago and illustrator of *The Indians' Book*, provided a more formal capsule assessment of the goals of education programs aimed at Native Americans:

The method of educating the Indian in the past was the attempt to transform him into a brown Caucasian within the space of five years or a little more. The educators made every effort to convince the Indian that any custom or habit that was not familiar to the white man showed savagery and degradation. A general attempt was made to bring him "up to date." The Indian, bound up as he is in tribal laws and customs, knew not where to make a distinction, not which of his natural instincts to discard, and the consequence was that he either became superficial and arrogant and denied his race, or he grew dispirited and silent. (De Cora 1907: 527)

Though she undoubtedly supported economic programs such as land allotment and endorsed the practical aspects of Indian education, Curtis was concerned about how assimilationist policies were exacting a toll on the Native arts of the Americas. In an article on the music of Laguna Pueblo, she sounded an alarm for the destruction of Native musical traditions. Laguna art, she warned, "is fast fading away, and the natural utterances of a healthy people, the unconscious birth of song is almost stilled." Invoking William Morris's connection between art and creative joy, she feared that Laguna lives were doomed to become "silent and colorless" due to "the deliberate crushing of every spark of native pride" (1904a: 35) through assimilationist policies which, as she noted in a later piece, paralleled the harsh measures used by the Spanish to eradicate the Native cultures of the Valley of Mexico four centuries earlier (1915a: 538). She roundly condemned the forces that she viewed as obliterating an artistic heritage: "No 'Huns' in Europe have destroyed art more deliberately and systematically than we in our own land, for the aboriginal race suffers a spiritual annihilation at our hands as ruthless as physical extermination" (1920a: 175).

Moved by her perception of the ultimately deleterious effects of the artistic implications of federal Indian education programs, Curtis undertook the task of salvaging the music of Native Americans, which she believed would disappear with the generation that was being educated at government schools. Like many collectors of traditional music and verbal art, especially that of American Indians, Curtis perceived her mission as a rescue operation, devoted to saving from oblivion a body of musical artistry that was facing extinction—"the remarkable music and poetry that is gradually being lost to the world through the decadence of Indian songs," as she put it during a lecture at Virginia's Hampton Institute in 1904 ([Curtis] 1904: 327). In what is apparently her first publication on American Indian music, an article that appeared in *Harper's* about a month after her visit to Theodore Roosevelt, Curtis articulated her motives: "I sought the Indian songs solely that I might reverently record and preserve what I could of an art that is now fast passing away beneath the influence of the Moody and Sankey hymn tunes and patriotic songs taught the Indians in the government schools" (1903: 626).

The visit to the president, though, marked an apparent watershed in her collecting efforts, and her perception of Roosevelt's response helps to clarify her own motivation. Over fifteen years after their conference in July 1903, Curtis recalled Roosevelt's words of encouragement:

"I am thoroughly in sympathy with the idea of preserving and, if possible, of developing the art, the music, the poetry of the Indian. . . . It fits in with all my policies of conservation, and I consider the question—the

conservation of Indian art in our education of Indians—important
enough to include in my next Message to Congress. I don't know anything about music, but the translations of Indian song-poems [which
Curtis showed him] show the native poetry to be of rare value, and a
movement to keep this song literature alive . . . has my immediate and
hearty support." (1919a: 399)

Within hours of Curtis's visit to Roosevelt, she received official noti-
fication that the attitude of federal authorities toward her music collecting was to change. Upon her return to the field, she recalled, "I could
not only assure the Indians who sang for me that their singing of Indian
songs would not get them into trouble with the agents, but these same
agents now strewed my path with courtesies and called on me before
breakfast with offers of help" (1919a: 399).

The "field" for Curtis was undoubtedly the Southwest, particularly
the pueblos at Laguna in New Mexico and on First and Third Mesas in
northeastern Arizona. Much of the material recorded from representatives of Indian groups outside the Southwest that appeared in *The Indians' Book* most likely was encountered at the Louisiana Purchase
Exposition in St. Louis during the first half of 1904. Curtis's field methods and the linguistic texts that they ultimately produced can effectively be examined by considering her activities among the Hopi, who
remained her "best-loved Indians," according to a eulogy prepared by
her friend Winfred Douglas for a memorial service at Hampton Institute
("Natalie Curtis" 1926: 140).

"To observe her among her beloved Indians was to witness a miracle,"
wrote conductor Kurt Schindler for the same service, "for with her utter
frankness and her beaming simplicity of approach she could make even
the most reticent ones among them talk and sing to her and explain the
mysteries of their legends." Schindler, visiting the Hopi community of
Walpi with Curtis in 1913, was amazed by her rapport with Hopi singers
and storytellers. He continued, "That strange mixture of child and
woman in her, which happens so rarely and which creates that thing
which we call 'genius,' made it possible for her to do what no wise man
or 'mere musician' could accomplish" ("Natalie Curtis" 1926: 136).

In the keynote address at the same ceremony, which was held some
five years after her death, New York City attorney Elbridge L. Adams
portrayed Curtis in the field:

When she undertook the tremendous task of collecting and recording the
folk-music of the American Indian she did not do it in an impersonal de-

tached way. No; she made herself one of the people whom she wanted to study and know; she entered into their very inmost lives; and soon they came to know that she was their friend and opened their hearts to her as they never would have done to the ordinary inquirer. . . . And so she sought not merely to discover and record the songs of the aboriginal American, as a scientist might have done, but she strove to do more than that—she wanted to understand and reveal the inner life of a primitive race. ("Natalie Curtis" 1926: 129)

Even though these eulogies were undoubtedly colored by the occasion at which they were presented, Curtis did try to establish an intimacy with many of the individuals whom she genuinely regarded as her collaborators in her task of salvage ethnography. The very fact that in *The Indians' Book*, the ultimate result of that salvage effort, she listed most of their names as sources for particular songs and stories suggests that Curtis credited Native singers and storytellers with the capacity for individual artistic achievement, a point of view that has not always been accepted by Euroamerican commentators on American Indian verbal art.[3] She took a much more personal approach and assumed a much more respectful stance toward what she wanted to collect and those from whom she wanted to collect it than fieldworkers who have actually been assigned the title "ethnologist" more readily than she.[4] For example, she believed—naively, though with good intentions—that her willingness to sing Indian songs herself helped potential collaborators to feel "though I had a white face I was somehow 'Indian inside' " (1913: 628).

The degree of Curtis's empathy with her collaborators is most evident in her fieldwork at Oraibi on Third Mesa. Most likely, it was her contact with Hopi verbal art and music there that first aroused her interest in Native American cultures. It certainly seems plausible that the Hopis' problems with government restrictions provided the primary impetus for Curtis to visit Theodore Roosevelt to enlist his presidential assistance for her project. Yet her contact with the Hopi, whom she revisited with Roosevelt and other Euroamerican luminaries in 1913, also reveals some of Curtis's misunderstanding brought on by her uncritical acceptance of cultural evolutionary theory and by her lack of appreciation of the complexity of Hopi relations with the Euroamerican power structure.

The first "Agent to the Moqui Reservation" was Charles Burton, who arrived in Arizona Territory in 1900. Following the guidelines of Bureau of Indian Affairs Superintendent William A. Jones, Burton instituted a rigorous policy of assimilation that required such drastically symbolic measures as haircuts for all men and boys (James 1974: 123). Curtis seems to have encountered Hopi ceremonial performances at about the same time. Probably in 1903, she paid an extensive visit to Oraibi, one that lasted "[m]any weeks" (1923: 490), during which she recorded songs from nine Hopi collaborators.

Upon her arrival after "a two days' drive across that Arizona wilderness of beauty known as the 'Painted Desert'" (1903: 626), Curtis established a "workshop" in a "government house" on the plain below Oraibi. "The government builds the foundations, and furnishes materials for walls and roofs," she wrote about the kind of structure she was temporarily inhabiting, "thus seeking to induce the Indians to leave their homes on the mesa for dwellings nearer the water-supply" (1903: 628). Here she had set up a phonograph that daily attracted a horde of curious Hopis, many of whom were eager to sing into her machine. At this early stage in her research, Curtis had not yet rejected the phonograph as a device for recording music in the field. She later found it too bulky and difficult to manage, though J. Walter Fewkes had successfully pioneered its use among the Passamaquoddy and the Zuni in the 1890s (Fewkes 1890a, 1890b).[5]

According to Curtis's account of her methodology, she typically began field research by approaching Native leaders of reservation communities to enlist their support for a project that would "keep for all time the songs and stories of their race" (1923: xxi). Then she attempted to contact a cross-section of potential singers, but "[e]specially sought out . . . the very oldest men" (1923: xxiii)—a procedure that reflected her deepest interest in materials least "corrupted" by encounter with Euroamericans. Among the Hopi, the individual whom Curtis believed to fit her concept of the ideal collaborator was Lololomai,[6] leader of the Bear Clan, who had become village chief of Oraibi possibly as early as 1880. Originally anti-Euroamerican in attitude, Lololomai profoundly altered his views after a trip to Washington, D.C. (perhaps in 1884), to ask for assistance in responding to territorial encroachments by the Navajo.[7] Accompanied by trader Thomas Varker Keams, the village chief met with President Chester A. Arthur and was so impressed by the advances made by Euroamerican civilization, which he attributed to its educational system, that he began to work toward influencing his people to educate their own children in the white man's schools. In 1887, as a result of petitioning by Lololomai and other "Friendlies"—as the faction he led at Oraibi came to be known, a school was established at Keams's trading post at the foot of First Mesa. Ironically, it was from this school that the Hopi children emerged singing "Marching Through Georgia," which gave Natalie Curtis one of her favorite examples of how federal education was robbing Indian children of their artistic heritage.

Lololomai apparently came to believe that the Euroamerican encounter had been foretold in Hopi creation mythology and, while he maintained his commitment to some traditional beliefs and practices, assumed an accommodationist stance. Many people at Oraibi, however, did not agree with his position, the result being intense factionalism that did not climax until after Lololomai's death, which probably occurred sometime around 1904 (Dockstader 1979: 526–529; James 1974: 130–132; Loftin 1991: 72–75; Rushforth and Upham 1992: 123–127). Curtis seems to have been oblivious to that factionalism and to Lololomai's complicity in Hopi moves toward assimilation.

Curtis recorded a song of the Wuwuchim Ceremony from Lololomai. Like her other collaborators, he chose what he would sing for her. Her account of her encounter with the Oraibi village chief—written, she claimed, soon after the event—related how she visited Lololomai, on whom "[e]ighty summers had shone," while he sat atop his house spinning (1923: 474). Through an interpreter (perhaps the Mennonite missionary H. R. Voth) she explained to him what she wanted:

> "[T]he Hopi children are going to school; they are learning new ways and are singing new songs—American songs instead of Hopi. Some of the children are very young—so young that there have been, perhaps, but three corn-plantings since they came into the world. These little ones will never sing the songs of their fathers. They will not sing of the corn, the bean-blossoms, and the butterflies. They will know only American songs. Hopi songs are beautiful; it is sad that they should be forgotten." (1923: 475)

The old man could not disagree with Curtis's assertions, but must have still been wondering where this was leading. So she continued,

> "[T]here is one thing in the school good for all to have and to know, and that is *books*. Books can be of many kinds, Hopi as well as English. As yet your people have no books nor do they read or write. That is why your songs will be forgotten, why even your language may some day pass away.
>
> "When you sing, your song is heard, then dies like the wind that sweeps the cornfields and is gone, none knows whither. But if you could write, you could put your song into a book, and your people, even to the children of their children, could know your song as if you yourself were

singing. They could look upon the written page and say: 'Thus sang Lololomai, our chief, in the long ago. Thus sings Lololomai to-day.' " (1923: 475)

Curtis then told Lololomai that she had come from her " 'far-distant home by the "great waters" in the East' " to make a record of Hopi songs so that they would not be " 'lost forever, like a wind-blown trail' " (1923: 475).

When Lololomai objected that the superintendent might be angry at her encouraging the Hopi to sing traditional songs, Curtis revealed to him that "the great chief in Washington" had given her written permission (presumably a copy of the letter that Theodore Roosevelt had written to endorse her project) to record the songs (1923: 475–476). Lololomai then consented to the undertaking and began to sing in "rhythmic monotone" while Curtis took notes. Apparently the phonograph that she had set up in her government home was too cumbersome to transport up the mesa and then to Lololomai's rooftop. Curtis insisted, though, that she noted the words and melodies (that of Lololomai and of other Native American singers) "exactly as sung by the Indians, as nearly as musical notation can record" (1923: xxvi). Like many singers and storytellers, Lololomai was affected by the slow pace of this method of recording. In response to his comment on the length of time it was taking her to record what it had only taken him a short time to sing, Curtis told him, " '[Y]ou know that when the Hopi sets a trap for the blackbird, sometimes it is long before he can catch his fluttering prey. Your song is a wild blackbird to me, and it may be that the sun will move far along the sky before I have captured it.' " When she finally finished and showed the transcription to him, Lololomai seemed impressed (1923: 477).

Curtis's expressed admiration for Lololomai was unreserved, and she apparently was unaware or chose to ignore the factionalism that his assimilationist tendencies had exacerbated. Though she depicted him as an almost prototypical Indian wise man and, in fact, included in *The Indians' Book* a picture painted by a Cochiti artist of "Lololomai's prayer," offered for "everything that has life" (1923: 94), some Hopi blamed him for the eventual disintegration of Oraibi, especially its ceremonialism. In addition to urging the establishment of the Keams Canyon Reservation School, he apparently had been instrumental in inviting the Mennonite H. R. Voth to found a mission at Oraibi, the first significant encroachment of Christianity there besides that of a few Mormons (Waters 1963: 291). Don Talayesva implicated Lololomai in the sale of Hopi sacred objects that were sacrilegiously displayed at the Field Museum in Chicago in the 1930s (Simmons 1942: 344). At the same time, though, Talayesva expressed an admiration for the Oraibi village chief that seems generally untempered: "One person held in high respect was Lolulomai [sic], the Village Chief (kikmongwi), who was the 'father' of all the people in Oraibi. Everybody was expected to look up to him and to obey his orders. He wanted to be friendly with the Whites, accept their gifts, and send us children to their school. He said that it was better to be educated and become civilized" (Simmons 1942: 68). However, Talayesva argued, much of Lololomai's appreciation of Euroamericans and their culture stemmed from practical expediency: "Our chief had to show respect to them and pretend to obey their orders, but we knew that he did it halfheartedly and that he put his trust in our Hopi gods." In fact, according to Talayesva, Lololomai did not really want Oraibi children to attend government schools, but sent them only because he was persuaded by the chiefs of other villages (Simmons 1942: 88–89). Obviously, whatever the truth about Lololomai's role in the loss of tradition at Oraibi and the introduction of Euroamerican influences, Curtis's idealized view of him was overly simplistic.

A similar rosy romanticism colored her view of another well known Hopi who provided material for *The Indians' Book*. It was certainly naive to characterize Tawakwaptiwa as "a Hopi untouched by foreign influences, the child of natural environment, spontaneous, alert, full of life and laughter" (1923: 480). As Lololomai's successor as leader of the "Friendlies" at Oraibi, though, Tawakwaptiwa definitely "felt that a compromise could be made with the representatives of Washington by which the Hopi could benefit without endangering their integrity as good Hopi—the children could attend school; American visitors could be met in friendly fashion; Hopi could avail themselves of wagons, metal, tools, and other helpful articles in exchange for labor" (James 1974: 132). But this view apparently led to a climax of village factionalism. On 8 September 1906, after Tawakwaptiwa had become village chief, the "Friendlies" and the "Hostiles" (those who opposed any compromise with Euroamerican influences) squared off physically against one another, the result being that 298 of the latter group left Oraibi and established the village of Hotevilla some seven miles away. The victory of the "Friendlies," though, was short-lived, for before the year was over, the federal government removed Tawakwaptiwa from his political position and sent him and his family to Sherman Institute in Riverside, California, to learn English and the Euroamerican way of life. Upon his return in 1910, he had become so embittered that he utterly

rejected moves toward assimilation and accommodation. Tawakwaptiwa gradually came to terms with his former adversaries and sometimes visited them at Hotevilla (James 1974: 132–145; Loftin 1991:
78–79; Rushforth and Upham 1992: 127–129). He was village chief of
Oraibi during the early 1930s during the ethnographic researches conducted by Mischa Titiev and others (Titiev 1972). Don Talayesva indicated that Tawakwaptiwa became a government policeman after his
return from Sherman Institute and worked for awhile as a cook for the
Santa Fe Railroad (Simmons 1942: 206, 337). By the time of his death in
1960, he had also become known for his Katcina carvings (Dockstader
1977: 288–290).

Curtis included one song recorded from Tawakwaptiwa, who was
probably much younger at the time than the tribal elder, her ideal
source. This was the text and tune of a composition of his own used in
the Poli Tiwa (Butterfly Dance).[8] Directed to him because, so she claims
(1923: 481), the Hopi told her that he "makes good songs" and "Everybody likes Tawakwaptiwa," Curtis elicited some information on the
composition process that confirmed her essentially romantic view of
the Native American as spontaneous oral poet. " 'When I am herding
my sheep, or away in the fields, and I see something that I like—then I
sing about it,' " Tawakwaptiwa told her (1923: 481).

Another of Curtis's Hopi collaborators provided material not only for
The Indians' Book, but for her first publication on a Native American
topic. In an article issued in the September 1903 issue of *Harper's*, Curtis had focused on Koianimptiwa, who had received the name "Thompson" while attending a government school. The essay also provides
additional insight into Curtis's field methods, since she describes how
she collected a Katcina song that Koianimptiwa had composed, the
words and melody of which also appear in *The Indians' Book* (1923:
484–485, 508–516).

One morning, Curtis recalls, "a graceful Hopi youth" who "spoke
English and wore American clothing, and was thus considered a 'civilized' Indian" appeared at her doorway and expressed a desire to sing the
song he had composed the previous day. No one else, he claimed, had
yet heard it. Curtis eagerly sat Koianimptiwa on an upturned box before
the phonograph and placed a rattle in his hand so that the rhythm for
the song would come through clearly. She "told him to shake it just as
he would if he were dancing." Curtis continues her description of the
situation: "The singing was indeed a solemn event to Koianimptiwa,
and we both awaited with keen interest the result on the phonograph. It
was a great success. Koianimptiwa flashed a smile as we listened, and I

was delighted, for I had been struck with the beauty of the song, and felt that with its associations it would always be one of my most prized records" (1903: 629). The singer-composer's motives for making the recording soon became clear when he asked Curtis if she would play the recording for other Hopi. She did so and elicited some evaluative comments from listeners who did not recognize the identity of the singer: " 'It is a fine song' " (1903: 629).

Several days later Curtis arranged a session with Koianimptiwa during which she transcribed the song's words in Hopi while he dictated slowly. "I strove to record in written symbols the strange melody of Hopi speech," she noted, "for the language has the vowel music of the Samoan, and yet the soft guttural strength of the Greek." Then she had Koianimptiwa attempt a translation into English, the "most difficult part of the task" (1903: 629). Next, she got the composer to describe the process by which he created the song. While his words reinforced Curtis's image of the Native American as natural poet, they may provide some insight into the oral creative process. Of special interest are Koianimptiwa's insistence that neither words nor music took precedence and his revelation that the process was indeed somewhat laborious, beginning shortly after dawn and continuing until a couple of hours before midday (1903: 631).

Curtis described one other interaction with Koianimptiwa. He and his mules were escorting her back to civilization, and she asked him to teach her to sing his song "just as you taught it to the men in the kivas." He responded by singing it over and over for the highly trained musician, who had to admit her inability to master it (an admission that raises questions about the accuracy of her transcriptions of other Native American songs). Their conversation led her to ask him if Hopis had as much difficulty learning to sing Euroamerican music as she was having with this song. His negative reply provided the opportunity for Curtis to digress on the "extraordinary musical aptitude" of the Hopi and of Native Americans in general (1903: 632). Curtis ends the *Harper's* article with a translation of Koianimptiwa's song:

> Yellow butterflies
> With pollen-painted faces
> Chase one another in brilliant throng
> Over the blossoming corn.
>
> Blue butterflies
> With pollen-painted faces

Chase one another in brilliant streams
Over the blossoming virgin beans.

Over the blossoming virgin corn
The wild bees hum:
Over the blossoming virgin beans
The wild bees hum.

Over your field of growing corn
All day shall come the thunder-cloud:
Over your field of growing corn
All day shall come the rushing rain.

(1903: 631)[9]

This differs in several respects from that published in *The Indians'*
Book four years later. The final lines of the first and second stanzas of
the 1903 translation have become the second lines of those stanzas in
the 1907 version. The third stanza has been reconfigured as follows:

Over the blossoming corn,
Over the virgin corn
Wild bees hum:
Over the blossoming beans,
Over the virgin beans,
Wild bees hum. (1923: 484–485)

In 1907 Curtis translated the verb rendered as "come" in the fourth
stanza as "hang." The orthography of the Hopi in the 1903 is slightly
different from that used in her anthology, and the former includes a
refrain in vocables that does not appear in either translation or in the
1907 rendering of the Hopi. The musical transcriptions are roughly the
same.

Curtis's other Hopi collaborators are not as easily identified as these
three, nor does she provide much information on how she managed to
collect material from them. Her spellings of their names do not represent even the consensus of her time, and later transliterations of Hopi
into the Roman alphabet result in varying ways of rendering Hopi
words, especially proper names.

However, some tentative suggestions can be made as to the identities
of a few of the seven other Hopi collaborators in *The Indians' Book*.
For example, Kavanghongevah, from whom Curtis recorded a song of

the Gray Flute Society, may be the person recalled by Don Talayesva, whose name Leo Simmons spells as "Kayahongnewa." In 1931, this person "knew most of the ceremonies, and people came to see him to check the songs in their memories" (Simmons 1942: 306). In his youth, he had been a prizewinning runner and could wrestle three people concurrently. A member of the Katcina, Wuwuchim, Soyal, Women's Ooqol, and Flute Societies, he was nearly blind at the time Talayesva characterized him.

Curtis's Masahongva could be Masahongneoma, the son of Talayesva's uncle. If so, Curtis would have been unlikely to know that "[h]e was called Nice Man by everyone now, because a prostitute in Winslow had praised him highly for his very long penis and had called him a 'nice man'" (Simmons 1942: 230). She recorded a Katcina song from Masahongva. Another source for a Katcina song was Lahpu, the brother of Tawakwaptiwa. Very likely this is "La-pu," a Hopi who, according to Belle Axtell Kolp, who had taught at the government school briefly in 1903, "lives, dresses and speaks 'American,'" but had been fined by Agent Burton "for leaving the reservation to earn money to support his family" (quoted in James 1974: 128). I will not hazard a guess as to the identity of Curtis's three other Hopi collaborators. She names them as Kuwanyisnim, Masaveimah, and Gashonienim (1923: 561).

Knowing from whom Curtis collected songs at Oraibi, how she went about doing the collecting, and the attitudes she brought with her to northeastern Arizona (particularly her apparent blindness to the factionalism there) are important because of Curtis's influence on the textualization and critical appreciation of Native American verbal art among the general public and upon literary enthusiasts for a score of years after *The Indians' Book* appeared in 1907. Her romanticization of her collaborators as figures untouched by the Euroamerican influences that were robbing them and their descendants, she believed, of a rich esthetic legacy has affected how many poets and literary critics have viewed Native American verbal art until the current ethnopoetics movement (Castro 1983). Undoubtedly, her idealistic ignoring of the conflicts at Oraibi, which had to have affected whom she interviewed and what they reported to her, arose also from motivations and ideologies that joined salvage ethnomusicology in shaping Curtis's work. Those were her acceptance of the theory of unilinear cultural evolution, her belief that Native American musical and verbal arts could provide a foundation for an indigenous American art heritage, and her endorsement of antimodernism.

Despite Curtis's somewhat enlightened view regarding Native American arts, she uncritically accepted the popular anthropology of her time. Moreover, she tempered that anthropology with what even the most ardent contemporary apologist must admit to be racism. Though Curtis deplored prohibitions on indigenous artistic expression, she accepted—and at least tacitly advocated—measures to ease the Indians' inevitable evolution from "primitive" to "civilized." Many contemporary anthropologists such as Franz Boas, to whom Curtis turned for informal mentoring throughout her career,[10] had for the most part rejected the cultural evolutionism espoused by their immediate intellectual ancestors, but Curtis accepted the idea that cultures everywhere evinced unilinear progression from savagery through barbarism to civilization. A generation after Daniel Garrison Brinton allowed cultural evolutionism to shape his textmaking philosophy, Curtis was doing the same thing. An ethnological survey of contemporary world societies, according to this view, would reveal the coexistence of representatives of each of the three stages of culture. The civilized Euroamerican fieldworkers whom John Wesley Powell commissioned for the BAE were thus, in a sense, confronting their own cultural forebears among American Indians, whose lifeways exemplified the savagery their ancestors in Europe had left behind many generations previously.

A common metaphor, which many took all too literally, held that cultures at the savage stage represented the "childhood" of humanity. For example, in an address to the National Education Association, Commissioner of Indian Affairs Francis Leupp, a Roosevelt appointee, ignored the metaphorical dimensions of the image: "The Indian is an adult child. He has the physical attributes of the adult and the mentality of about our fourteen-year-old boy" (1907: 71). And Curtis herself employed the image in her introduction to *The Indians' Book*, identifying "primitive races" such as Native Americans as "child races" (1923: xxx). "Enlightened" sympathizers with the Indians such as Curtis and Leupp believed that if left alone, the cultural "child" would evolve through many generations into a civilized cultural "adult." But they also thought the process could be hastened through well-conceived programs such as land allotment that emphasized economic development to "Americanize" Native Americans while maintaining a degree of Indian identity through preservation and encouragement of Native arts and music. Curtis drew upon an image borrowed from Leupp when she wrote, "As the young Indian becomes educated, he will leave barbarous customs behind him of his own free will, like a tadpole which sheds its tail" (1915b: 480). However, she elsewhere noted, Native American art must be preserved and encouraged because, like all primitives, Indians use art to express their "aspirations": "If we close to him this outlet we crush in him his spirit's life, and the result must ever be a degradation of the real man. But if all that is best in the Indian—his aspiration toward the good, the true, and the beautiful—be developed along natural lines . . . then shall we have gained when the Indian becomes a citizen and the red man not have lost" (1904c: 450). In short, to prevent "discouragement," "moral disintegration," "hopelessness," and "bewilderment," Curtis asserted, "Indian songs should be encouraged" (1915b: 480). In 1913 she summarized her somewhat paradoxical concept of progress combined with artistic conservation: "We may provide the undeveloped races with the means of adjustment to the life of modern industry and with the mechanical processes of self-expression, but . . . we should at least recognize the inborn racial ideas and inherited art impulses" (1913: 625).

Hence, her interest in salvaging Native American traditional music and verbal art did not stem simply from her fears of the material's being lost—a theme, though, that reverberates throughout her writings on the subject. She also recognized the place of Native arts in the assimilationist social agenda whose principal intellectual foundation lay in cultural evolutionism. Consequently, what she represented in her texts had to be the "best" that Native American cultures had to offer, since it would contribute to those cultures' progress toward civilization.

Curtis noted, "We believe that for the Indian's sake, for his legitimate human needs, as well as in the interests of American literature and music, Indian songs should be encouraged"(1920b: 666). The seemingly casual interpolation, "as well as in the interests of American literature and music," suggests another source of Curtis's concern for Native American arts. She explained to the Indian women at Laguna whose corn-grinding songs she collected that her efforts would have implications beyond the immediate cultural context: " 'I shall write these songs on paper, just as you have seen songs written in books in the schools. Then people will know that Indian songs are beautiful, and the songs will never wholly be lost, or forgotten" (1904a: 37). Curtis saw in Native American music something of value for American culture in general. A thoroughgoing nationalist despite her European education, she consistently argued for a truly American art, independent as far as possible from foreign influences. "We echo Europe," she complained, "whereas we might develop a decorative art truly American" (1919b: 389).

A persistent theme in American intellectual life since its beginnings has been how art, science, and letters in the United States could assert their distinctiveness, declare their independence from their European forebears. The "truly American" art that Curtis advocated represented a goal toward which intellectuals in the United States had been striving for generations. Like many of her forerunners, Curtis believed that such an art could find at least some of its inspiration in those forms indigenous to the western hemisphere—in the Native American pottery, textiles, basketry, verbal art, and music which she identified as "the artistic heritage of America" (1905a: 544).

Though a variety of influences might have turned Curtis toward this idea, an important factor must have been Arthur Farwell, founder of the Wa-Wan Press, which had published Curtis's musical settings for Robert Louis Stevenson's children's poems in 1902. Farwell established the Wa-Wan Press primarily to afford an outlet to American composers who were developing distinctively American themes. In "A Letter to American Composers" written in 1903, he articulated his philosophy of American music:

> Such an art will not be a mere echo of other lands and times, but shall have a vital meaning for us, in our circumstances, here and now. While it will take the worthier traditions of the past for its point of departure, it will derive its convincing qualities of color, form, and spirit from our nature-world and our humanity.
>
> No other country has matured, musically, without creating such an art for itself,—an expression of the temper of its land and people; and we feel that America will not be an exception to this universal way of healthful artistic life and growth. (1970: xvii)

Farwell had already demonstrated that one inspiration for an American music could be found in the musical traditions of Native Americans. Perhaps even before the turn of the century, he had composed "American Indian Melodies," a series of ten short pieces for piano that used material collected and published by Alice Cunningham Fletcher. The Wa-Wan Press (which took its name from an Omaha ceremony documented by Fletcher) published the series in 1901.

Farwell also wrote extensively on how American composers might use Native American songs "in place of borrowed European melodies ... as the basis of various musical art-works of considerable dimensions" (1902: 212). Moreover, American Indian culture, especially mythology and ceremonialism, might provide Euroamerican artists with a foundation for a national art. In myth, Farwell claimed, a "race" embodies "its view of the universe, and of human life in its relation to superhuman forces." Mythology establishes a society's "intellectual, moral and political character, and leave[s] to future ages . . . a record of its place and meaning in history" (1904: 47). Although Greek mythology had performed these services for the European heritage, "the informing spirit of modern life in America" required new material in "forms not already too inflexibly crystallized." Farwell believed that the mythos of the Indian would point American artists "to the heights of a Paracelsus, an Oedipus or a Parsifal" (1904: 49).

Natalie Curtis took up Farwell's cause and perhaps was influenced by the founder of the Wa-Wan Press in setting for herself the task of documenting the Native American musical traditions that would provide the source material for a distinctive American art. She strongly believed that if American Indian artistry in various media would "be eventually absorbed into the art expression of our country, we shall have woven into the fabric of our national culture a strand of color, instead of adding to the monotone of grey" (1904c: 450). She also suggested that "Anglo-Saxon" "mechanical and inventive genius" lacked "sincere and spontaneous art inpulses [sic]"—a deficiency that could be remedied by the "undeveloped talents native to aboriginal America" (quoted in Castro 1983: 11). Whatever dismay she felt at the educational system's discouraging of Native artistry became compounded when she considered the impact of that policy not only on American Indians' vanishing cultures and their evolutionary potential, but also how the loss of that artistry would affect the development of a distinctive Euroamerican art heritage.[11] If the texts with which she intended to represent this artistic foundation were really to be useful to Euroamerican poets, they had to evince an accessibility that placed them toward the Identity pole of the continuum.

Farwell derived some of his inspiration from the philosophy and practice of William Morris, the Victorian English artist whose medievalism combined high standards of workmanship with a consciousness of artistic expression as one of life's necessities. Antimodernism, the point of view advocated by Morris's disciples in the United States, was undoubtedly another influence on Curtis's interest in Native American music. In its most usual form in this country, antimodernism represented a "recoil from an 'overcivilized' modern existence to more intense forms of physical or spiritual existence supposedly embodied in medieval or Oriental cultures" (Lears 1981: xiii). The practical dimension of the antimodernist movement focused on the premodern artisan as the role model for a return to a "primal authenticity of thought, feeling, and action" (Lears 1981: 91). This resulted in a belief that craftsmanship rooted in a "primitive" sense of community could revitalize modern men and women spiritually enervated by the loss of touch with essential nature. Sylvester Baxter articulated how contact with "primitive" esthetic ideas and practices could be put to active use by antimodernist artists and craftspersons:

> . . . the student goes back to the primitive beginnings of an art, and is shown how to put himself in place of the ancient worker, so far as possible; doing the thing as it was done in the beginning and, by following the primal instincts for art, to develop his work according to natural indications and without the sophistication that comes with beginning a lesson in the middle. Knowing what we know, we cannot, of course, return to the primitive state of mind and feeling, and hence do things in just that same way, any more than the grown man can return to childhood. But while from our twentieth century civilization we may not return to the childhood of the race, we can in great measure bring into play the primitive springs of thought, impulse, and action that exist in every human being and so put ourselves *en rapport* with the primitive state of mind and primitive view of things, just as the adult can bring himself into sympathetic relations with the child. (quoted in Lears 1981: 91–92)

A principal activist in and spokesperson for the arts and crafts movement connected with antimodernism was Gustav Stickley, who propagandized his views by editing a periodical, *The Craftsman*, from 1901 through 1916. Natalie Curtis contributed regularly to Stickley's magazine, writing fifteen articles over an eleven-year period between 1904 and 1914. Seven of these pieces dealt with Native American music and art, but Curtis also wrote on such subjects as architecture, music settlement schools, and Franz Liszt. In the September 1910 issue of *The Craftsman*, an unsigned article, presumably written by editor Stickley, appeared under the title "People Who Interest Us: Natalie Curtis, the 'Friend of the Indians' " ([Stickley] 1910). Accompanied by a studio photograph of its subject, the brief essay clearly identified Curtis with the aims espoused by Stickley. Moreover, Curtis frequently mentioned William Morris and John Ruskin, intellectual forebears of antimodernism, in her writings, especially those on Native American music and art.

The connection between at least some of the Natives of the Americas and the idealized preindustrial artisan admired by antimodernists had apparently occurred to several of Curtis's contemporaries. A late-twentieth-century commentator on antimodernism has noted that the movement's proponents "sought a wider selfhood by embracing the 'childlike' or 'feminine' aspects of premodern character" (Lears 1981:

57). Given the metaphorical language of cultural evolutionists, one could expect to find the "childlike" and perhaps the "feminine" in cultures such as those of Native Americans that had not yet attained sophisticated "maturity." The Pueblos of the Southwest held special appeal, and antimodernism contributed to the vogue for the region that emerged around the turn of the century, when Natalie Curtis was collecting music and verbal art in Hopiland. Artists who flocked to Santa Fe and Taos during the first two decades of the twentieth century came in part because they sought the pastoral primitivism represented by the Pueblos (Evans 1988: 261–262; Gibson 1983). Antimodernism contributed an esthetic of simplicity to Curtis's textmaking; anything but simplicity would violate the antimodernist perception of what was needed spiritually to resuscitate twentieth-century humanity.

In a letter written to Franz Boas in 1903, Curtis made explicit the connection between her evolutionary interest in the culture of the Hopis (whom she referred to with the unwitting ethnic slur "Moquis") and the medievalism advocated by Morris and Ruskin. She began by asking Boas, whom she was contacting apparently for the first time, whether an ethnologist would be able to determine the hypothetical line of evolutionary development that the Hopi communities would take if left to themselves. Then she refers to the city of Rothenburg where civic decree dictates preservation of the medieval flavor by forbidding construction of buildings not in keeping with that flavor. Why, she wonders, could not the same thing be done in the Hopi communities, thus providing America with the same kind of attraction that lures its citizens as tourists to Europe?[12]

This letter, which shows the influence of antimodernistic medievalism on Curtis's thinking about American Indians, also reflects her nationalism and her concerns about federal Indian policy that would interfere with the Hopis' natural cultural evolution. The four major influences on Curtis's interest in collecting Native American music and verbal art coalesce into a more-or-less coherent rationale that affected her textualization of that music and art. She unquestioningly accepted the image of the Indian as "vanishing American." While her evolutionary stance compelled her to accept the necessity of change in Native cultures and to endorse efforts to facilitate such change on an economic level, she also insisted that cultural evolution—which someday would inevitably result in assimilation—should be gradual and naturally build upon the positive features of Native cultures, especially the arts. As Native American arts provided the foundation for American Indian cultures, they could also provide the basis for a truly indigenous

Euroamerican esthetic culture, one that developed the raw material of the Indians into a distinctive artistic heritage. A turn away from the hollow sophistication of modern European-derived art and toward artistic expression rooted in the authenticity of human experience as represented among American Indians could provide vitality that would otherwise be absent from an American artistic tradition.

This set of ideas clearly influenced Curtis's approach to fieldwork at Oraibi in 1903 and consequently the kind of material she recorded. It contributed to her seeking out "uncorrupted" performers and to her ignoring (or glossing over) any evidences of their having been affected by contacts with Euroamerican culture and of the factionalism such contacts might occasion. Textualizations of the material she collected from these idealized Hopis that would fulfill the goals of Curtis's ambitious program for Native American arts had to meet several criteria.

First, they had to be faithful to the originals. If the texts were actually to preserve a vanishing artistry, they should represent that artistry as it actually emerged from the performances of those who knew it in its oldest and most pristine form. Curtis's recognition of the effects of federal education policy on the Hopi made it essential that she be as accurate as she possibly could in preserving what was about to be lost.

Second, the textualizations should accurately reflect the "best" in Native cultures. Since the material she recorded and textualized was intended, in part at least, to contribute to Indians' inevitable progress toward civilization, as defined by the scenario of unilinear cultural evolution, Curtis had to make sure that she collected and textualized only material that documented the values that would contribute to such progress. Recording verbal expressions from individuals whose art had become corrupted by contacts with Euroamericans would dilute the actual Hopi contribution to their own evolution.

Third, her texts had to be accessible to a Euroamerican readership. Unlike Boas and others who saw the text principally as data source for scholars, Curtis viewed her texts as part of a program for establishing a truly American art. American artists, whether in music or literature, had to be able to appreciate the material that would serve as the foundation for their own development of an indigenous American art heritage.

Fourth, the texts should evince simplicity, since they represented premodern artistic values. Nor should they reflect anything that might suggest that the stresses of modern life had had an impact on her Hopi collaborators. Hence, she had another reason for ignoring the conflicts at Oraibi.

Factoring in Curtis's lack of training in the study of Native American languages and her deep involvement in the musical heritage of European civilization, we should expect that her success in accomplishing these four goals varied. On one hand, as modern students of Hopi have pointed out (e.g., Shaul 1992), Curtis clearly did not achieve much accuracy in texts made from the singing of her collaborators. She was certainly not as successful in this regard as her predecessors and contemporaries in the anthropological community who insisted foremost on linguistic accuracy in textualization. Moreover, her idea of what was "best" in Hopi and other Native American cultures reflected what even her most ardent apologists and certainly her critics have to recognize at best as "benign" racism (e.g., Krupat 1992b: 9). On the other hand, she did achieve considerable accessibility in her texts—a fact attested to by their inclusion in anthologies directed toward general readers of American poetry (e.g., Untermeyer 1931: 696) and by the influence she exerted on the enthusiasm for American Indian verbal art during the 1910s and 1920s (Castro 1983: 8–12). Yet Curtis attained accessibility not through Schoolcraftian embellishments; after all she was interested in Native American music and verbal art as potential, not as fully realized "literature" in the Euroamerican sense. Instead, omission might be a better characterization of her approach, since she tended to ignore such frequently notable features of Native American verbal art as vocables and repetition.

The presentation of Natalie Curtis's linguistic texts (occasionally with enough characterization of expressive situations to approach ethnographic textualization) in *The Indians' Book* affected the way in which Native American verbal art has entered the popular consciousness throughout most of the twentieth century. Following the lead of Curtis's 1907 book, the intercultural anthology has become a principal vehicle for publishing texts—for the most part, though, without her forays into ethnographic textualization.

CHAPTER NINE

THE ANTHOLOGY AS MUSEUM OF VERBAL ART

Most of us have probably seen an exhibition of American Indian (or other "primitive"/"tribal") objects displayed as "art." Even if they appear in a venue other than an art museum, displays of the pottery, baskets, beadwork, ceremonial masks, and other manifestations of what Natalie Curtis called the "art impulse" of Native Americans usually follow the same pattern. An object—let's say a Hopi Katcina figure—appears in a freestanding Plexiglass case that allows the viewer to circumambulate it in order to see it from all perspectives. Perhaps a special light shines on the object, and there's usually a card attached to the case:

HOPI KATCINA DOLL   c. 1910
This figure representing the Antelope Katcina provided a visual image of the spirit world for Hopis who depended upon the ancestral spirits to bring rain to their fields in the northeastern Arizona desert.
Artist unknown.

Usually I will read the card, walk around the display case, and decide whether I "like" the figure. Maybe I'll comment on it to a companion before we move on to the next item, which is displayed in much the same "minimalist installation style" (Kirshenblatt-Gimblett 1991: 391–392). If I have a copy of the exhibit catalog, perhaps I'll read more about the piece than the card attached to the exhibit presents, but usually I don't acquire the catalog until after I've toured the exhibit and then will read it at home with only photographs to remind me of what I've seen.

I have to confess that after I've punctiliously read the exhibit cards for a few of the items, I'm likely to become increasingly too lazy to continue doing so and begin only to glance to see what an item's identity is supposed to be: "Hopi Katcina Doll," "Tlingit Blanket," or "Maidu Basket." I come out of the exhibit, though, with a sense that I've had an esthetic experience, one that compares, I believe at the time, to that of touring an exhibit of works by contemporary Spanish sculptors or late eighteenth-century French painters.

But are those experiences really comparable? Though I know nothing specific about contemporary Spanish sculpture or late eighteenth-century French painting, I do share a common heritage with them: that of the Judaeo-Christian West. A portrait of a French aristocrat by Jacques-Louis David addresses the cultural baggage with which a half century of socialization within that heritage has burdened me—especially the ideas that certain kinds of material expression fall within a distinctive category of objects called "art," that one way in which this so-called "art" has traditionally manifested itself is in painted representations of specifically identifiable individuals, that such representations are often stylized rather than photographically realistic, and that one function of such representations is to adorn the walls of art galleries and museums so that people like me can walk by them in our quest for esthetic experience. Though I may need to read the exhibit card to find out who painted the portrait, when it was painted, and whom it is supposed to depict, and though I may need to study the exhibit catalog (or maybe some art history textbook) to understand the portrait's precise place in the history of Western art, I still bring some general assumptions to the portrait that don't require any special study.

This is not so for American Indian "art" (the quotation marks here reflect the tentativeness—at least in conventional Western terms—of the term's relevance to Hopi Katcina figures, Tlingit blankets, and Maidu baskets). If I am really to appreciate these objects, I must know more about them than a museum or art gallery can possibly provide me on an exhibit card or even in an exhibit catalog, except in those instances when an exhibit focuses on only a limited range of objects (for example, "Basketry of the California Tribes"). For either me or the museum/gallery to assume that a Western-socialized viewer can appreciate these objects when they are displayed like Spanish sculpture or French paintings presumes too much. It diminishes them by suggesting they they are so elemental, so simple, so *primitive,* so reflective of "esthetic universalism" (Krupat 1992a: 180) that one doesn't need to bring to them specific cultural perspectives such as those that enter into an appreciation of Spanish sculpture or French painting. Being a Westerner in search of esthetic experience and sensitive enough to recognize it when encountered is apparently enough. A few simple facts, which many of us may not bother to read anyway, suffice to allow us to appreciate these materials as art.

In a review of several exhibitions of "tribal" art that appeared in New York City in the mid-1980s, James Clifford has expressed concerns regarding the apparent understanding of both ethnography and esthetics on the parts of the museums or galleries. The assumptions underlying most of the exhibitions, especially that at the Museum of Modern Art entitled " 'Primitivism' in 20th Century Art: Affinity of the Tribal and the Modern," were that the creations of Western artists share important qualities with the work of artists from "tribal" or "primitive" cultures, that Western gallery-goers could appreciate those shared qualities in such a way that required no special insight into the cultural milieus involved, that a Kwakiutl mask and detail from Picasso's *Girl Before a Mirror* could be appreciated in the same terms. As Clifford suggests, though, these assumptions raise "ambiguous and disturbing questions about aesthetic appropriation of non-Western others, issues of race, gender, and power" (1988: 197; cf. Torgovnick 1990: 119–137). This essentially appropriative spirit allowed a Westerner like Picasso to tour the Paris Musée d'Ethnographie and—according to Marianna Torgovnick in an essay similar to Clifford's—"cleverly pick out its 'best' and 'worst' pieces" (1990: 82).

These assumptions also seem to equate "an ignorance of cultural context" with "artistic appreciation," since the catalogs for the exhibits emphasize formal qualities of the displayed objects instead of their use, symbolic valences, and functions (Clifford 1988: 200). In a related essay, Clifford, in fact, stresses the different emphases in displaying artifacts on the parts of ethnographic and art museums, the latter suggesting that the object's "place in everyday cultural practices . . . is irrelevant to its essential meaning" (1988: 227; cf. Torgovnick 1990: 81). One of his examples points to displayed objects that would have "religious" significance in their original contexts as now in the art gallery evincing "no individual 'power' or mystery—qualities once possessed by 'fetishes' [using a nineteenth-century catch-all for non-Western religious objects] before they were reclassified in the modern system as primitive art or cultural artifact." For an object in a museum display, its "specific power or sacredness is relocated to a general aesthetic realm" (1988: 226).

One is reminded of the Aztec mask that the Medicis set with rubies and mounted in a gilded, enameled copper frame, an instance of how objects brought from the Americas "were absorbed into a particular European world and were as culturally insignificant as the mermen or unicorn horns to be found in the same *Wunderkammern*" (Pagden 1993: 33). This represents the shift from "cult value" to "exhibition value" that reduces a way of life to "mere artifacts and snippets of disconnected information" (Sarris 1993: 52). Applying the process to Pomo basketry, Greg Sarris has written,

> It seems that this shift from "cult value" to "exhibition value" displaces the basket's historical testimony and subsequent authority, and this displacement not only maintains a separation of the spectator from the world and history out of which the baskets were created but also precipitates a closed cycle of presentation and discussion about the basketry itself. (1993: 54)

When one views a Pomo basket in a museum, Sarris argues, it is like viewing a close-up photograph of water: "[I]t could be water anywhere, or nowhere" (1993: 56).

Clifford lists features of tribal art works (and artists) that museum catalogs suggest as being also present in the works of their twentieth-century Modernist parallels: "a use of rough or 'natural' materials, a ritualistic attitude, ecological concern, archaeological inspiration, certain techniques of assemblage, a conception of the artist as shaman, and some familiarity with 'the mind of primitive man' " (1988: 212). Moreover, Torgovnick adds, the exhibits tend to present tribal art in a sort of eternal present, oblivious and untainted by the processes of history, especially those generated by contact with the very Western cultures that have appropriated that art for the stasis of museum display (1990: 121). Noting the political implications of the situation—implications that have become increasingly apparent to students of the West's contact with the tribal Other (e.g., Boon 1982; Greenblatt 1991; McGrane 1989; Wolf 1982), Clifford concludes his review, "The relations of power whereby one portion of humanity can select, value, and collect the pure products of others need to be criticized and transformed" (1988: 213).

Though not an exclusively Western activity in the same sense as museum display may be (if we allow examples of "preliterate" textualization such as the "sand stories" of the Walbiri of north-central Australia [Munn 1986], rock art among the Zuni [Young 1988], and Ojibwa bark drawings [Densmore 1910]), textmaking can represent a similar selection, valuation, and collection of the products of others by cultural outsiders. Most published texts of Native American verbal art are, of course, the work of Euroamericans responding to Euroamerican needs—whether politically, scientifically, or artistically imperialistic. Some of the venues in which those texts have been published foreground their museological effect, especially when those venues suggest—like the New York City art exhibits—the "universal" artistic qualities that do not depend upon their cultural contexts and when the texts record only the linguistic product of oral expression, not the totality of the event. The anthology of Native American "literature" is the most obvious of such venues. This chapter looks at several such anthologies and emphasizes some ways in which their displays of verbal art texts parallel the presentation of material art in many museums and galleries. This "art museum" approach (or equally apt: "jewelry store" approach [Torgovnick 1990: 78, 114, 116]) to presenting texts of Native American verbal art implies that Westerners don't need to reorient themselves culturally to appreciate the texts, that those texts can (and should) be presented in ways that make them as accessible to the Western reader as possible without detracting from their indigenous values, that the verbal art of "primitives" exists in an eternal present that does not reflect the specifics of time and place of creation, that the linguistic component of an expressive event is all that matters, and that it can pass "the litmus test" of being "stripped of contingency and still hold[ing] up" (Kirshenblatt-Gimblett 1991: 391). Before considering some more or less contemporary anthologies that present linguistic texts of American Indian verbal expression as literature, we will consider some of the history of anthologizing of such materials.

In a letter written in 1907 to Franz Boas, Natalie Curtis explained that *The Indians' Book*, the anthology that she viewed as the culminating product of her self-appointed task in salvage ethnomusicology that had begun among the Hopis, was partially intended to make Native American verbal and musical materials available for use in government educational programs for Indians. She also informed Boas that her principal intent was to preserve the verbal art she collected as faithfully as possible and to offer only such commentary as her Native collaborators had provided.[1] In fact, though, *The Indians' Book* was fulfilling a long-stated Euroamerican interest: enthusiasts for Native Americana had been calling for an intercultural anthology of American Indian verbal art for over half a century before Curtis's book was published.

In 1829, James Athearn Jones had put together a volume of verbal material—translated and rewritten according to the Euroamerican literary esthetic of the era, as suggested in chapter 5—from various Native groups (Jones 1829). Passing quickly into literary oblivion, Jones's volume had apparently been forgotten by mid-century when William Gilmore Simms, second only to Longfellow in the exploitation of Native American materials in his own literary work, recommended "to some of our clever compilers . . . the plan of an Indian miscellany, in which choice specimens of their oratory, their fable, their poetry" might be published (1962: 142).

No one acted on Simms's suggestion, so a generation later John Reade, addressing the Royal Society of Canada, again emphasized the possibilities of a cross-cultural anthology: "If the best of the scattered productions of northern [hemisphere] genius were . . . collected and properly exhibited, they might form no contemptible anthology" (1884: 29). Apparently Daniel G. Brinton, who was at the time publishing his "Library of Aboriginal American Literature," had a plan for such a collection in preparation when Reade delivered his talk, for the Canadian mentioned the eager anticipation of "Dr. Brinton's promised work," which was to include materials from North American Indians in addition to the Middle American literature that was becoming Brinton's specialty (1884: 29). Moreover, at the end of his booklet *Aboriginal American Authors and Their Productions,* Brinton appended an advertisement for an "ABORIGINAL AMERICAN ANTHOLOGY," which he would edit. The work would be a "collection of songs, chants and metrical compositions of the Indians, designed to display the emotional and imaginative powers of the race and the prosody of their languages" (1883a: [67]).

Brinton's projected anthology never materialized, and in 1900 Andrew Lang, the Victorian gentleman scholar with strong interests in folklore and evolutionary anthropology, commented, "[I]t would be a pleasant task for some American man or woman of letters to give us an anthology of Red Indian poetry and prose," drawing especially upon the materials published in the BAE Annual Reports and Bulletins (Lang 1900: 163).

Although Natalie Curtis probably knew nothing of these attempts to promote an intercultural anthology of Native North American verbal art, she must have known Alice Cunningham Fletcher's *Indian Story and Song from North America,* published the same year as Lang's suggestion. Although an anthology, Fletcher's book did not completely fulfill the hopes for such a work, since it focused almost entirely on the Native cultures of the northern Plains, especially of the Omaha. While *The Indians' Book* also reflects a regional interest (in the Southwest), its eighteen groups represent a range of North American culture areas: Northeast (Abnaki), Midwest (Winnebago), Plains (Dakota, Pawnee, Cheyenne, Arapaho, and Kiowa), Northwest Coast (Kwakiutl), and

Southwest (Pima, Apache, Mojave, Yuma, Navajo, Zuni, San Juan, Acoma, Laguna, and Hopi). Perhaps it is not too much to claim for *The Indians' Book* the distinction of being the first truly cross-cultural anthology of Native American verbal art, a kind of fulfillment of the ideas and plans of Simms, Reade, Brinton, Lang, and others. Certainly its influence was apparent in many other anthologies that have appeared since 1907 in its "art museum" method of presenting materials and in its compiler's assumption that those materials were not only easily accessible to, but in fact eminently usable, by Euroamerican readers.

Though Curtis did provide some very general ethnographic data on the groups whose verbal art she anthologized, she seldom placed specific texts in fully described contexts or expressive situations. Instead, she clearly viewed the materials she was presenting as "art," one of whose functions was to serve as the basis for a distinctly American esthetic heritage. In this respect, Curtis was "typical of the Western tradition" in "positing the importance of primitive productions . . . in terms of their relationship to modern art" (Torgovnick 1990: 122). The section on the Kiowa (1923: 221–240) provides an example of how Curtis presented verbal art in *The Indians' Book*. She begins with a sketchy historical and cultural overview of the group, including a paragraph paying tribute to Apiatan, "the head chief of the Kiowas," whose interest in her project helped to ensure "that all the songs contributed then and afterwards by the Kiowas are some of the oldest now remembered by the tribe" (1923: 222–223)—a concern that reflects the salvage orientation of Curtis's work. Characterized by others as "a careful man and a thinking man," Apiatan (or Wooden Lance) had been a principal factor in the Kiowas' failure to participate in the Ghost Dance movement. He had been sent by his people to visit Wovoka, the Ghost Dance prophet, in Nevada in 1890 or 1891 and returned thoroughly disillusioned. He also traveled to Washington to protest the allotment of tribal lands under the Jerome Agreement in 1894. At the time Curtis came into contact with him—probably at the Louisiana Purchase Exposition in 1904—he was in his mid-forties (Dockstader 1977: 339–340; Marriott 1945: 196–205; Mayhall 1971: 206, 313, 319). Curtis, though, presents none of this information about one of her most important Kiowa collaborators.

The Kiowa section of *The Indians' Book* includes eight Kiowa songs with accompanying translations and, in most cases, some comments about the circumstances when each might be naturally performed. About "Koalda Daagya. Begging-Song," for example, Curtis writes, "Sometimes twenty or thirty children go at night to the tipi of some people who have one dearly loved child. They stand outside the tipi and make songs about the child, begging that for love of the little one the parents will throw them something to eat" (1923: 225). Transcriptions for the melodies of all songs follow, and Curtis resists the temptation to provide the melodies with the harmonized settings that she had created for some earlier publications of Native American traditional music (e.g., 1905b). But she does use standard Euroamerican notation without indicating ways in which Kiowa singers may not have conformed to the alien scales. Curtis also provides a key signature for each melody and indicates its tempo in terms of beats per minute.

The section on the Kwakiutl (1923: 297–307) also begins with a general description, but the verbal art presented from this Northwest Coast culture includes a prose narrative ("The Story of Wakiash and the First Totem-Pole") as well as the songs and musical material. Curtis handles the material from each tribe as she does that of the Kiowa and the Kwakiutl, though the amount of non-song material varies and some musical transcriptions add appropriate instrumental accompaniment such as drums or rattles. Never does she provide more than a couple of pages of general cultural background or more than a brief paragraph depicting the specific situations that produced a song. Clearly, she believed the reader could appreciate the universal esthetic features of the verbal art with only a minimum of cultural knowledge.

Published in 1918, George W. Cronyn's *The Path on the Rainbow: An Anthology of Songs and Chants from the Indians of North America* was the first anthology to follow the lead set by Curtis's volume. As evidence of the artistic thrust of the anthology, the editor cited *Poetry* magazine as his principal inspiration (1918: vii–viii).[2] Most of the translations and re-translations as well as the commentaries on Native American verbal art that had appeared in that magazine during the previous decade had been influenced by Curtis's book. Moreover, the Curtis influence is clear in the specific material chosen for the collection by Cronyn: ten of the seventeen items that comprise the Southwest section come from Curtis. Yet though clearly indebted to Curtis's work, *The Path on the Rainbow* carried the "art museum" approach to anthologizing farther than its predecessor. For example, Cronyn added materials from the Eastern Woodlands (specifically from the Delawares and Cherokees), California (represented by Wintun and Yuma materials, the latter of which Curtis had presented as Southwestern), and the Arctic to Curtis's coverage, thus creating an even more diffuse effect. He also placed more stress on the accessible artistic features of the material by presenting linguistic texts totally devoid of any information about cultural context. The volume contains absolutely no notes except for bibliographic acknowledgments, and seldom does anything besides the unadorned linguistic text appear. The reader thus confronts the following without even the benefit of the anthology equivalent of a museum exhibit card:

VENGEANCE SONG
(Micmac)

Death I make, singing
Heh-yeh! heh-yeh! heh-yeh! heh-yeh!
Bones I hack, singing
Heh-yeh! heh-yeh! heh-yeh! heh-yeh!
Death I make, singing
Heh-yeh! heh-yeh! heh-yeh! heh-yeh!
(Cronyn 1918: 7)

Moreover—in a move resembling the Museum of Modern Art's juxtaposition of Kwakiutl mask with Picasso painting—Cronyn stresses the essential kinship between orally expressed verbalization such as this (from the translation of Silas T. Rand) and modern American poetry by appending to the material from Native American oral traditions a collection of poetic "interpretations" of Indian themes, composed with one exception (Pauline Johnson) by Euroamerican poets. Thus, items like the Micmac "Vengeance Song" have apparent relatives such as "Feast of Wolves" by Frank S. Gordon, whose work has been assessed as an attempt to represent "the very lyric energy of southwestern tribal chants" (Castro 1983: 31):

Ho, oh-o-o
Come ye shades, shadows come
Ho, oh-o-o
Come ye shades, shadows come
Come ye shades, oh-o-o, ho, oh-o-o
Ye night ghosts and dance ye
What—dark!
Ho, oh-o-o
Come ye wolves, wolf-howls come
Ho, oh-o-o
Come ye wolves, wolf-howls come
Come ye wolves, oh-o-o, ho, oh-o-o
Ye singers merry feast ye

What—bark!
Ho, oh-o-o
Come ye crows, crow-bills come
Ho, oh-o-o
Come ye crows, crow-bills come
Come ye crows, oh-o-o, ho, oh-o-o
Ye black robes and flap ye
What—hark!
Ho, oh-o-o
Come ye bones, bone-grins come
Come ye bones, oh-o-o, ho, oh-o-o
What—stark! (Cronyn 1918: 236)

Other Euroamerican poets whose "interpretations" (by which was apparently meant compositions much farther removed from any Native American originals than Jerome Rothenberg's "workings" or Brian Swann's "versions") appear in *The Path on the Rainbow* are Constance Lindsay Skinner, Alice Corbin Henderson, and Mary Austin.

The introduction to the anthology, written by Austin, emphasizes the universality of the "poetic faculty" that the material in the volume illustrates. She notes that the volume's purpose (not all that different from the exhibitions critiqued by Clifford and Torgovnick) was to establish "some continuity with the earliest instances" of poetic response in the Americas in order to ensure that the new "American poetic genius has struck its native note" (Cronyn 1918: xiii)—articulating one of the very points that had informed the work of Natalie Curtis. But Austin also casts the study and presentation of American Indian verbal art in less narrowly nationalist terms: "For such illuminating gleams that Indian poetry can throw on the genesis of inspired literature, its study would be worth while, even if without the renewal of our native stock of poetic forms and figures" (Cronyn 1918: xxiv).

The Path on the Rainbow is an American Indian verbal art gallery, exhibited partially because it demonstrates in their most primitive manifestations the universal fundamentals of poetic expression (especially imagery, figurative tropes, and rhythm) and partially because it provides a foundation for a uniquely (Euro)American literary tradition. The assumption underlying this anthology implies that the verbal artistry of Native America is literarily transparent enough that those without specific cultural knowledge can easily appreciate its esthetic qualities. That artistry is available for appropriation by readers who need not bother with cultural background and by artists who respond to the stimuli of their environments with the same genius as the unnamed Native American creators of the works that Cronyn has displayed.

Other anthologies have succeeded Cronyn's, most of them providing considerably more in the way of cultural background for the materials and less in the way of facile comparisons with Euroamerican poetic consciousness. Yet they convey the same messages about the accessibility of a simplistic art form to sophisticated Euroamerican readers. Particularly important have been Nellie Barnes's *American Indian Love Lyrics* (1925), Margot Astrov's *The Winged Serpent* (1946), A. Grove Day's *The Sky Clears* (1951), and Jerome Rothenberg's *Shaking the Pumpkin* (1972). Though not as egregiously imperialistic in their assumptions as Cronyn's collection, each of these suffers from such common failings of anthologies as selectivity, downplaying the role of the individual in the creation of Native American verbal art (see Hymes 1987), and ignoring the status of oral expression as event. Moreover, they also suggest that sensitive Euroamerican readers without much grounding in the relevant cultural contexts can identify what is artful in non-Western verbal art.

In 1971 (reprinted in 1991) an anthology appeared that marked so blatant a return to the imperialistic assumptions that inform *The Path on the Rainbow* that it is difficult to reconcile it with a later work by its editor dealing with some of those assumptions (Brandon 1986). *The Magic World: American Indian Songs and Poems*, edited by William Brandon, includes linguistic texts of about eighty "poems," most coming from North American sources. Brandon presents each item totally without cultural background, the only notes being an identification of culture group and the bibliographic source from which he has "adapted" (sometimes "freely adapted") the material. His apologia for this contextless presentation argues, "The poems can speak for themselves. They are presented here not as ethnological data but strictly as literature. There should be no more need to talk about the 'cultures' of the various American Indian groups than to preface Catullus with a discourse on ancient Rome" (1991: n. p.). Most of his introduction to the collection defends this stance by suggesting that some transcendent poetic identity emerges from the poems, an identity that requires no familiarity with the culture to understand.

The analogy with the poems of Catullus with which Brandon begins his defense seems a particularly unfortunate choice. The Roman poet is best known for the series of poems addressed to "Lesbia" in which he treats the development of his love affair with Clodia, wife of a provincial Roman governor. Though Brandon is correct in suggesting that we don't need a disquisition on ancient Roman society and history to appreciate Catullus's poetry, most Western readers coming to his Lesbia series bring some familiarity with the amatory tradition of which the poems are a part. We know the conceits of Western love poetry, many of which Catullus may have been the first to articulate, but which have figured into Western popular culture so forcefully that they are recognizable even for those readers with no specialized knowledge of the Roman poet's work or his society. Everyone who has seen *Gone with the Wind* or *Casablanca*, read romance novels, or watched television soap operas has the cultural background to respond to Catullus. Our cultural background enables us to bring to his poems recognitions and awarenesses similar to that which I or another Western viewer of a French portrait or a Spanish statue might bring. Without more specific information about Catullus, his times, and his predecessors in the writing of love lyrics (especially Sappho), we miss some of the subtleties, but we can appreciate the ideas that inform Catullus's work. And we realize that lyric poetry is an appropriate medium for the expression of such ideas.

As Talal Asad has written, "[T]he opposition between a 'contextual interpretation' and one that is not contextual is entirely spurious. Nothing has meaning 'in isolation.' The problem is always, what kind of context?" (1986: 151). So we do not come to the material in Brandon's anthology devoid of all "contingencies" and able to appreciate their universal esthetic qualities (Kirshenblatt-Gimblett 1991: 391). We bring contexts of our own, which may have little relevance for these poems.

Brandon's claim that the linguistic texts that he presents as poetry "can speak for themselves" ignores the fact that all communication—artistic and otherwise—expresses itself within specific situations and contexts. When those change, the import of the communication changes (cf. Bauman 1993). One might compare the way in which some African carvers appreciate sacred masks—an appreciation that arises from their context of use. Torgovnick concludes, "Since their role in performance counts more than their appearance in repose, masks . . . could not (for traditional Africans) be judged at all in typical Western contexts—on a wall in a museum or gallery—but only as they were perceived or experienced in a performance, in specific kinds of light, from specific angles, and from within a group's set of traditions" (1990: 132). Esthetic evaluation, in this case, derives principally from context of use, not from "contextless" form.

What, though, does the reader who appreciates that lyric poetry is the proper medium for the dramatization of certain kinds of ideas make of a poem identified by Brandon as "PAPAGO: Elegy Dream Song"?

> In the great night my heart will go out
> darkness will come toward me
> > with a sound of rattling
> in the great night my heart will go out
>
> I am running toward a range of low mountains
> from those mountain tops I will see the dawn
>
> I die and lie dead here
>
> I die and lie dead here! (1991: 42)

Brandon notes that this has been "Adapted" from Frances Densmore's collection of Papago songs that appeared as the ninetieth BAE Bulletin. This is his only comment about the material, which he believes can speak for itself even to a Western reader with no knowledge of the culture of the Tohono O'odham.

The material that Brandon characterizes as one "elegy song" actually consists of parts of three different songs, all of which were used by Juana Manuel (Owl Woman) in healing. Manuel had received her healing songs from the spirits of non-Christian Tohono O'odham, who had gone to "the spirit land," learned the songs there, and then returned to teach them to her. The healer then taught the songs to Savariano Garcia, who did the actual singing while Manuel administered treatment. Customarily, Garcia sang four songs before Manuel brushed the patient's body with owl feathers sprinkled with ashes. Usually, the pair would stay with a sick person throughout the night, and certain songs were designed for certain parts of the night (Densmore 1929: 114–116).

Densmore recorded the songs from Garcia, who was prompted by Manuel during the recording process. The first of the songs upon which Brandon's text is based had been taught to Juana Manuel by the spirit of Jose Garcia. Neither Densmore nor her Tohono O'odham collaborators found the songs taught by Garcia's spirit particularly interesting. In fact, Densmore transcribed the music for only one of them, and Manuel dismissed Garcia's songs by saying, " 'Jose was not a lively boy, he was slow and sleepy headed' " (1929: 126). Densmore's translation of the words of the song that provides the source for the first stanza of Brandon's text are these:

> In the great night my heart will go out,
> Toward me the darkness comes rattling,
> In the great night my heart will go out.

Densmore notes that these words "are of unusual poetic beauty" (1929: 126). This song was intended to be performed before midnight during an all-night healing vigil.

The second song that provides a source for Brandon came to Manuel from the spirit of Francisco Pablo. It is the first of a series of four songs (the standard number for a song sequence during healing) which would be performed between midnight and early morning. Densmore translated it freely:

> A low range of mountains, toward them I am running.
> From the top of these mountains I will see the dawn.
>
> (1929: 129)

The repeated final line of Brandon's text comes from still another of Juana Manuel's songs, this one learned from the spirit of "a man who met his death by falling in a well." It would be sung as third in the sequence that included the song learned from the spirit of Francisco Pablo. Densmore's translation includes a line omitted by Brandon's reworking:

> I am dead here, I die and lie here,
> I am dead here, I die and lie here,
> Over the top of *Vihuhput* I had my dawn.

Densmore notes that the "dawn" in this song and in that above learned from Pablo's spirit refers to "the light seen by the spirits." The place name in the last song refers to the site where the man had died (1929: 130).

The problems with Brandon's handling of this material should be apparent. Though the comments given here remain insufficient to appreciate the cultural significance of this material, they suggest that a context-free presentation has considerable potential for misrepresentation, especially when the material is mislabeled an "elegy dream song" and when three songs, which come from two different times in the healing ritual, are converted into one linguistic text. No matter what he claims in his introduction, Brandon's loose handling of sources suggests that he doesn't really believe the material "can speak" for itself.

Meanwhile, contextual information does not transform the material from literature into ethnological data, as Brandon claims. Instead it affords the songs taught to Juana Manuel some of the same respect that Catullus's poetry has. For the reader really to give this composite text the respect it deserves, he or she should become thoroughly familiar with Tohono O'odham song magic and healing practices (Underhill 1993). Moreover, orally expressed verbal art is by nature much more bound to a particular situation and context than is its written counterpart, since the former exists only in a performance that occurs in a specific time and place. Though they reflect a particular event and period, Catullus's poems are not responses to specific and immediate environmental stimuli in the way that any oral expression is.

Furthermore, though Densmore's translations are free adaptations of the originals in O'odham, Brandon's reworkings are not intended to restore anything original to them. While he writes nothing about specific poems that he has adapted, he suggests something about his "respect" for the esthetics of the originals in his comments about the "problem of repetition" in some Native American oral poetry:

> Some images otherwise beautiful *to us* are buried all but out of sight in repetition, perhaps each line being repeated as many as half a dozen times. *Our* ears can get the same effect of hypnotic repetition with considerably less actual repeating. . . . *We* only want the feeling of the earnest repetition, the feeling of the hypnosis, of the marvelous emerging, the feeling of the magic. All that *we* want from any of it is the feeling of its poetry. (1991: n.p., emphasis added)[3]

It is harder to imagine a more blatant admission of esthetic appropriation than this substitution of what "we" want for what appears in the original. Though one may disagree with the methods of such contemporaries of Brandon's as Jerome Rothenberg and Dennis Tedlock in representing Native American oral expression, both have made genuine efforts to represent the indigenous oral esthetic as much as possible. Even more gratuitously than Schoolcraft and other early nineteenth-century textmakers (who may have been unconscious of what they were doing), Brandon has undermined the real poetry of the originals through his assumptions that his own Western esthetic can replace those of the originals.

The Magic World represents the worst in literary museology, since it totally ignores what is needed for understanding the exhibited materials on their own terms and brazenly substitutes a Western way of looking at literature that conflicts with and destroys what is actually there. It goes farther than the museum exhibits reviewed by Clifford and Torgovnick, for not only is there an assumption that tribal art can be accessible to a Western audience who do not have the specific cultural knowledge, but Brandon exercises the self-proclaimed right to re-work the tribal art if it is not as accessible as he thinks it should be. The MOMA catalog juxtaposed Picasso painting and Kwakiutl mask. What Brandon does amounts to a recarving of the mask so that it resembles the Picasso as nearly as possible.

Brandon's anthology foregrounds some of the most egregious abuses of the art museum approach to presenting Native American linguistic texts, but these same problems are noticeable in some of the other anthologies that have capitalized on the late-twentieth-century Native American literary renaissance (Lincoln 1983). Most anthologies that have appeared recently concentrate on literature written by contemporary American Indian authors and often have a generic focus on short fiction or poetry (e.g., Lesley 1991). However, at least one well-known anthology attempts to survey both oral and written verbal art. Alan Velie's *American Indian Literature: An Anthology*, first published in 1979 and revised in 1991, commits itself in its selections of oral materials and its commentaries upon them to demonstrating the accessibility of this material to Western audiences with as little ethnographic background as possible.

In his general introduction to the collection, Velie clearly articulates his philosophy of selection: "The principle I have used in selecting works from both [oral and written] traditions is literary quality. All selections in this anthology are to be judged as serious literature" (1991: 9). While this is a valid sentiment, it soon becomes clear that the standard of literary quality by which even the oral materials are measured is Western. This becomes evident in almost every headnote, where Velie compares the oral material to something from the Western literary heritage. For example, in his introduction to a version of the Acoma origin myth (his single example of a cosmogonic myth from the diverse Native cultures of North America) he observes:

> Another interesting feature is the impregnation of Nautsiti, which seems to combine elements of virgin birth and original sin. Tempted by an evil spirit in the shape of a serpent, Nautsiti lies on her back and "receives" rain, which makes her pregnant. This incident is treated as sin in the Acoma account—the original sin, in fact—but it seems reminiscent not only of Jove's taking Danae in a shower of gold but also of Luke's account of the impregnation of Mary: "The Holy Ghost shall come upon thee, and the power of the Highest shall overshadow thee." (1991: 14)

The "High Horse's Courting" section of *Black Elk Speaks* is presented as "a classic short story of the type O. Henry used to write" (1991: 33).

The character of Meadow Lark Woman in a Clackamas Chinook story resembles "the fairy godmother of European folk tales" (1991: 38). The Winnebago Trickster cycle begins *in medias res* "like a Homeric epic" (1991: 45). Moreover, though he does not go so far as Brandon, Velie does adjust some of the material he has anthologized: "I have taken out the meaningless vocables put in for rhythmical purposes" (1991: 74). The total effect is to produce a highly selective sampling of linguistic textualizations of oral artistry in a way that assumes that little if any cultural background is necessary and that comparisons from the Western literary heritage provide a more meaningful context than the actual verbal traditions from which the artistry emerged.

My final exhibit in this rogues' gallery of anthologies that fail to take into account the necessary cultural backgrounds or performance situations of the linguistic texts they present is perhaps the most widely known contemporary collection of Native American oral narratives. *American Indian Myths and Legends,* selected and edited by Richard Erdoes and Alfonso Ortiz (1984), seems very promising on first glance. The first editor attained recognition and respect for his editing the autobiography of Lakota holy man John Fire (Lame Deer) (Fire and Erdoes 1972). The second editor, himself a Tewa from San Juan Pueblo and an anthropologist, has published an important study of the Tewa world view (Ortiz 1969) and edited the volume on the Pueblos in the Smithsonian Institution's *Handbook of North American Indians* (Ortiz 1979). Their impressive credentials contribute to their anthology's respectability as does the fact that—unlike Brandon and Velie—they themselves have apparently recorded much of the material in *American Indian Myths and Legends* themselves.

But the book's positive qualities are something of an illusion. For the materials that they recorded, Erdoes and Ortiz give a minimum of data about the situation when the stories were told. For example, for an Ojibway narrative, their note about the source reads only: "Told by David Red Bird in New York City, 1974, and recorded by Richard Erdoes. David Baker Red Bird is a young Green Bay Indian with a great sense of humor. He is a well-known singer and musician" (Erdoes and Ortiz 1984: 151). As far as cultural background is concerned, the reader may turn to the back of the book and read a brief paragraph of eight lines on the Ojibway (1984: 511). What results, of course, is a linguistic text that has too little information about matters not included in that text to allow the reader to apply anything much beyond his or her own culturally determined preconceptions to the story.

Another problem with this anthology lies in the linguistic texts themselves. Dell Hymes has punctiliously demonstrated how Erdoes and

Ortiz ignore indigenous esthetic considerations in presenting their stories (Hymes 1987). Like Hymes, the editors of American Indian Myths
and Legends have drawn from previously published sources for much of
the material included in the anthology. Furthermore, like Hymes, they
have usually reworked that material from its original translated form.
But unlike Hymes, Erdoes and Ortiz have not gone back to original
Native-language texts to reproduce their artistry. Instead, they have
retold the stories from the translations themselves. Typical source
notes for stories in the Erdoes-Ortiz anthology read, "Retold from several nineteenth-century sources" (1984: 65); "Based on a story reported
in 1905 by H. R. Voth" (1984: 117); "Retold from English source, 1883"
(1984: 193); and "Based on two stories told in 1899 and 1903" (1984: 314).
The editors justify their reworking of the previously published material
by noting that it was "embellished in the somewhat artificial style
typical of the period." They, in turn, "have retold these tales to restore
them to a more authentic and less stilted form" (1984: xv). Though these
retellings may occasionally draw upon the editors' knowledge of a community's verbal artistry—Ortiz's handling of Tewa tales, for example—
often the editors seem to apply their perception of what late-twentieth-
century readers of the material will tolerate and respond to. In no case is
there any evidence that Erdoes and Ortiz have returned to a Native-
language original with the purpose of restoring the artistry it lost when
it was first translated into English.

That appreciation of Native American verbal art as linguistic text and
expressive event depends upon cultural context has received endorsement from many commentators, both literary and ethnographic. A hit-
and-miss survey of opinion might include the comments of Eda Lou
Walton, who wrote in Poetry magazine (an unlikely forum for such
opinion), "Navaho songs, especially those of a ceremonial nature, consist of a series of predications. One can connect these predications only
after learning the entire traditional background of the tribe" (1924: 43).
More recent testimony comes from a review of an anthology of Native
American verbal art from the Northwest (i.e., Jarold Ramsey's Coyote
Was Going There, which, in fact, is less guilty than most anthologies of
the sins against context treated here): "Without sufficient information
on their narrative conventions and on the ways Oregon Indians con-
strue their social universe, we cannot possibly hope to discover for
ourselves how 'richly imaginative and expressive' their folktales are,
nor can we hope to grasp the meanings of their tales in any but the most
superficial and naive fashion" (Kendall 1979: 98). Richard Dauenhauer
and Nora Marks Dauenhauer, translators and textualizers of Tlingit

verbal art, reiterate this point: "When the story is read by a person outside the culture of the story teller, the cultural context is lost. Information and assumptions shared by the composer and original audience may no longer be shared. Many things may no longer be understood" (1987: 7–8). Andrew Wiget adds, "[A]n informed reading [of Native American verbal art texts] requires much more information than one customarily expects, and texts that suggest—through lack of notes, introductions, and other material, or through overt appeals to supposedly universal features of human nature—that naked, naive readings can be deeply satisfying are misleading" (1990: 84). And Arnold Krupat, who has been cited frequently in these pages, lists as one criterion for a literary criticism of Native American verbal art "a knowledge of the cultures whose concerns Native American literatures—like any literatures the world over—address and express" (1992a: 179).

The art museum (or jewelry store or—to use William Bevis's analogy —Wild West show [1974: 699]) approach to the presentation of verbal art exhibits the following traits: focus only on the linguistic component of oral expression, minimal presentation of context (since that context is deemed unimportant), a wide range of materials (since the universal poetic qualities transcend the particulars of any one culture), elimination of indigenous features of the material that might obscure what the presenter perceives as their artistry, and an emphasis on what the material shares with the familiar Western tradition. These features should be added to "distortions inherent in the anthology form"—especially the necessity of excerpting from longer verbalizations (Bevis 1974: 694).

In her comments on the display of "primitive" objects in ethnographic and art museums, Marianna Torgovnick has noted what the move to the latter meant in terms of attitudes toward those objects:

> [T]he "elevation" of primitive objects into art is often implicitly seen as the aesthetic equivalent of decolonization, as bringing Others into the "mainstream" in a way that ethnographic studies, by their very nature, could not. Yet that "elevation" in a sense reproduces, in the aesthetic realm, the dynamics of colonialism, since Western standards control the flow of the "mainstream" and can bestow or withhold the label "art." (1990: 82)

Moreover, this elevation into "art" becomes "a European game with high cultural stakes, a game in which primitives are pawns, unable to grasp the rules and unable to win" (1990: 96). Torgovnick's comments, which seem as applicable to the anthologies of linguistic texts that have been considered above, return us to the continuum that has provided one of the frameworks for this study since chapter 1. Fredric Jameson's distinction between viewing the Other in terms of "Identity" or in terms of "Difference" suggests the tension that has colored the contact of Europeans (and Euroamericans) with the Other (exoticized by space, time, or both) since our earliest records of such contact. Emphasizing "Identity" seems the more humane approach. It seems to counteract the ideologies that divide people from people, such as racism, polygeneticism, and ethnocentrism. But too facile an assumption of Identity can do as much harm as the assumption of Difference. We may all be humans, but we are humans in different ways. That is nowhere more apparent than in verbal art. Artistic expression in words is a universal phenomenon, but it manifests itself in markedly different ways from era to era, from place to place. Attempting to subsume the Other's verbal art in terms of our age's and our place's specific manifestation of this universal phenomenon disserves that art. Torgovnick asserts that we must "resist the temptation to translate differences into similarities" (1990: 130). Differences exist; our representations of those differences should present them accurately. Every oral expression of verbal art is unique; our representation of each such expression should demonstrate that uniqueness.

EPILOGUE

 The ideal text represents oral expression. Since oral expression is an event, that text should be what has been called in these pages an "ethnographic" text, one that characterizes the totality of a communicative situation. Such a situation includes, of course, what is said and how paralinguistic and kinesic devices enhance its message (in other words, what has been called in these pages a "linguistic" text), but it also involves such things as setting (time and place), participants (both verbalizer and audience), and cultural and psychological contexts. Unfortunately, there are few examples of such ideal texts in the history of representation of Native American (or, in fact, any other) oral expression. So, in one sense, as I warned the reader in the introduction, this study has been a history of failure—failure occasioned by insufficient technology to record accurately oral expression in its conventional contexts; by an inability to transcend presuppositions about the "savage" Other and the nature of verbal art; by too narrow a focus on only the linguistic component of oral expression; and by assumptions that orally performed "literature" can be comprehended without considering its contexts of generation.

In addition to the continuum between Identity and Difference, another set of terms seems to define this history. Though they should really be incorporated into the same ethnographic text, "text" and "context" (including expressive situation) often seem to be at odds. On one hand, textualizers like Franz Boas and his students, who scrupulously represented what they heard down to the least phoneme, produced linguistic texts that remain exemplary in many respects—and from which later textualizers and translators such as Dell Hymes and his students have produced texts that are even more exemplary. But Boasians did not record context, except to note very briefly and at most when, where, and by whom a particular oral expression was related. On the other hand, the Jesuits, the early nineteenth-century explorers and travelers, and even Henry Rowe Schoolcraft might provide quite full descriptions of the situations in which oral expressions occurred and even include some cultural background information. To call their descriptions exemplary certainly overstates, but they offered essential information for an event-oriented approach to the textualization of oral expression that is absent from the Boasian records. Of course, their linguistic texts usually depart from the mark of accuracy so far that little of the original is left but the content and perhaps some figurative tropes that caught their fancies.

Ethnographic textualization should do what the Boasians did (and more) for the linguistic aspect of oral expression *and* should do what the Jesuits and the others did (and more) for the situational and contextual aspects of oral expression. Thus, the text-context tension that has characterized the textualization of Native American verbal art emerges from a false dilemma. Even in the 1990s no efforts have completely mastered the complex process of representing the expressive event in an ethnographic text, but developments by textualizers during the last third of the twentieth century point in some hopeful directions.

Though they still maintain their focus principally on the linguistic text, many participants in the ethnopoetics movement are clearly aware that oral expression is an event. Moreover, their linguistic texts, which may be as punctiliously faithful to the material they represent as the work of Boas, attempt to go beyond the Boasians by organizing their representations in ways that reflect the indigenous esthetic as accurately as possible. Several methods of textual organization have developed among poets, translators, and linguists (Woodbury 1987: 176), and separately or in combination, these methods have been providing guidance for textmakers. One of the most successful of these methods is the "pause phrasing" that Dennis Tedlock used in presenting the narrative poetry of the Zunis and which is treated in chapter 1. Tedlock assumed that oral narratives could be segmented into lines, like those of written poetry, that reflected the way a narrator paced the tale. Pauses ranging from one-half to three-fourths of a second signaled to Tedlock where line divisions should occur in his linguistic text. He also suggested other features of oral delivery through manipulation of typography (1972: xv–xxxv). Another method for representing the organization of linguistic texts ethnopoetically is that of Dell Hymes, who favors the use of syntactic markers, especially changes in predicate, to determine line divisions (1981; 1982: 140). Using a methodology called "verse analysis," Hymes also organizes his texts into larger poetic units. Based upon such clues as linguistic parallelism and culture-specific pattern numbers, lines are grouped into verses, several of which may constitute a stanza. A scene consists of several stanzas, and acts, the largest units of the text, are composed of several scenes (Hymes 1985a: 409). While the ethnopoetic approach used by Tedlock requires the translator to have aural recordings with which to work, Hymes has been able to reanalyze, retextualize, and retranslate published materials collected in Native languages by Boas, Melville Jacobs, and others.

Both these approaches to ethnopoetic organization of linguistic texts have attracted adherents, but the most promising development for the future may be attempts to resolve seeming differences between pause phrasing and verse analysis. For example, using both approaches on a tape-recorded Karok myth, William Bright found that pacing and syntactics yielded the same line organizations ninety percent of the time and that ambiguities in determining lines by one approach might be resolved by consulting the other (1982: 173–174). Joel Sherzer, working in the field with Kuna storytellers in Central America, discovered that line markers (the basic feature of this approach to ethnopoetic organization) might include either syntactic devices, pauses, or both (1987: 105).

The real issue separating the approaches of Tedlock and Hymes seems to be the determination of where the artistry of oral expression lies. For Tedlock, that artistry emerges in each expression; one might call his approach a discourse-centered approach (cf. Urban 1991). Hymes perceives an artistry that transcends the specifics of any expressive event, even one in which that artistry is suppressed. Using verse analysis, he has identified esthetic patterns even in dictated materials such as those recorded by Boas. Tedlock's view may work when we have audio recordings of specific expressions, but to recover the artistry of traditions represented only in the collections of Boas and his students, we must rely on Hymes's method.

Another recent approach to ethnopoetic textualization and translation may be seen in the work of Anthony Mattina (1985). His presentation of "The Golden Woman," a linguistic text in Colville, a Salishan language, made from a tape-recording of storyteller Peter J. Seymour telling a redaction of a European folktale, appears with an interlinear translation with English vocabulary provided by Native consultant Madeline DeSautel and a "continuous translation" adapted from De-

Sautel's English translation. These materials foreground an important feature of much of the textualization and translation of American Indian oral expression that has occurred over the past four centuries. That feature is the role of the Native consultant, for the continuous translation—which is all that most readers of the Mattina-Seymour-DeSautel volume will read—derives not directly from the Salishan original, but from DeSautel's translation of it. The result is a narrative presented in what Mattina calls "Red English"—the version of English spoken by DeSautel (and apparently by Seymour). The continuous translation represents how Seymour probably would have told the story if he had narrated in English.

While I am not entirely comfortable with Mattina's decision to use Red English, since it may not represent very accurately the tone, style, or performance qualities that Seymour actually used in Colville, I believe that Mattina's work is a breakthrough, partly because of his stress on the role of DeSautel, a Native consultant who corresponds to a long line of such figures from Henry Timberlake's John McCormack to Henry Rowe Schoolcraft's Jane Johnston to Franz Boas's Charles Cultee to many others. I am also impressed with how forthcoming Mattina has been about the processes that produced the volume containing the materials collected and translated from Seymour (see Mattina 1987b). Mattina clearly describes the situation when, where, and why Seymour told the story. During the summer of 1968, Mattina, who did not understand Colville at the time, was eliciting vocabulary and grammatical patterns from Seymour, who, tiring of this drudgery, suggested that he tell stories. Over three different days, Seymour told "The Golden Woman" into Mattina's tape recorder, fully aware that the linguist did not understand what he was saying. "Seymour's only audience was the tape," as Karl Kroeber has commented (1987: 62). Mattina also goes through in detail how and what was represented in the textualization process and how and why he decided to use DeSautel's Red English in the continuous translation. His thorough presentation of the methodology from recording situation through final translation that produced the linguistic text points this work toward the ethnographic text ideal. As Mattina has written of the presentation of linguistic texts without the ethnographic context,

Narratives on the printed page are museum artifacts, just as arrowheads in a museum case are spent projectiles. A transcript of a narrative has no more sound than a musical score. The understanding which readers gain from the script is in direct proportion to what they know about the tradition and the context of the text, and mythographers [i.e., textmakers] should facilitate the reading of texts by providing whatever they can toward that goal. (1987a: 143)

Mattina's attention to the role of both Seymour and DeSautel in the production of *The Golden Woman* leads me to another hopeful development in current work in the textualization of Native American oral expression. That is the growing interest by American Indians in textualizing and translating oral expressions from their own communities. Chapter 2 reiterated the view, articulated by many other commentators (e.g., Sarris 1993: 22), that the very presence of an outsider, whether an anthropologist recording materials by means of dictation or a casual observer who textualizes the performance situation ("context") that he or she witnesses, may interfere with the realization of authentic performance in an oral expression. One way (though certainly not an infallible one) to enhance the full performance potential of materials to be recorded involves Native researchers, whose less intrusive presence and fuller grasp of the conventional dynamics of situation and context, may yield texts that are artistically richer because they represent expressions that are artistically richer. The history of the study of Native American verbal expression, of course, includes the work of many Indians. Some such as Ojibwa George Copway (1860), Nakota Gertrude Bonnin (Zitkala-Ša) (Zitkala-Ša 1901), and Okanagan Mourning Dove (Hu-mis-hu-ma) (1934) lacked ethnological training and produced linguistic texts that reflected a Euroamerican literary esthetic much more than the relevant Native artistic criteria. Others such as Nez Perce Archie Phinney (1934) were influenced by the documentary emphasis of their training in linguistic anthropology in the records they produced. But the current literary renaissance in Indian America (Lincoln 1983) encourages Native Americans to attempt to textualize what they encounter in relatively natural performance contexts not according to preconceptions from either Euroamerican literature or linguistic theory and method, but from the indigenous esthetic.

A good example is the work of Felipe Molina, a Yaqui who has collaborated with Larry Evers on several studies—including textualizations that achieve almost full ethnographic potential—of Yaqui songs. Molina's principal publication has been a book-length treatment of Yaqui deer songs (Evers and Molina 1987; see also Evers and Molina 1989), which meticulously provides descriptions of the songs' performance as well as carefully worked-out linguistic texts, presented in Yaqui with English translations. Both Yaqui and English reflect the indigenous esthetic through layout and line length, use of repetition and parallelism, and the representation of vocables.

Similar work is being done with Tlingit verbal art by Native Tlingit-speaker Nora Marks Dauenhauer. In collaboration with Richard Dauenhauer, she has published several collections of her culture's traditional oral expression, the two most important being books on oral narratives (Dauenhauer and Dauenhauer 1987) and oratory (Dauenhauer and Dauenhauer 1990). Both volumes present Tlingit and English linguistic texts, which replicate as far as possible the ways in which the material was realized orally. Dauenhauer and Dauenhauer have placed the narratives and orations within their contexts of situation and culture to produce what amount to ethnographic textualizations of Tlingit verbal art.

Finally, an important development that bodes well for future work in linguistic and ethnographic textualization of Native American oral expression is the development of a body of literary criticism that addresses the esthetic values of American Indian verbal art on its own terms. Not only does this criticism look at published materials from indigenous perspectives (e.g., Rice 1989; 1991), but it also brings some of the most recent developments in literary analysis to bear upon the material (e.g., Krupat 1987; 1992). The result is a growing corpus of work that takes American Indian oral expression very seriously as art and that does not appear to be merely one of the periodic "cycles of appreciation" (Evers 1983) that have characterized Euroamerican interest in Native Americana throughout the history of contact.

Brian Swann's recent anthology, *Coming to Light* (1994), offers a generous sampling of the results of these contemporary trends in the textualization of Native American oral expression—the ethnopoetics movement; the tendency toward openness about the processes of recording, textualization, and translation; the involvement of indigenous textualizers; and the applications of contemporary literary critical theories to Native American verbal art. The book is "intended to showcase the state of contemporary Native American translation" (1994: xiv). The reader of the anthology confronts short representations of the verbal art of Native groups from throughout North America on their own terms. For the most part the translators work directly from Native-language sources, either material from the documentary records of Boasian anthropology or performances they themselves have recorded. The translations reflect the indigenous artistry—often through the methodologies of Tedlock or Hymes—without sacrificing Native esthetics for the sake of Euroamerican literary standards.

Unlike the anthologies castigated in chapter 9, Swann's volume manages to avoid the most serious pitfall of this genre: the presentation of the material as if it could be understood without the benefits of cultural background knowledge. Introductory notes to each selection provide at least enough cultural background to understand the basics of the narratives or lyrics, and many of the translators explain how they went about their work. Swann's general introduction correctly notes that this feature distinguishes *Coming to Light* from its predecessors (1994: xiv). Many of the pieces name a Native collaborator as cotranslator, and several pieces have been recorded and translated purely through the efforts of a member of the group.

Another way in which the verbal art textualized in Swann's anthology differs from that represented in other collections is its contemporaneity. Swann and many of the translators make clear that the tradition represented by the oral expressions "has survived and continues to thrive" (1994: xx). Unlike *The Indians' Book*, the anthology to which Swann feels his book has most affinity, *Coming to Light* does not represent salvage work. As a series of "photographs" of ongoing verbal art traditions, it very literally is a work in progress.

Coming to Light is not flawless: some of the translators are less successful than others in producing ethnographic texts that represent the goals of accuracy and thoroughness; the selection of material is diffuse, heavily weighted toward Arctic, Sub-Arctic, and Northwest Coast culture groups (particularly at the expense of the Southeast, which is represented only by the Koasati—an imbalance Swann hopes to correct in future editions [1994: xxxvi]); Native-language texts are not included; and the anthology format precludes the inclusion of longer examples of Native American verbal art such as complete chantway myths from the Navajo. Yet Swann's anthology amply validates this epilogue's optimism, while showing that an anthology can be successful at exhibiting verbal art as *art* without taking the museum approach of similar collections.

If the present and the future in the study of Native American verbal art seem essentially rosy, I believe that its past has not been as bleak as a superficial consideration from the vantage of modern ethnopoetics might suggest. And that recalls the purpose of this study: to demonstrate that something of value can be recovered by digging through the melange of ideas and influences that shaped (and undoubtedly corrupted) how the stories, songs, speeches, and ritual discourse of Native Americans made their way into print during the centuries that preceded our present enlightenment.

NOTES

INTRODUCTION

1. Mark Wallace (1994) has recently treated the nature of the "voice" projected through Black Hawk's autobiography.

2. The idea that figurative language resulted from a primitive, childlike inability to articulate in abstract terms was a commonplace in the cultural evolutionism that dominated anthropology and its intellectual forebears until the early twentieth century. The idea's sources lie in the foundations of modern social science. Giambattista Vico, for instance, writes in the *New Science* (1744): "Now the sources of all poetic locution [i. e., concrete figures] are two: poverty of language and need to explain and be understood" (Vico 1970: 6). The idea that figures were necessary to supplement lacunae in primitive languages also appears in Alcuin's *Rhetoric* (Cheyfitz 1991: 119). See also C. M. Bowra's comments about "primitive" languages: "[T]hey lack words for general and abstract ideas. . . . [S]uch a language is a poor instrument for the expression of ideas, [but] it is admirably suited for emotions and sensations and impressions" (1962: 22). As David Murray points out, the limited nature of American Indian languages became an excuse for difficulties in translating them into the "higher" tongues of Europe (1991: 8).

3. The view that texts should simply record events has come to be recognized as simplistic, given the complexity of factors involved in what Bauman and Briggs conceive as "recontextualization" from oral original to written or printed representation (1990: 75–78). Moreover, the notion that there exists some sort of "intertextual transparency" between the oral expression and its textual record has encouraged textmakers to subterfuges that conceal the effects of writing and printing in their products (Briggs 1993). Of course, textualization is a "powerful act of interpretation" (Briggs 1988: 55), a point that is demonstrated throughout this study. Sherzer and Urban

(1986: 11) note that textualization is essentially an analytical enterprise that foregrounds "some facet of the discourse."

4. Of course, many Native American communities are using texts as the basis for language instruction. And one motive behind at least some text collection and publication has been to provide a record for the people themselves. This is an obvious example of what Sarris seems to intend when he writes, "[A] text is not just a representation of an interaction but also an occasion for interaction" (1993: 185). Robin Ridington has suggested an analogy between a tape recording of an oral expression and a documentary photograph (in Swann 1994: 177).

5. Cf. Murray's comments on the conceptualization of Native American myths as "literature" and on the implications of the term "myth" (1991: 98–99).

CHAPTER 1. ZUNI VERBAL ART

An earlier version (1991) of this chapter appeared as " 'Identity' and 'Difference' in the Translation of Native American Oral Literatures: A Zuni Case Study," *Studies in American Indian Literatures* 3(3): 1–13. I appreciate the advice of the journal's editor, Helen Jaskoski, and of the article's anonymous reviewers.

1. Cf. Anthony Pagden's description of the "principle of attachment" that colored early documents treating European encounters with the Americas (1993: 17–49)

2. Of particular relevance to issues of translation and parallel to Jameson's Identity-Difference continuum may be two views of the nature of language described by George Steiner. The "universalist" view (cf. "Identity") holds that "the underlying structure of language is universal and common to all men." Linguistic disparities occur "essentially on the surface." Translation requires one "to descend beneath the exterior disparities of two languages in order to bring into vital play their analogous and . . . common principles of being" (1975: 73). The "monadist" view (cf. "Difference"), on the other hand, assumes that though the deep structures of language may be universal, they are so remote or abstract as to be meaningless. Meanwhile, actual occurrences of language "are so diverse, they manifest so bewilderingly complicated a history of centrifugal developments, they pose such stubborn questions as to economic and social function" that translation becomes elusive. "What passes for translation," according to this view, "is a convention of approximate analogies" (1975: 74). See also Cheyfitz (1991: 105–106) and Murray's "quintessential and mythical poles" in relations between American Indians and Euroamericans: "those of encounter with the incomprehensible other and of transparent intelligibility" (1991: 14).

3. Murray (1991: 133–146) has also chosen ethnographic work at Zuni as a

case study of monologism and dialogism in anthropological research and writing. He deals principally with Cushing, Tedlock, and Benedict.

4. Biblical style often figures in textualizations and translations of Native American oral expression. For example, Ruth Underhill told Gretchen M. Bataille and Kathleen Mullen Sands that she tried to keep the prose of the autobiography of Maria Chona, a Tohono O'odham woman, " 'vivid' like Old Testament writing, perhaps her way of suggesting the dignity and complexity of the original oral form" (Bataille and Sands 1984: 58). For an earlier example, see the often-stated analogy between Native American verbal art and the Hebrew Psalms in the anonymous essay "North American Indians," which appeared in *Southern Literary Messenger* in 1840. See also the comments about parallelism in chapter 5.

5. M. Jane Young has retranslated the Zuni ritual song sequence recorded by Bunzel that contains these lines (in Swann 1994: 570–579).

6. Yet his texts do not fully convey what that picture is. They remain *linguistic* texts. Tedlock doesn't provide much in the way of either context of situation or context of culture—essential elements for a comprehensive *ethnographic* text.

7. Further study of Zuni allowed Tedlock to translate the conventional opening formula as "Now we are taking it up" and the closing formula as "Enough, the word is short" (1983b: 65–66).

CHAPTER 2. SITUATIONS AND PERFORMANCES

A small portion of this chapter comes from a previously published essay (1981): "Faking the Pumpkin: On Jerome Rothenberg's Literary Offenses," *Western American Literature* 16(3): 193–204.

1. Ekkehart Malotki draws a similar distinction between renderings of Hopi oral storytelling tradition by two categories of narrators, "storytellers" and "story rememberers." He uses the distinction, though, as a justification for "improving" the verbal materials he heard from representatives of the latter category (1985: xi). One might also compare C. W. von Sydow's differentiation between "active" and "passive" bearers of tradition (1964: 231). Presumably "storytellers" or "active" bearers would be the more likely sources of "authentic" performances. Also, we should note that the term "authentic" does not refer to *texts*, but to *performances* and that the criteria for authenticity are emic and culture specific.

2. Julian Rice has noted several analogues for this story: Around Him 1983: 23; Deloria 1932: 261–262, 266–268.

3. Cf. Greg Sarris's comments that any understanding of the Pomo narratives collected by Robert Oswalt must be "predicated on the presence" of the fieldworker (1993: 22). Writing specifically about the verbal art of the Yucatec Maya, Allen F. Burns has similarly stressed the importance of the

fieldworker/translator's influence: "Narrators select stories . . . with the audience in mind. . . . The task of the translator is to participate in the oral literature events, recognize the historical and social meaning of the texts, and bring both the esthetics of the tale and the historic context into another language and culture" (1992: 404). Though dealing with research among African storytellers rather than American Indian raconteurs, Lee Haring's important treatment of this issue (1972) remains a crucial articulation of how the presence of a researcher affects what and how a verbal artist performs.

4. For more information on the source of this formula and analyses of other formulas, see Mooney and Olbrechts 1932.

5. We should note that Rothenberg attempts to enlist Mooney's support for his ethnopoetic rendering by misquoting Mooney's commentary so that his (Rothenberg's) wording appears to be Mooney's (Rothenberg 1972: 413). Moreover, in *Technicians of the Sacred,* where "The Killer" had previously appeared, Rothenberg's commentary stresses the importance of color symbolism and suggests parallels between the "Cherokee" use of blue in this texts and that color's appearance in Diane Wakoski's "Blue Monday (1965)" (Rothenberg 1968: 433–436), the point being that "The Killer" clearly reflects Rothenberg's Euroamerican poetic sensibility more than features of Cherokee oral performance.

6. When Rothenberg revised *Shaking the Pumpkin,* he omitted this Winnebago-derived material. However, he did include his "working" of the Cherokee formula (1986: 60).

CHAPTER 3. NATIVE CANADIAN VERBAL ART

An earlier version (1994) of this chapter appeared as "The Jesuit Foundations of Native North American Literary Studies," *American Indian Quarterly* 18: 43–59. I appreciate the suggestions of the journal editor, Morris W. Foster, and of anonymous readers who commented upon the paper.

1. Reuben Gold Thwaites's edition of *The Jesuit Relations and Allied Documents,* which appeared in seventy-nine volumes between 1896 and 1901, remains the most accessible source for most of the primary materials used in this chapter. Subsequent references to Thwaites 1959 in this chapter will be abbreviated as *JR.*

2. Since a principal concern here is with the accuracy of textualizations of Native American verbal art, I have left "texts" of orations, songs, and stories in the French of the Jesuit reporters (providing my own English translations when lack of contextual clues or the length of the texts required them). Including only English translations would create an additional step between orally expressed originals and printed texts.

3. Though material on Native North American verbal art may have been

published before the earliest reports of the Jesuit missionaries, my argument for their primacy stresses the extensiveness and relatively systematic approach to recording Native culture in the Jesuit documents.

4. Drawing upon recent archeological and ethnohistorical data, Trigger (1985) has reassessed the "heroic age" of New France, including the presence of the Jesuits, by stressing Native perspectives more fully than many of his predecessors.

5. In fact, the Jesuits attributed a catalog of "brutish" qualities to the North American Natives to support their portrayal of an "Iroquois menace" during the mid-seventeenth century: "their exclusive concern with earthly affairs and with the present; their restriction to hunting, fishing, and collecting food supplies and their culinary limitations; their nudity; their lack of permanent housing; their lack of government and civic administration" (Jaenen 1976: 18).

6. This approach to missionizing—that is, transferring existing forms of worship to the Christian deity—had long been a practice of missionaries, beginning in northern Europe. As early as 601, Pope Gregory had expressed the policy that instead of destroying indigenous places of worship, missionaries should use them for Christian exercises "so that the people, not seeing their own temples destroyed, may displace error from their hearts, and recognise and adore the true God, meeting in the familiar way at the accustomed places" (quoted in Smith 1972: 162). One is also reminded of Father Paul in Leslie Marmon Silko's short story "The Man to Send Rain Clouds," who sprinkles holy water at a traditional Laguna Pueblo funeral, though other Roman Catholic procedures have been eschewed (Silko 1981: 182–186). See also Jaenen 1976: 50.

7. The Jesuits' frequent analogy between certain aspects of *sauvage* behavior and European carnival is relevant here. On one hand, it served as a device of familiarization to clarify Native behavior. At the same time, it could be used to reproach the licentiousness of carnivals back in Europe. But the analogy also suggested the essential humanity of the Natives—their behavior being an example of what happens when natural reason becomes perverted. It follows that when Christianity is introduced and restores natural reason to its proper course, the *sauvages* will become like contemporary Europeans—among whom savagery persists in some carnivalesque activities. See Walsh 1982.

8. Motif A812 (Thompson 1955–58: 1:161). For a survey of the distribution of this myth throughout North America, see Rooth 1957. Analyses of Earth Diver include Count 1952, Dundes 1962, and Köngas 1960.

9. For a glossary of tropes reported as being used by Iroquois orators, see Jennings et al. 1985: 115–124.

10. Foster (1985) examines the use of wampum belts by Iroquois orators.

11. Indeed, the Jesuit missionaries were accomplished linguists. For an appreciation of their contributions to the early study of American Indian languages, see Hanzeli 1969.

CHAPTER 4. HENRY TIMBERLAKE'S CHEROKEE WAR SONG

1. That Timberlake's memoir contains the first English translation of the words of a Native American song seems to have become common knowledge among students of American Indian verbal art (e.g., Krupat 1992a: 176). Though such claims of primacy are always a little risky, I have found nothing to dispute this one. Even if an earlier translation were discovered, the priority of Timberlake's work (like that of the Jesuits) would remain because of its influence and, as I will suggest in this chapter, its establishing a pattern for textualizations and translations of Native American oral poetry in the years to come. In 1791 William Bartram published what may be the Timberlake translation's first successor, a song from a Europeanized part-Choctaw: "All men must surely die, / Tho' no one knows how soon, / Yet when the time shall come, / The event may be joyful" (Harper 1958: 322).

2. A survey of some of Timberlake's Euroamerican predecessors among the Cherokees appears in Rothrock 1929.

3. This is motif B101.7, "Serpent with jewel in head" in Thompson 1955–58: 1:375.

4. The major difficulty in corroborating the song's depiction of Cherokee war practices involves avoiding circularity. Most twentieth-century works treating the eighteenth-century Cherokees and other southeastern groups draw upon Timberlake's ethnography (e.g., Hudson 1976; Swanton 1946). Moreover, contemporary chroniclers provided little extensive treatment of Native American warfare (Randolph 1973: 159).

5. A painting by Joshua Reynolds of the Cherokee delegation that Timberlake accompanied to London in 1762 includes in its title part of a "War Whoop": "Woach Woach ha ha hoch Waoch" (Jacobs 1967: facing 50).

6. My colleague Jerry Ball suggested the relevance of the Ossianic vogue to Timberlake's work.

7. The existence of these songs predating Timberlake's publication does not necessarily undermine the claim that his translation is the first of an American Indian song into English. They both seem to be original compositions based upon Indian themes, the sort of thing that Longfellow would produce almost a century later in *The Song of Hiawatha*.

CHAPTER 5. THE EARLY NINETEENTH CENTURY

A version of this chapter appeared as " 'Tokens of Literary Faculty': Native American Literature and Euroamerican Translation in the Early Nineteenth Century," in Brian Swann, ed., *On the Translation of Native American Literatures* (Washington: Smithsonian Institution Press, 1992): 33–50. I appreciate suggestions from Frances Malpezzi and Brian Swann regarding both stylistic and substantive features of the original version.

1. This was undoubtedly one of the motives that generated the publication of Black Hawk's autobiography, the textualization of Native American verbal expression that introduces the problem addressed in this study. See Wallace 1994.

2. Cf. Edward Said's comments on the processes by which people deal with the "Other": "[All] cultures impose corrections upon raw reality, changing it from free-floating objects into units of knowledge. The problem is not that conversion takes place. It is perfectly natural for the human mind to resist the assault on it of untreated strangeness; therefore cultures have always been inclined to impose complete transformations upon other cultures, receiving these other cultures not as they are but as, for the benefit of the receiver, they ought to be" (1978: 67).

3. A commitment to "improving" texts was not exclusive to those dealing with Native American verbal art at the time. Consider the case of the Brothers Grimm, whose reworking of the *Märchen* and *Sagen* that they had collected in Germany has received considerable attention recently (e.g., Bottigheimer 1988; Briggs 1993). See, for instance, the Grimms' comment in the foreword to their collection of *Sagen* that the texts' "innermost essence must never be violated, not even in trivial details, and all circumstances must be faithfully recorded. It has thus been our task to follow the exact words as faithfully as was feasible, *but not necessarily to adhere slavishly to them*" (Ward 1981: 1:4–5, my emphasis).

4. For a recent description of this guessing game, see Black Bear and Theiz 1976: 133. (I am grateful to Julian Rice for this reference.)

5. Hoffman may have been influenced by Schoolcraft, with whom he had a close relationship, in producing the Native-language version with literal translation. Schoolcraft provided similar materials occasionally when he presented Ojibwa poetry, and some of the free translations that appear in Schoolcraft's work—especially *Oneóta* (retitled *The Indian in His Wigwam* [1848])—came from the pen of Hoffman. Hoffman's "literal" translation of "Indian Serenade" was republished as "Calling-One's-Own" in George W. Cronyn's early-twentieth-century anthology of American Indian poetry, *The Path on the Rainbow* (1918: 12–13).

6. I am grateful to Julian Rice for these references.

7. Or consider what may seem a more prosaic example, that of the Ozark folktale collector Vance Randolph, who customarily claimed to have "set down the tales as accurately as I could," at the same time admitting to revisions in sentence structure and deletions of profanity (1952: xvi–xvii). In doing so, Randolph apparently believed that he was representing Ozark

folktales accurately as *literature,* even if he had to adapt them somewhat to the esthetics of mid-1950s printed prose.

8. Whether this piece was ever orally expressed remains questionable. In Longfellow's letter to Freiligrath, he says that it was *"written* by a Choctaw" and translated by the Mississippian (Longfellow 1966–1982: 2:516, my emphasis). And whether Longfellow actually meant to be taken literally or was using "written" in the loose sense of "composed" is unclear. I have found nothing like these lines in major published collections of Choctaw songs (either original-language versions or translations).

CHAPTER 6. SCHOOLCRAFT AS TEXTMAKER

An earlier version of this chapter appeared in *Journal of American Folklore* 103 (1990): 177–192. I appreciate the recommendations of the journal's editor, Bruce Jackson, and its anonymous readers.

1. The best book-length treatment of Schoolcraft's life and work is Bremer 1987. The author's death prevented the publication of John F. Freeman's (1960) dissertation on Schoolcraft. Another important unpublished source is the chapter on Schoolcraft in McNeil 1980: 102–144. Published works on Schoolcraft include Osborn and Osborn 1942, which contains a biography so uncritical and laudatory that its uses are limited, a collection of letters to and from Schoolcraft (originals deposited in the Public Library of Sault Ste. Marie), and the most complete bibliography of Schoolcraft's writings available. More useful in terms of biography and evaluation of Schoolcraft's work are Hays 1964: 3–14; Freeman 1965; Marsden 1976; Zumwalt 1976; Bremer 1982; Bieder 1986: 146–193; Ruppert 1991; and McNeil 1992. An uncritical summary of Schoolcraft's *Notes on the Iroquois* appears in Newton 1954. Some assistance in untangling the complexity of Schoolcraft's bibliography is afforded in Hallowell 1946.

2. A brief biography of Jane Johnston Schoolcraft appears in Stone-Gordon 1994.

3. This is motif A2611.1, "Corn from body of slain person" in Thompson's catalog (1955–1958: 1:331). For a listing of some analogous Native American narratives, see the note to tale xxii in Thompson 1929: 293–294. Longfellow reworked the story to form Book Five in *The Song of Hiawatha* (1901: 48–57).

4. Whether *Algic Researches* fulfilled these goals for Schoolcraft can be inferred from publication figures. Two thousand copies were printed, of which 1,062 were sold within three years. Schoolcraft apparently lost a little from the process, and in 1848 the publisher still had about seven hundred unsold copies (Bremer 1987: 249).

5. According to Freeman (1959), *Oneóta* appeared in eleven variant edi-

tions with five different titles between 1844 and 1853. I have used the incarnation entitled *The Indian in His Wigwam* (Schoolcraft 1848).

CHAPTER 7. LINGUISTIC TEXTS AS DATA SOURCES

1. Other Native American authors who produced historical works before 1900 include Hendrick Aupaumut (1982), a Mohegan who wrote c. 1790; David Cusick (Beauchamp 1892), a Tuscarora who published a history of the Six Nations in the 1820s; George Copway (1860), an Ojibwa convert to Christianity who first published a history of his people in 1850; and Elias Johnson (1881), another Tuscarora whose book focused on his own group's role in the history of the Six Nations.

2. Biographical information on Warren appears in Vizenor 1984: 56–59.

3. Huddleston (1967) shows that most of these theories (and more) were current as early as the sixteenth and seventeenth centuries, especially among Spanish writers.

4. The most important study of Brinton's life and career is Darnell 1988. Assessments that focus on particular aspects of his work (but not his text-making to any significant extent) include McNeil 1980: 217–243 and Vorpagel 1983.

5. Müller's most important work was "Comparative Mythology" (1909), first published in 1856. A summary of his approach to myth appears in Dorson 1968: 160–186.

6. Writers who preceded Brinton in such "literary criticism" include Schoolcraft, whose "Indian Music, Songs, and Poetry" appeared in *Oneóta* in 1844. See chapter 6.

7. Gatschet issued the material for the second volume under the auspices of the Saint Louis Academy of Science (Gatschet 1888).

8. Book-length studies of Boas's career are Herskovits 1953 and Hyatt 1990. See also the collection of essays edited by Goldschmidt (1959). The most comprehensive treatment of Boas as textmaker appears in McNeil's unpublished dissertation (1980: 866–926). Evaluations and re-evaluations of Boas's contributions to various aspects of the study of Native American verbal art include Berman 1992; Codere 1966; Darnell 1990; Goldman 1980; Hymes 1981; Kinkade 1992; Krupat 1992a: 81–100; Rohner and Rohner 1969; and Stocking 1992: 60–113.

9. Boas had used a phonograph in the field as early as 1897, when he and James Teit recorded songs in British Columbia (Rohner 1969: 202–203).

10. It may be ironic that Schoolcraft, of whose work Boas was critical, had actually used this approach to text presentation. Though inconsistently and without the punctilious attention to linguistic detail that developed in Boa-

sian anthropology, Schoolcraft did occasionally include Native-language texts with literal and free translations throughout his voluminous published work.

CHAPTER 8. NATALIE CURTIS IN HOPILAND

1. I have encountered no sources written or published during Curtis's lifetime that explain the origins of her Native American interests. Most later sources agree with the suggestion advanced here, a notable exception being Charles Haywood (1986: 1:557), who claims that she first encountered Native Americans at the Louisiana Purchase Exposition in St. Louis in 1904. But she had already paid her visit to Theodore Roosevelt and published an essay on Hopi music the previous year! The fullest published biography of Curtis (Bredenberg 1994) essentially avoids the question of the origins of her interests. Though quite uncritical of Curtis's work, Bredenberg's essay should contribute to her becoming more well known as an early advocate of "multiculturalism."

2. See also a Hopi's own description of his experience in a government reservation school (Simmons 1942: 88–113).

3. We need not go very far back in the study of Native American verbal art to encounter denials and minimizations of individual creativity. In 1933, translator of Tewa song texts Herbert J. Spinden, for instance, claimed that American Indian poetic expression lacked "the individual point of view," asserting, though, that "the world is richer by reason of this lack which leaves the social mode uncompromised" (1933: 62). Eighteen years later, in an anthology of Indian poetry, A. Grove Day was equally assertive about the "community-minded" Indian verbal artist's lack of creative individuality: "The romantic or egotistical exhibition of his personal impressions of the world was foreign to his nature, and such an act would have been looked upon by his fellow tribesmen not only as impractical, but as dangerously anti-social" (Day 1951: 176). Even Melville Jacobs, whose experience hearing dozens of Clackamas Chinook narratives told by a single storyteller, Victoria Howard, should have convinced him of the importance of the individual, equated oral art with "the creative expression of a people, not of a unique individual or of a series of so-called geniuses" (1959: 21).

4. Compare, for example, the description of John Gregory Bourke's behavior at a Snake Dance at the Hopi community of Walpi as reported by himself in *The Snake-Dance of the Moquis* (1884) and in Porter's biography (1986: 95–111).

5. Curtis did make a number of recordings of Native American music. For example, ten cylinders of Hopi music that she recorded in 1903 were transferred from the Museum of the American Indian to the Bureau of American

Ethnology (Brady et al. 1984: 41). Curtis also used a phonograph to record African and African American songs a decade later.

6. Variations occur in the spellings of Hopi proper names. Despite the advances in linguistics and orthography represented by more recent spellings, I am using those of Curtis.

7. Authorities differ on many of the details of Lololomai's conversion—as well as on other aspects of Hopi history leading up to the "Oraibi split" in 1906. For a summary of some of those differing views and a reinterpretation of this period in Hopi history, see Rushforth and Upham 1992: 123–148.

8. For a structural analysis that reveals the importance of music in the textualization of this song, see Shaul 1992.

9. David Leedom Shaul has retranslated this song in Swann 1994: 685.

10. Correspondence between Boas and Curtis dating from 1903 until shortly before her death in 1921 is preserved among the Boas professional papers at the American Philosophical Society.

11. Curtis was particularly gratified when her teacher Ferruccio Busoni used melodies from *The Indians' Book* as the basis for his *Red Indian Fantasy* (op. 44), first performed in 1914, and at least two other compositions. (See Beaumont 1985: 190–203 and Curtis 1915a.) Curtis herself drew upon Native American music to create her own musical compositions. The Music Division, Library of Congress, contains three manuscript compositions by Curtis: "Dawn Song, Based on a Cheyenne Indian Song" (dated 1920), "Victory Song (Pawnee Indian)" (also 1920), and "American Indian Dance Pageant" (1921). For some of the ways in which twentieth-century American poets have used Indian verbal art as a foundation for their works, see Castro 1983. More recently, Jarold Ramsey has lamented the failure of Euroamerican writers—especially those in the nineteenth century—to take advantage of the indigenous verbal arts of Native North America (1990: 52–55).

12. This letter appears among the Boas papers at the American Philosophical Society. It was dated 15 August 1903 and mailed to Boas in New York City from the Curtis home on Long Island.

CHAPTER 9. THE ANTHOLOGY AS MUSEUM OF VERBAL ART

1. This letter appears among the Boas papers at the American Philosophical Society. It was dated 6 March 1907 and mailed to Boas from Curtis's home on West 69th Street in New York City.

2. The contribution of this anthology to the development of Euroamerican poetic interest in American Indians has been treated by Castro (1983: 19–22). In a letter written to Franz Boas, dated 17 June 1917, and preserved among the Boas papers in the American Philosophical Society, editor

Cronyn wrote, "We are trying to make a truly worthy book." Certainly, as Arnold Krupat has argued, *The Path on the Rainbow* did much to forge the connection between Native American verbal art and a distinctively American literature.

3. Compare Bevis's treatment of the way in which Brandon has reworked Pawnee material, originally translated and published by Alice Cunningham Fletcher (1974: 694–698).

REFERENCES

Adams, David Wallace. 1979. "Schooling the Hopi: Federal Indian Policy Writ Small, 1887–1917." *Pacific Historical Review* 48:335–356.

Alexander, Hartley Burr. 1916. *North America. The Mythology of All Races.* Vol. 10. Boston: Marshall Jones.

Andresen, Julie Tetel. 1990. *Linguistics in America 1769–1924: A Critical History.* London: Routledge.

Around Him, John. 1983. *Lakota Ceremonial Songs.* Trans. Albert White Hat, Sr. Rosebud, S.Dak.: Sinte Gleska College.

Asad, Talal. 1986. "The Concept of Cultural Translation in British Social Anthropology." In *Writing Culture: The Poetics and Politics of Ethnography,* ed. George E. Marcus and James Clifford, 141–164. Berkeley: University of California Press.

Astrov, Margot, ed. 1946. *The Winged Serpent: American Indian Prose and Poetry.* New York: John Day.

Aupaumut, Hendrick. 1982. "History of the Muh-he-con-nuk Indians." In *The Elders Wrote: An Anthology of Early Prose by North American Indians, 1768–1931,* ed. Bernd Peyer, 25–33. Berlin: Dietrich Reimer Verlag.

Barlow, William, and Daniel O. Powell. 1986. " 'The Late Dr. Ward of Indiana': Rafinesque's Source of the Walam Olum." *Indiana Magazine of History* 82(2): 185–193.

Barnes, Nellie, ed. 1925. *American Indian Love Lyrics and Other Verse from the Songs of the North American Indians.* New York: Macmillan.

Bascom, William R. 1955. "Verbal Art." *Journal of American Folklore* 68: 245–252.

Bassnett-McGuire, Susan. 1980. *Translation Studies.* London: Methuen.

Bataille, Gretchen M., and Kathleen Mullen Sands. 1984. *American Indian Women: Telling Their Lives.* Lincoln: University of Nebraska Press.

Baudet, Henri. 1965. *Paradise on Earth: Some Thoughts on European Images of Non-European Man.* Trans. Elizabeth Wentholt. New Haven: Yale University Press.

Bauman, Richard. 1984. *Verbal Art as Performance.* Prospect Heights, Ill.: Waveland.

———. 1993. "The Nationalization and Internationalization of Folklore: The Case of Schoolcraft's 'Gitshee Gauzinee.'" *Western Folklore* 52:247–269.

Bauman, Richard, and Charles L. Briggs. 1990. "Poetics and Performance as Critical Perspectives on Language and Social Life." *Annual Review of Anthropology* 19:59–88.

Beauchamp, W. M. 1892. *The Iroquois Trail, or Foot-Prints of the Six Nations, in Customs, Traditions, and History, in Which Are Included David Cusick's Sketches of Ancient History of the Six Nations.* Fayetteville, N.C.: H. C. Beauchamp.

Beaumont, Anthony. 1985. *Busoni the Composer.* Bloomington: Indiana University Press.

Ben-Amos, Dan. 1993. "'Context' in Context." *Western Folklore* 52:209–226.

Benjamin, Walter. 1968. *Illuminations.* Ed. Hannah Arendt. Trans. Harry Zohn. New York: Schocken.

Berkhofer, Robert F., Jr. 1978. *The White Man's Indian: Images of the American Indian from Columbus to the Present.* New York: Knopf.

Berman, Judith. 1992. "Oolachan-Woman's Robe: Fish, Blankets, Masks, and Meaning in Boas's Kwakw'ala Texts." In Swann 1992: 125–162.

Bevis, William. 1974. "American Indian Verse Translations." *College English* 35:693–703.

Bidney, David. 1953. *Theoretical Anthropology.* New York: Columbia University Press.

———. 1954. "The Idea of the Savage in North American Ethnohistory." *Journal of the History of Ideas* 15:322–327.

Bieder, Robert E. 1986. *Science Encounters the Indian, 1820–1880: The Early Years of American Ethnology.* Norman: University of Oklahoma Press.

Bierhorst, John. 1969. *The Fire Plume: Legends of the American Indians Collected by Henry Rowe Schoolcraft.* New York: Dial.

Bitterli, Urs. 1989. *Cultures in Conflict: Encounters Between European and Non-European Cultures, 1492–1800.* Trans. Ritchie Robertson. Stanford, Calif.: Stanford University Press.

Black Bear, Ben, Sr., and R. D. Theiz. 1976. *Songs and Dances of the Lakota.* Rosebud, S.Dak.: Sinte Gleska College.

Black Hawk. 1834. *Life of Ma-ka-tai-me-she-kia-kiak or Black Hawk* . . . Boston: n.p.

Boas, Franz. 1901. *Kathlamet Texts*. Bureau of American Ethnology Bulletin 26. Washington, D.C.: GPO.

——. 1902. *Tsimshian Texts*. Bureau of American Ethnology Bulletin No. 27. Washington, D.C.: GPO.

——. 1912. "Tsimshian Texts (New Series)." *Publications of the American Ethnological Society* 3:65–285.

——. 1916. *Tsimshian Mythology*. Thirty-First Annual Report of the Bureau of American Ethnology, 29–1037. Washington, D.C.: GPO.

——. 1917. "Introductory." *International Journal of American Linguistics* 1(1): 1–8.

——. 1928. *Bella Bella Texts*. Columbia University Contributions to Anthropology, no. 5. New York: Columbia University Press.

——. 1935. *Kwakiutl Culture as Reflected in Mythology*. Memoirs of the American Folklore Society, no. 28. New York: G. Stechert.

——. 1940. *Race, Language, and Culture*. Chicago: University of Chicago Press.

Boon, James A. 1982. *Other Tribes, Other Scribes: Symbolic Anthropology in the Comparative Study of Cultures, Histories, Religions, and Texts*. Cambridge: Cambridge University Press.

Bottigheimer, Ruth B. 1988. "From Gold to Guilt: The Forces Which Reshaped *Grimms' Tales*." In *The Brothers Grimm and the Folktale*, ed. James M. McGlathery, 192–204. Urbana: University of Illinois Press.

Bourke, John Gregory. 1884. *The Snake-Dance of the Moquis of Arizona: Being a Narrative of a Journey from Santa Fe, New Mexico, to the Villages of the Moqui Indians of Arizona*. New York: Scribner's.

Bowra, C. M. 1962. *Primitive Song*. Cleveland: World.

Bradbury, John. 1819. *Travels in the Interior of America, in the Years 1809, 1810, and 1811*. 2d ed. London: Sherwood, Neely, and John.

Brady, Erika, et al. 1984. *The Federal Cylinder Project: A Guide to Field Cylinder Collections in Federal Agencies*. Vol 1. *Introduction and Inventory*. Washington, D.C.: GPO.

Brandon, William. 1986. *New Worlds for Old: Reports from the New World and Their Effect on the Development of Social Thought in Europe, 1500–1800*. Athens: Ohio University Press.

——, ed. 1991. *The Magic World: American Indian Songs and Poems*. Athens: Ohio University Press.

Bredenberg, Alfred R. 1994. "Natalie Curtis Burlin (1875–1921): A Pioneer in the Study of American Minority Cultures." *Connecticut Review* 16(1): 1–15.

Bremer, Richard G. 1982. "Henry Rowe Schoolcraft: Explorer in the Mississippi Valley." *Wisconsin Magazine of History* 66(1): 40–59.

——. 1987. *Indian Agent and Wilderness Scholar: The Life of Henry Rowe Schoolcraft*. Mount Pleasant, Mich.: Clark Historical Library.

Briggs, Charles L. 1988. *Competence in Performance: The Creativity of Tradition in Mexicano Verbal Art*. Philadelphia: University of Pennsylvania Press.

———. 1993. "Metadiscursive Practices and Scholarly Authority in Folkloristics." *Journal of American Folklore* 106:387–434.

Bright, William. 1982. "Poetic Structure in Oral Narrative." In *Spoken and Written Language: Exploring Orality and Literacy*, ed. Deborah Tannen, 171–184. Norwood, N.J.: Ablex.

———. 1984. *American Indian Linguistics and Literature*. Berlin: Mouton.

Brinton, Daniel G. 1859. *Notes on the Floridian Peninsula: Its Literary History, Indian Tribes and Antiquities*. Philadelphia: Joseph Sabin.

———. 1876. *The Myths of the New World: A Treatise on the Symbolism and Mythology of the Red Race of America*. 2d ed. New York: Henry Holt.

———. 1883a. *American Aboriginal Authors and Their Productions; Especially Those in the Native Languages: A Chapter in the History of Literature*. Philadelphia: n.p.

———. 1883b. *The Maya Chronicles*. Brinton's Library of Aboriginal American Literature, no. 1. Philadelphia: Daniel G. Brinton.

———. 1884. *The Lenâpé and Their Legends, with the Complete Text and Symbols of the Walam Olum: A New Translation, and an Inquiry into Its Authenticity*. Brinton's Library of Aboriginal American Literature, no. 5. Philadelphia: Daniel G. Brinton.

———. 1885. *The Annals of the Cakchiquels: The Original Text, with a Translation, Notes and Introduction*. Brinton's Library of Aboriginal American Literature, no. 6. Philadelphia: Daniel G. Brinton.

———. 1890. *Essays of an Americanist*. Philadelphia: Porter and Coates.

———. 1891. *The American Race: A Linguistic Classification and Ethnographic Description of the Native Tribes of North and South America*. New York: N.D.C. Hodges.

———. 1892. "Primitive American Poetry." *Poet Lore* 4:329–331.

Brown, Elizabeth Gaspar. 1953. "Lewis Cass and the American Indian." *Michigan History* 37:286–298.

Bunzel, Ruth L. 1932a. *Zuñi Origin Myths*. Forty-Seventh Annual Report of the Bureau of American Ethnology, 545–609. Washington, D.C.: GPO.

———. 1932b. *Zuñi Ritual Poetry*. Forty-Seventh Annual Report of the Bureau of American Ethnology, 611–835. Washington, D.C.: GPO.

———. 1933. *Zuñi Texts*. Publications of the American Ethnological Society, no. 15. New York: Stechert.

Burns, Allan F. 1992. "Modern Yucatec Maya Oral Literature." In Swann 1992: 387–405.

Casagrande, Joseph B. 1954. "The Ends of Translation." *International Journal of American Linguistics* 20:335–340.

Cass, Lewis. 1822. "Indian Customs." *The Columbian Star* 20 (April): 1–2.

——. 1826. Review of *Manners and Customs of Several Indian Tribes,* by John D. Heckewelder; and *Historical Notes Respecting the Indians of North America,* by John Halkett. *North American Review* 22:53–119.

Castro, Michael. 1983. *Interpreting the Indian: Twentieth-Century Poets and the Native American.* Albuquerque: University of New Mexico Press.

Catlin, George. 1841. *Letters and Notes on the Manners, Customs, and Condition of the North American Indians* . . . 2 vols. London: By the Author.

Chamberlain, Alexander F. 1899. "In Memoriam: Daniel Garrison Brinton." *Journal of American Folklore* 12:215–225.

Channing, Walter. 1815. "Essay on American Language and Literature." *North American Review* 1:307–314.

Cheyfitz, Eric. 1991. *The Poetics of Imperialism: Translation and Colonization from The Tempest to Tarzan.* New York: Oxford University Press.

Chicken, George. 1928. "Colonel Chicken's Journal." In Williams 1928: 93–106.

Clements, William M., ed. 1986. *Native American Folklore in Nineteenth-Century Periodicals.* Athens: Ohio University Press.

Clifford, James. 1988. *The Predicament of Culture: Twentieth-Century Ethnography, Literature, and Art.* Cambridge, Mass.: Harvard University Press.

Codere, Helen. 1966. Introduction to *Kwakiutl Ethnography,* by Franz Boas, ed. Helen Codere, xi–xxxii. Chicago: University of Chicago Press.

Coltelli, Laura, ed. 1989. *Native American Literatures.* Pisa: SEU.

Copway, George. 1860. *Indian Life and Indian History, by an Indian Author; Embracing the Traditions of the North American Indians Regarding Themselves, Particularly of That Most Important of All the Tribes, the Ojibways.* Boston: Albert Colby.

Corkran, David H. 1962. *The Cherokee Frontier: Conflict and Survival, 1740–62.* Norman: University of Oklahoma Press.

——. 1969. Introduction to Alexander Long, "A Small Postscript on the ways and manners of the Indians called Cherokees . . . " *Southern Indian Studies* 21:3–49.

Count, Earl W. 1952. "The Earth-Diver and the Rival Twins: A Clue to Time Correlation in North-Eurasiatic and North American Mythology." In *Indian Tribes of Aboriginal America: Selected Papers of the XXIXth International Congress of Americanists,* ed. Sol Tax, 55–62. Chicago: University of Chicago Press.

Cronyn, George W. 1918. *The Path on the Rainbow: An Anthology of Songs and Chants from the Indians of North America.* New York: Boni and Liveright.

Cuming, Alexander. 1928. "Journal of Sir Alexander Cuming." In Williams 1928: 115–146.

Curtis, Natalie. 1903. "An American-Indian Composer." *Harper's* 107:626–632.

———. 1904a. "A Bit of American Folk-Music: Two Pueblo Indian Grinding Songs." *The Craftsman* 7:35–41.

———. 1904b. "The Shepherd Poet: A Bit of Arizona Life." *Southern Workman* 33:145–148.

———. 1904c. "The Value of Indian Art." *Southern Workman* 33:448–450.

———. 1905a. "Hampton's Double Mission." *Southern Workman* 34:543–545.

———. 1905b. *Songs of Ancient America: Three Pueblo Indian Corn-Grinding Songs from Laguna, New Mexico.* New York: G. Schirmer.

———. 1913. "The Perpetuating of Indian Art." *The Outlook* 105:623–631.

———. 1915a. "Busoni's Indian Fantasy." *Southern Workman* 44:538–544.

———. 1915b. "Folk Song and the American Indian." *Southern Workman* 44:476–480.

———. 1919a. "Mr. Roosevelt and Indian Music: A Personal Reminiscence." *The Outlook* 122:399–400.

———. 1919b. "Our Native Craftsmen." *Southern Workman* 48:389–396.

———. 1920a. "A Plea for Our Native Art." *Musical Quarterly* 6:175–178.

———. 1920b. "Saving Indian Music and Legend from Annihilation." *The Etude* 38:666.

———, ed. 1923. *The Indians' Book: An Offering by the American Indians of Indian Lore, Musical and Narrative, to Form a Record of the Songs and Legends of Their Race.* 2d ed. New York: Harper and Brothers.

[Curtis, Natalie.] 1904. "Indian Music at Hampton Anniversary." *Southern Workman* 33:327–328.

Cushing, Frank Hamilton. 1896. *Outlines of Zuñi Creation Myths.* Thirteenth Annual Report of the Bureau of American Ethnology, 332–462. Washington, D.C.: GPO.

———. 1901. *Zuñi Folk Tales.* New York: Putnam.

Darnell, Regna. 1988. *Daniel Garrison Brinton: The "Fearless Critic" of Philadelphia.* University of Pennsylvania Publications in Anthropology, no. 3. Philadelphia: Department of Anthropology, University of Pennsylvania.

———. 1990. "Franz Boas, Edward Sapir, and the Americanist Text Tradition." *Historigraphia Linguistica* 17:129–144.

Dauenhauer, Richard, and Nora Marks Dauenhauer. 1987. *Haa Shuká, Our Ancestors: Tlingit Oral Narratives.* Seattle: University of Washington Press.

——. 1990. *Haa Tuwunaagu Yís, for Healing Our Spirit: Tlingit Oratory.* Seattle: University of Washington Press.

Davis, Richard Beale. 1978. *Intellectual Life in the Colonial South, 1585– 1763.* Knoxville: University of Tennessee Press.

Day, A. Grove. 1951. *The Sky Clears: Poetry of the American Indians.* New York: Macmillan.

De Caro, Francis A. 1986. "Vanishing the Red Man: Cultural Guilt and Legend Formation." *International Folklore Review* 4:74–80.

De Cora, Angel. 1907. "Native Indian Art." *Southern Workman* 36:527– 528.

Deloria, Ella. 1932. *Dakota Texts.* Publications of the American Ethnological Society, no. 14. New York: Stechert.

DeMallie, Raymond J., ed. 1984. *The Sixth Grandfather: Black Elk's Teachings Given to John Neihardt.* Lincoln: University of Nebraska Press.

Demos, John. 1972. Review of *Shaking the Pumpkin,* edited by Jerome Rothenberg. *Library Journal* 1 (March): 879.

Densmore, Frances. 1910. *Chippewa Music.* Bureau of American Ethnology Bulletin 45. Washington, D.C.: GPO.

——. 1913. *Chippewa Music—II.* Bureau of American Ethnology Bulletin 53. Washington, D.C.: GPO.

——. 1929. *Papago Music.* Bureau of American Ethnology Bulletin 90. Washington, D.C.: GPO.

DeVorsey, Louis, Jr., ed. 1971. *De Brahm's Report on the General Survey in the Southern District of North America.* Columbia: University of South Carolina Press.

Dickason, Olive Patricia. 1984. *The Myth of the Savage and the Beginnings of French Colonialism in the Americas.* Edmonton: University of Alberta Press.

Dippie, Brian W. 1982. *The Vanishing American: White Attitudes and U.S. Indian Policy.* Middletown: Wesleyan University Press.

Dockstader, Frederick. 1977. *Great North American Indians: Profiles in Life and Leadership.* New York: Van Nostrand Reinhold.

——. 1979. "Hopi History, 1859–1940." In Ortiz 1979: 524–532.

Dorson, Richard M. 1968. *The British Folklorists: A History.* Chicago: University of Chicago Press.

Druke, Mary A. 1987. "Linking Arms: The Structure of Iroquois Tribal Diplomacy." In *Beyond the Covenant Chain: The Iroquois and Their Neighbors in Indian North America, 1600–1800,* ed. Daniel K. Richter and James H. Merrell, 29–39. Syracuse, N.Y.: Syracuse University Press.

Duignan, Peter. 1958. "Early Jesuit Missionaries: A Suggestion for Further Study." *American Anthropologist* 60:725–732.

Dundes, Alan. 1962. "Earth-Diver: Creation of the Mythopoeic Male." *American Anthropologist* 64:1032–1051.

——, ed. 1964a. *The Study of Folklore*. Englewood Cliffs, N.J.: Prentice-Hall.

——. 1964b. "Text, Texture, and Context." *Southern Folklore Quarterly* 28:251–265.

——. 1985. "Nationalistic Inferiority Complexes and the Fabrication of Fakelore: A Reconsideration of Ossian, the *Kinder- und Hausmärchen*, the *Kalevala*, and Paul Bunyan." *Journal of Folklore Research* 22:5–18.

Eastman, Mrs. Mary. 1849. *Dahcotah; or, Life and Legends of the Sioux Around Fort Snelling*. New York: John Wiley.

Elder, William. 1871. "The Aborigines of Nova Scotia." *North American Review* 112:1–30.

Erdoes, Richard, and Alfonso Ortiz, eds. 1984. *American Indian Myths and Legends*. New York: Pantheon.

Evans, E. Raymond. 1976. "Notable Persons in Cherokee History: Ostenaco." *Journal of Cherokee Studies* 1:41–54.

Evans, Timothy H. 1988. "Folklore as Utopia: English Medievalists and the Ideology of Revivalism." *Western Folklore* 47:245–268.

Evers, Lawrence J. 1973. Review of *Shaking the Pumpkin*, edited by Jerome Rothenberg. *Prairie Schooner* 47:79–80.

——. 1983. "Cycles of Appreciation." In *Studies in American Indian Literature: Critical Essays and Course Designs*, ed. Paula Gunn Allen, 23–32. New York: Modern Language Association.

Evers, Lawrence, and Felipe S. Molina. 1987. *Yaqui Deer Songs/Maso Bwikam*. Tucson: University of Arizona Press.

——. 1989. "Coyote Songs." In Coltelli 1989: 9–37.

Fairchild, Hoxie Neale. 1961. *The Noble Savage: A Study in Romantic Naturalism*. New York: Russell and Russell.

Farwell, Arthur. 1902. "Aspects of Indian Music." *Southern Workman* 31:211–217.

——. 1904. "The Artistic Possibilities of Indian Myth." *Poet Lore* 15:46–61.

——. 1970. "A Letter to American Composers." In Lawrence 1970: 1:xvii–xix.

Fewkes, J. Walter. 1890a. "A Contribution to Passamaquoddy Folk-Lore." *Journal of American Folklore* 3:257–280.

——. 1890b. "On the Use of the Phonograph Among the Zuñi Indians." *American Naturalist* 24:687–691.

Fine, Elizabeth C. 1984. *The Folklore Text from Performance to Print*. Bloomington: Indiana University Press.

Fire, John (Lame Deer), and Richard Erdoes. 1972. *Lame Deer, Seeker of Visions*. New York: Simon and Schuster.

Fletcher, Alice Cunningham. 1900. *Indian Story and Song from North America*. Boston: Small Maynard.

Foreman, Carolyn Thomas. 1943. *Indians Abroad, 1493–1938*. Norman: University of Oklahoma Press.

Foster, Michael K. 1985. "Another Look at the Function of Wampum in Iroquois-White Councils." In Jennings et al. 1985: 99–114.

Franklin, Wayne. 1979. *Discoverers, Explorers, Settlers: The Diligent Writers of Early America*. Chicago: University of Chicago Press.

Freeman, John Finley. 1959. "Pirated Editions of Schoolcraft's *Oneóta*." *Papers of the Bibliographical Society of America* 53:252–261.

——. 1960. "Henry Rowe Schoolcraft." Ph.D. diss., Harvard University.

——. 1965. "Religion and Personality in the Anthropology of Henry Schoolcraft." *Journal of the History of the Behavioral Sciences* 1:301–313.

Friedman, Albert B. 1961. *The Ballad Revival: Studies in the Influence of Popular on Sophisticated Poetry*. Chicago: University of Chicago Press.

Frisbie, Charlotte J., and David P. McAllester, eds. 1978. *Navajo Blessingway Singer: The Autobiography of Frank Mitchell, 1881–1967*. Tucson: University of Arizona Press.

Gatschet. Albert S. 1884. *A Migration Legend of the Creek Indians, with a Linguistic, Historic and Ethnographic Introduction*. Vol. 1. Brinton's Library of Aboriginal American Literature, no. 4. Philadelphia: Daniel G. Brinton.

——. 1888. "Tchikilli's Kasi'hta Legend in the Creek and Hitchiti Languages." *Academy of Science of St. Louis Transactions* 5:33–239.

Gearing, Fred. 1962. *Priests and Warriors: Social Structures for Cherokee Politics in the 18th Century*. American Anthropological Association Memoir 93. Menasha, Wis.: American Anthropological Association.

Gibson, Arrell Morgan. 1983. *The Santa Fe and Taos Colonies: Age of the Muses, 1900–1942*. Norman: University of Oklahoma Press.

Gilbert, William H., Jr. 1943. "The Eastern Cherokees." In *Anthropological Papers*. No. 23, 169–413. Bureau of American Ethnology Bulletin 133. Washington, D.C.: GPO.

Gingerich, Willard. 1983. "Critical Models for the Study of Indigenous Literature: The Case of Nahuatl." In Swann 1983: 112–125.

Goldman, Irving. 1980. "Boas on the Kwakiutl: The Ethnographic Tradition." In *Theory and Practice: Essays Presented to Gene Weltfish*, ed. Stanley Diamond, 331–345. The Hague: Mouton.

Goldschmidt, Walter, ed. 1959. *The Anthropology of Franz Boas: Essays on the Centennial of His Birth*. San Francisco: American Anthropological Association.

Goody, Jack. 1977. *The Domestication of the Savage Mind*. Cambridge: Cambridge University Press.

Grant, Frances. 1921. "World Loses Ardent Seeker of Truth in Natalie Curtis-Burlin." *Musical America* 35(2): 47.

Grant, Ludovick. 1909. "Historical Relation of Facts Delivered by Ludovick

Grant, Indian Trader, to His Excellency the Governor of South Carolina." *South Carolina Historical and Genealogical Magazine* 19:54–68.

Greenblatt, Stephen. 1991. *Marvelous Possessions: The Wonder of the New World*. Chicago: University of Chicago Press.

Gumperz, John J., and Dell Hymes, eds. 1964. *The Ethnography of Communication*. Washington, D.C.: American Anthropological Association.

Hale, Horatio. 1883. *The Iroquois Book of Rites*. Brinton's Library of Aboriginal American Literature, no. 2. Philadelphia: Daniel G. Brinton.

Hallowell, A. Irving. 1946. "Concordance of Ojibwa Narratives in the Published Works of Henry R. Schoolcraft." *Journal of American Folklore* 59:136–153.

Hanzeli, Victor Egon. 1969. *Missionary Linguistics in New France: A Study of Seventeenth- and Eighteenth-Century Descriptions of American Indian Languages*. The Hague: Mouton.

Haring, Lee. 1972. "Performing for the Interviewer: A Study of the Structure of Context." *Southern Folklore Quarterly* 36:383–398.

Harper, Francis, ed. 1958. *The Travels of William Bartram: Naturalist's Edition*. New Haven: Yale University Press.

Harrington, John P. 1940. "Boas on the Science of Language." *International Journal of American Linguistics* 11:97–99.

Hays, H. R. 1964. *From Ape to Angel: An Informal History of Social Anthropology*. New York: Capricorn.

Haywood, Charles. 1986. "Curtis (Burlin), Natalie." In *The New Grove Dictionary of American Music*, ed. H. Wiley Hitchcock and Stanley Sadie, 1:557. New York: Macmillan.

Healy, George R. 1958. "The French Jesuits and the Idea of the Noble Savage." *William and Mary Quarterly*, 3d ser., 15:143–167.

Heckewelder, Rev. John. 1876. *History, Manners, and Customs of the Indian Nations Who Once Inhabited Pennsylvania and the Neighbouring States*. Philadelphia: Historical Society of Pennsylvania.

Hegeman, Susan. 1989. "Native American 'Texts' and the Problem of Authenticity." *American Quarterly* 41:265–283.

Henderson, Alice Corbin. 1917. "Aboriginal Poetry III." *Poetry* 9:256.

Herskovits, Melville J. 1953. *Franz Boas: The Science of Man in the Making*. New York: Scribner's.

Hinsley, Curtis M., Jr. 1981. *Savages and Scientists: The Smithsonian Institution and the Development of American Anthropology, 1846–1910*. Washington, D.C.: Smithsonian Institution Press.

Hodgen, Margaret T. 1964. *Early Anthropology in the Sixteenth and Seventeenth Century*. Philadelphia: University of Pennsylvania Press.

Hoffman, Charles Fenno. 1835. *A Winter in the West; By a New-Yorker*. 2 vols. New York: Harper and Brothers.

Hollis, Christopher. 1968. *The Jesuits: A History.* New York: Macmillan.

Huddleston, Lee. 1967. *Origins of the American Indians: European Concepts, 1492–1729.* Austin: University of Texas Press.

Hudson, Charles. 1976. *The Southeastern Indians.* Knoxville: University of Tennessee Press.

Hyatt, Marshall. 1990. *Franz Boas, Social Activist: The Dynamics of Ethnicity.* New York: Greenwood.

Hymes, Dell. 1975. "Folklore's Nature and the Sun's Myth." *Journal of American Folklore* 88:345–369.

———. 1981. *"In Vain I Tried to Tell You": Studies in Native American Ethnopoetics.* Philadelphia: University of Pennsylvania Press.

———. 1982. "Narrative Form as a 'Grammar' of Experience: Native Americans and a Glimpse of English." *Journal of Education* 164:121–142.

———. 1985a. "Language, Memory, and Selective Performance: Cultee's 'Salmon's Myth' as Twice Told to Boas." *Journal of American Folklore* 98:391–434.

———. 1985b. "Verse Analysis of a Kathlamet Chinook Text Preserved by Franz Boas: Charles Cultee's 'Southwest Wind's Myth.'" In *Aims and Prospects of Semiotics: Essays in Honor of Algirdas Julien Greimas,* ed. Herman Parret and Hans-George Reprecht, 953–978. [Amsterdam]: John Benjamins.

———. 1987. "Anthologies and Narrators." In Swann and Krupat 1987: 41–84.

———. 1992. "Use All There Is to Use." In Swann 1992: 83–124.

———. 1994. "Ethnopoetics, Oral-Formulaic Theory, and Editing Texts." *Oral Tradition* 9:330–370.

"Indian Eloquence." 1828. *The Ariel* 27 (December): 142.

"Indian Eloquence." 1831. *The Ariel* 5(9): 144.

Indiana Historical Society. 1954. *Walam Olum or Red Score, The Migration Legend of the Lenni Lenape or Delaware Indians: A New Translation, Interpreted by Linguistic, Historical, Archaeological, Ethnological, and Physical Anthropological Studies.* Indianapolis: Indiana Historical Society.

Jacobs, Melville. 1959. *The Content and Style of an Oral Literature: Clackamas Chinook Myths and Tales.* Chicago: University of Chicago Press.

Jacobs, Wilbur R., ed. 1967. *The Appalachian Indian Frontier: The Edmond Atkin Report and Plan of 1755.* Lincoln: University of Nebraska Press.

Jaenen, Cornelius J. 1976. *Friend or Foe: Aspects of French-Amerindian Culture Contact in the Sixteenth and Seventeenth Centuries.* New York: Columbia University Press.

———. 1982. "'Les Sauvages Ameriquains': Persistence into the 18th Century of Traditional French Concepts and Constructs for Comprehending Amerindians." *Ethnohistory* 29:43–56.

Jakobson, Roman. 1959. "On Linguistic Aspects of Translation." In *On Translation*, ed. Reuben A. Brower, 232–239. Cambridge: Harvard University Press.

James, Edwin. 1823. *Account of an Expedition from Pittsburgh to the Rocky Mountains, Performed in the Years 1819 and '20* . . . 2 vols. Philadelphia: H. C. Carey and I. Lea.

James, Harry C. 1974. *Pages from Hopi History*. Tucson: University of Arizona Press.

Jameson, Fredric. 1979. "Marxism and Historicism." *New Literary History* 11:41–73.

Jennings, Francis. 1975. *The Invasion of America: Indians, Colonialism, and the Cant of Conquest*. Chapel Hill: University of North Carolina Press.

Jennings, Francis, et al. 1985. *The History and Culture of Iroquois Diplomacy: An Interdisciplinary Guide to the Treaties of the Six Nations and Their League*. Syracuse: Syracuse University Press.

Johnson, Elias. 1881. *Legends, Traditions and Law, of the Iroquois, or Six Nations, and History of the Tuscarora Indians*. Lockport, N.Y.: Union.

Jones, James Athearn. 1829. *Tales of an Indian Camp*. London: Colburn and Bentley.

Kaiser, Rudolph. 1987. "Chief Seattle's Speech(es): American Origins and European Reception." In Swann and Krupat 1987: 497–536.

Kendall, Martha B. 1979. Review of *Coyote Was Going There: Indian Literature of the Oregon Country*, by Jarold Ramsey. *International Journal of American Linguistics* 45:97–99.

Kennedy, J. H. 1950. *Jesuit and Savage in New France*. New Haven: Yale University Press.

Kinkade, M. Dale. 1992. "Translating Pentlatch." In Swann 1992: 163–175.

Kirshenblatt-Gimblett, Barbara. 1991. "Objects of Ethnography." In *Exhibiting Cultures: The Poetics and Politics of Museum Display*, ed. Ivan Karp and Steven D. Lavine, 386–443. Washington, D.C.: Smithsonian Institution Press.

Köngas, Elli Kaija. 1960. "The Earth Diver (Th. A 812)." *Ethnohistory* 7: 151–180.

Kroeber, Karl. 1983. "The Wolf Comes: Indian Poetry and Linguistic Criticism." In Swann 1983: 98–111.

——. 1987. "Oral Narrative in an Age of Mechanical Reproduction." *Studies in American Indian Literatures* 11(2): 61–90.

——. 1989. "American Ethnopoetics: A New Critical Dimension." *Arizona Quarterly* 45(2): 1–13.

Krupat, Arnold. 1983. "Identity and Difference in the Criticism of Native American Literature." *Diacritics* 13:2–13.

——. 1985. *For Those Who Come After: A Study of Native American Auto-biography*. Berkeley: University of California Press.

——. 1987. "Post-Structuralism and Oral Literature." In Swann and Krupat 1987: 113–128.

——. 1989. *The Voice in the Margin: Native American Literature and the Canon*. Berkeley: University of California Press.

——. 1992a. *Ethnocriticism: Ethnography, History, Literature*. Berkeley: University of California Press.

——. 1992b. "On the Translation of Native American Song and Poetry: A Theorized History." In Swann 1992: 3–32.

Lafitau, Father Joseph François. 1974–1977. *Customs of the American Indians Compared with the Customs of Primitive Times*. Ed. and trans. William N. Fenton and Elizabeth L. Moore. 2 vols. Toronto: Champlain Society.

Lang, Andrew. 1900. "The Red Indian Imagination." *The Independent* 52: 163–165.

Lawrence, Vera Brodsky, ed. 1970. *The Wa-Wan Press, 1901–1911*. 5 vols. New York: Arno.

Lears, T. J. Jackson. 1981. *No Place of Grace: Antimodernism and the Transformation of American Culture 1880–1920*. New York: Pantheon.

Lesley, Craig, ed. 1991. *Talking Leaves: Contemporary Native American Short Stories*. New York: Dell.

Leupp, Francis E. 1907. "Indians and Their Education." *National Education Association Journal of Proceedings and Addresses* 45:70–74.

Lienhardt, Godfrey. 1954. "Modes of Thought." In *The Institutions of Primitive Society*, ed. E. E. Evans-Pritchard et al., 95–107. Oxford: Basil Blackwell.

Lincoln, Kenneth. 1983. *Native American Renaissance*. Berkeley: University of California Press.

Loftin, John D. 1991. *Religion and Hopi Life in the Twentieth Century*. Bloomington: Indiana University Press.

Longfellow, Henry Wadsworth. 1901. *The Song of Hiawatha*. Boston: Houghton Mifflin.

——. 1966–1982. *The Letters of Henry Wadsworth Longfellow*. Ed. Andrew Hilen. 6 vols. Cambridge: Harvard University Press.

Lord, Albert Bates. 1991. *Epic Singers and Oral Tradition*. Ithaca: Cornell University Press.

Lurie, Nancy Oestreich. 1966. "The Lady from Boston and the Omaha Indians." *American West*. 3(4): 31–33, 80–85.

Malotki, Ekkehart. 1985. *Gullible Coyote/Una'ihu: A Bilingual Collection of Hopi Coyote Stories*. Tucson: University of Arizona Press.

Marcus, George E., and Michael M. J. Fischer. 1986. *Anthropology as Cultural Critique: An Experimental Moment in the Human Sciences.* Chicago: University of Chicago Press.

Mark, Joan. 1988. *A Stranger in Her Native Land: Alice Cunningham Fletcher and the American Indians.* Lincoln: University of Nebraska Press.

Marriott, Alice. 1945. *The Ten Grandmothers.* Norman: University of Oklahoma Press.

Marsden, Michael T. 1976. "Henry Rowe Schoolcraft: A Reappraisal." *The Old Northwest* 2:153–182.

Mattina, Anthony, ed. 1985. *The Golden Woman: The Colville Narrative of Peter J. Seymour.* Tucson: University of Arizona Press.

——. 1987a. "North American Indian Mythography: Editing Texts for the Printed Page." In Swann and Krupat 1987: 129–148.

——. 1987b. "On the Transcription and Translation of *The Golden Woman*." *Studies in American Indian Literatures* 11(2): 92–101.

Mayhall, Mildred P. 1971. *The Kiowas.* 2d ed. Norman: University of Oklahoma Press.

Mays, John Bentley. 1973. "The Flying Serpent: Contemporary Imaginations of the American Indian." *Canadian Review of American Studies* 4(1): 32–47.

McAllester, David P. 1983. "The Tenth Horse Song of Frank Mitchell." In Rothenberg and Rothenberg 1983: 393–398.

McCutchen, David. 1993. *The Red Record, The Wallam Olum: The Oldest Native North American History.* Garden City Park, N.Y.: Avery.

McGrane, Bernard. 1989. *Beyond Anthropology: Society and the Other.* New York: Columbia University Press.

McGuire, Joseph D. 1901. "Ethnology in the Jesuit Relations." *American Anthropologist* 3:257–269.

McNeil, W. K. 1980. "A History of American Folklore Scholarship Before 1908." Ph.D. diss., Indiana University.

——. 1992. New Introduction to *Algic Researches: Indian Tales and Legends, Volumes I & II,* by Henry Rowe Schoolcraft, 1–18. Baltimore: Clearfield.

Mooney, James. 1891. *The Sacred Formulas of the Cherokees.* Seventh Annual Report of the Bureau of American Ethnology, 301–397. Washington, D.C.: GPO.

Mooney, James, and Franz M. Olbrechts. 1932. *The Swimmer Manuscript: Cherokee Sacred Formulas and Medicinal Prescriptions.* Bureau of American Ethnology Bulletin 99. Washington, D.C.: GPO.

Moore, James T. 1982. *Indian and Jesuit: A Seventeenth-Century Encounter.* Chicago: Loyola University Press.

Mourning Dove. 1934. *Coyote Stories*. Ed. Hester Dean Guie. Caldwell, Idaho: Caxton.

Müller, Max. 1909. *Comparative Mythology*. London: Routledge.

Munn, Nancy D. 1986. *Walbiri Iconography: Graphic Representation and Cultural Symbolism in a Central Australian Society*. Chicago: University of Chicago Press.

Murphy, Peter T. 1986. "Fool's Gold: The Highland Treasures of Macpherson's Ossian." *ELH* 53:567–591.

Murray, David. 1991. *Forked Tongues: Speech, Writing, and Representation in North American Indian Texts*. Bloomington: Indiana University Press.

Myrsiades, Kostas, and Linda Myrsiades. 1983. "Texts and Contexts: A Primer for Translating from the Oral Tradition." *Translation Review* 11: 45–59.

Nash, Gary B. 1972 "The Image of the Indian in the Southern Colonial Mind." *William and Mary Quarterly*, 3d ser., 29:197–230.

——. 1974. *Red, White, and Black: The Peoples of Early America*. Englewood Cliffs, N.J.: Prentice-Hall.

"Natalie Curtis." 1926. *Southern Workman* 55:127–140.

Newton, Hilah Foote. 1954. "Schoolcraft on the Iroquois." *New York Folklore Quarterly* 10:127–132, 176–188.

Nichols, John D. 1991. " 'Chant to the Fire-fly': A Philological Problem in Ojibwe." In *Linguistic Studies Presented to John L. Finlay*, ed. H. C. Wolfart. Algonquian and Iroquoian Linguistics Memoir, no. 8, 113–126. Winnipeg: Algonquian and Iroquoian Linuistics.

Niles, John D. 1993. "Understanding *Beowulf*: Oral Poetry Acts." *Journal of American Folklore* 106:131–155.

"North American Indians." 1840. *Southern Literary Messenger* 6:190–192.

Ong, Walter J. 1982. *Orality and Literacy: Technologizing the Word*. London: Methuen.

——. 1988. "Before Textuality: Orality and Interpretation." *Oral Tradition* 3:259–269.

Ortiz, Alfonso. 1969. *The Tewa World: Space, Time, and Becoming in a Pueblo Society*. Chicago: University of Chicago Press.

——, ed. 1979. *Handbook of North American Indians*. Vol. 9. *Southwest*. Washington, D.C.: Smithsonian Institution.

Osborn, Chase, and Stellanova Osborn. 1942. *Schoolcraft—Longfellow—Hiawatha*. Lancaster, Pa.: Jaques Cattell.

Pagden, Anthony. 1982. *The Fall of Natural Man: The American Indian and the Origins of Comparative Ethnology*. Cambridge: Cambridge University Press.

——. 1993. *European Encounters with the New World from Renaissance to Romanticism*. New Haven: Yale University Press.

Palmer, R. R. 1961. *Catholics and Unbelievers in Eighteenth Century France.* 2d ed. New York: Cooper Square.

Pandey, Triloki Nath. 1972. "Anthropologists at Zuni." *Proceedings of the American Philosophical Society* 116:321–327.

Parker, Rev. Samuel. 1838. *Journal of an Exploring Tour Beyond the Rocky Mountains, under the Direction of the A.B.C.F.M. Performed in the Years 1835, '36, and '37* . . . Ithaca: By the Author.

Parkman, Francis. 1983. *The Jesuits in North America in the Seventeenth Century.* In *France and England in North America.* Vol. 1, 331–712. New York: Library of America.

Pearce, Roy Harvey. 1952. "The 'Ruines of Mankind': The Indian and the Puritan Mind." *Journal of the History of Ideas* 13:200–217.

———. 1988. *Savagism and Civilization: A Study of the Indian and the American Mind.* Berkeley: University of California Press.

Phinney, Archie. 1934. *Nez Perce Texts.* Columbia University Contributions to Anthropology, no. 25. New York: Columbia University Press.

Porter, Joseph C. 1986. *Paper Medicine Man: John Gregory Bourke and His American West.* Norman: University of Oklahoma Press.

Pound, Louise. 1976. *Nebraska Folklore.* Westport, Conn.: Greenwood.

Powell, John Wesley. 1883. "Report of the Director." *Second Annual Report of the Bureau of Ethnology,* xv–xxxvii. Washington, D.C.: GPO.

Radin, Paul, ed. 1963. *The Autobiography of a Winnebago Indian.* New York: Dover.

Ramsey, Jarold. 1983. *Reading the Fire: Essays in the Traditional Indian Literatures of the Far West.* Lincoln: University of Nebraska Press.

———. 1990. "Thoreau's Last Words—and America's First Literatures." In Ruoff and Ward 1990: 52–61.

Randolph, J. Ralph. 1973. *British Travelers Among the Southern Indians, 1660–1763.* Norman: University of Oklahoma Press.

Randolph, Vance. 1952. *Who Blowed Up the Church House? and Other Ozark Folktales.* New York: Columbia University Press.

Reade, John. 1884. "The Literary Faculty of the Native Races of America." *Publications and Transactions of the Royal Society of Canada,* 1st ser., 2(2): 17–30.

Review of *An Account of the History, Manners and Customs of the Indian Nations . . .* , by John Heckewelder. 1819. *Western Review and Miscellaneous Magazine* (September): 65–74.

Review of *Algic Researches . . .* , by Henry Rowe Schoolcraft. 1838. *North American Review* 49:354–372.

Review of *Report on the Census of the Iroquois Indians in the State of New York . . .* , by Henry Rowe Schoolcraft. 1847. *North American Review* 64:292–314.

Review of *Shaking the Pumpkin*, edited by Jerome Rothenberg. 1972. *Choice* (July/August): 654–655.

Rice, Julian. 1989. *Lakota Storytelling: Black Elk, Ella Deloria and Frank Fools Crow*. New York: Peter Lang.

———. 1991. *Black Elk's Story: Distinguishing Its Lakota Purpose*. Albuquerque: University of New Mexico Press.

———. 1992. "Narrative Styles in *Dakota Texts*." In Swann 1992: 276–292.

Richardson, William. 1931. "An Account of the Presbyterian Mission to the Cherokees, 1757–1759." *Tennessee Historical Magazine*, ser. 2, 1:125–128.

Ricoeur, Paul. 1973. "The Model of the Text: Meaningful Action Considered as Text." *New Literary History* 5(1): 91–117.

Rink, Henry. 1875. *Tales and Traditions of the Eskimo, with a Sketch of Their Habits, Religion, Language, and Other Peculiarities*. Trans. Robert Brown. Edinburgh: Blackwood.

Robbins, Richard Howard. 1973. Review of *Shaking the Pumpkin*, edited by Jerome Rothenberg. *American Anthropologist* 75:1062.

Rohner, Ronald P., ed. 1969. *The Ethnography of Franz Boas: Letters and Diaries of Franz Boas Written on the Northwest Coast from 1886 to 1931*. Trans. Hedy Parker. Chicago: University of Chicago Press.

Rohner, Ronald P., and Evelyn C. Rohner. 1969. "Introduction: Franz Boas and the Development of North American Ethnology and Ethnography." In Rohner 1969: xiii–xxx.

Roosevelt, Theodore. 1951. *The Letters of Theodore Roosevelt*. Ed. Elting E. Morison. 8 vols. Cambridge: Harvard University Press.

Rooth, Anna Birgitta. 1957. "The Creation Myths of the North American Indians." *Anthropos* 52:497–508.

Rothenberg, Jerome, ed. 1968. *Technicians of the Sacred: A Range of Poetries from Africa, America, Asia & Oceania*. Garden City, N.Y.: Anchor Doubleday.

———, ed. 1972. *Shaking the Pumpkin: Traditional Poetry of the Indian North Americas*. Garden City, N.Y.: Anchor Doubleday.

———. 1983. "Total Translation: An Experiment in the Presentation of American Indian Poetry." In Rothenberg and Rothenberg 1983: 381–393.

———. 1986. *Shaking the Pumpkin: Traditional Poetry of the Indian North Americas*. Rev. ed. Albuquerque: University of New Mexico Press.

———. 1992. " 'We Explain Nothing, We Believe Nothing': American Indian Poetry and the Problematics of Translation." In Swann 1992: 64–79.

Rothenberg, Jerome, and Diane Rothenberg, eds. 1983. *Symposium of the Whole: A Range of Discourse Toward an Ethnopoetics*. Berkeley: University of California Press.

Rothrock, Mary U. 1929. "Carolina Traders Among the Overhill Chero-kees." *East Tennessee Historical Society's Publications* 1:3–18.

Rowbotham, Arnold H. 1956. "The Jesuit Figurists and Eighteenth-Century Religious Thought." *Journal of the History of Ideas* 17:471–485.

Rowe, John Howland. 1965. "The Renaissance Foundations of Anthropology." *American Anthropologist* 67:1–20.

Ruoff, A. LaVonne Brown, and Jerry W. Ward, Jr., eds. 1990. *Redefining American Literary History.* New York: Modern Language Association.

Ruppert, James. 1991. "Henry Rowe Schoolcraft: The Indian Expert and American Literature." *Platte Valley Review* 19(1): 99–128.

Rushforth, Scott, and Steadman Upham. 1992. *A Hopi Social History: Anthropological Perspectives on Sociocultural Persistence and Change.* Austin: University of Texas Press.

Sage, Rufus P. 1846. *Scenes in the Rocky Mountains, and in Oregon, California, New Mexico, Texas, and the Grand Prairies . . .* Philadelphia: Carey and Hart.

Said, Edward W. 1978. *Orientalism.* New York: Pantheon.

Sarris, Greg. 1993. *Keeping Slug Woman Alive: A Holistic Approach to American Indian Texts.* Berkeley: University of California Press.

Schoolcraft, Henry Rowe. 1825. *Travels in the Central Portions of the Mississippi Valley: Comprising Observations on Its Mineral Geography, Internal Resources, and Aboriginal Population.* New York: Collins and Hannay.

——. 1828. Review of *Le Decouverte des Sources du Mississippi . . . ,* by J. C. Beltram. *North American Review* 27:89–114.

——. 1837. Review of *Archaeological Americana: Transactions and Collections of the American Antiquarian Society. . . North American Review* 45:34–59.

——. 1839. *Algic Researches: Comprising Inquiries Respecting the Mental Characteristics of the North American Indians. First Series. Indian Tales and Legends.* 2 vols. New York: Harper and Brothers.

——. 1848. *The Indian in His Wigwam, or Characteristics of the Red Race of America.* New York: W. H. Graham.

——. 1851a. *Personal Memoirs of a Residence of Thirty Years with the Indian Tribes on the American Frontiers: with Brief Notices of Passing Events, Facts, and Opinions, A. D. 1812 to A. D. 1842.* Philadelphia: Lippincott, Grambo.

——. 1851b. *Historical and Statistical Information, Respecting the History, Condition and Prospects of the Indian Tribes of the United States: Collected and Prepared under the Direction of the Bureau of Indian Affairs, per Act of Congress of March 3d, 1847, Part I.* Philadelphia: Lippincott, Grambo.

——. 1852. *Information Respecting the History, Condition and Prospects of the Indian Tribes of the United States . . . Part II.* Philadelphia: Lippincott, Grambo.

——. 1853. *Information Respecting the History, Condition and Prospects of the Indian Tribes of the United States . . . Part III.* Philadelphia: Lippincott, Grambo.

——. 1854. *Information Respecting the History, Condition and Prospects of the Indian Tribes of the United States . . . Part IV.* Philadelphia: Lippincott, Grambo.

——. 1855. *Information Respecting the History, Condition and Prospects of the Indian Tribes of the United States . . . Part V.* Philadelphia: J. B. Lippincott.

——. 1856. *The Myth of Hiawatha, and Other Oral Legends, Mythologic and Allegoric, of the North American Indians.* Philadelphia: J. B. Lippincott.

——. 1857. *History of the Indian Tribes of the United States: Their Present Condition and Prospects, and a Sketch of Their Ancient Status. Part VI.* Philadelphia: J. B. Lippincott.

——. 1953. *Narrative Journal of Travels Through the Northwestern Regions of the United States Extending from Detroit Through the Great Chain of American Lakes to the Sources of the Mississippi River in the Year 1820.* Ed. Mentor L. Williams. East Lansing: Michigan State College Press.

——. 1956. *Schoolcraft's Indian Legends.* Ed. Mentor L. Williams. East Lansing: Michigan State University Press.

——. 1986. "Mental Character of the Aborigines." In Clements 1986: 52–60.

Shaul, David Leedom. 1992. "A Hopi Song-Poem in 'Context.'" In Swann 1992: 228–241.

Shaw, R. Daniel. 1987. "The Translation Context: Cultural Factors in Translation." *Translation Review* 23:25–29.

Sheehan, Bernard. 1980. *Savagism and Civility: Indians and Englishmen in Colonial Virginia.* Cambridge: Cambridge University Press.

Sherzer, Joel. 1987. "Poetic Structuring of Kuna Discourse: The Line." In Sherzer and Woodbury 1987: 103–139.

Sherzer, Joel, and Greg Urban, eds. 1986. *Native South American Discourse.* Berlin: Mouton de Gruyter.

Sherzer, Joel, and Anthony C. Woodbury, eds. 1987. *Native American Discourse: Poetics and Rhetoric.* Cambridge: Cambridge University Press.

Silko, Leslie Marmon. 1979. "An Old-Time Indian Attack in Two Parts." In *The Remembered Earth: An Anthology of Contemporary Native American Literature,* ed. Geary Hobson, 211–216. Albuquerque: University of New Mexico Press.

———. 1981. *Storyteller*. New York: Seaver Books.

Simmons, Leo, ed. 1942. *Sun Chief: The Autobiography of a Hopi Indian*. New Haven: Yale University Press.

Simms, William Gilmore. 1962. *Views and Reviews in American Literature and Fiction*. Ed. C. Hugh Holman. Cambridge: Harvard University Press.

Smart, J. S. 1905. *James Macpherson: An Episode in Literature*. London: David Nutt.

Smith, Henry Nash. 1950. *Virgin Land: the American West as Symbol and Myth*. Cambridge, Mass.: Harvard University Press.

Smith, Robert Jerome. 1972. "Festivals and Celebrations." In *Folklore and Folklife: An Introduction*, ed. Richard M. Dorson, 159–172. Chicago: University of Chicago Press.

Snelling, W. J.. 1835. "Life of Black Hawk." *North American Review* 40:68–87.

Spinden, Herbert Joseph. 1933. *Songs of the Tewa*. New York: Exposition of Indian Tribal Arts.

Squier, E. G. 1849. "Historical and Mythological Traditions of the Algonquins; with a Translation of the 'Walam-Olum,' or Bark Record of the Linni-Lenape." *American Review* 9:173–193.

Staub, Michael E. 1991. "(Re)Collecting the Past: Writing Native American Speech." *American Quarterly* 43:425–456.

Steiner, George. 1975. *After Babel: Aspects of Language and Translation*. London: Oxford University Press.

Stensland, Anna Lee. 1975. "Traditional Poetry of the American Indian." *English Journal* 64(6): 41–47.

Stevenson, Robert. 1973. "English Sources for Indian Music Until 1882." *Ethnomusicology* 17:399–442.

[Stickley, Gustav]. 1910. "People Who Interest Us: Natalie Curtis, the 'Friend of the Indians.'" *The Craftsman* 18:678–679.

Stocking, George W., Jr. 1992. *The Ethnographer's Magic and Other Essays in the History of Anthropology*. Madison: University of Wisconsin Press.

Stone-Gordon, Tammy. 1994. "The Other Schoolcraft." *Michigan History* 78:24–29.

Strachey, William. 1849. *A Historie of Travaile into Virginia Brittania . . .* Ed. R. H. Major. London: Hakluyt Society.

Swann, Brian, ed. 1983. *Smoothing the Ground: Essays on Native American Oral Literature*. Berkeley: University of California Press.

———, ed. 1992. *On the Translation of Native American Literatures*. Washington, D.C.: Smithsonian Institution Press.

———. 1993. *Song of the Sky: Versions of Native American Song-Poems*. Rev. ed. Amherst: University of Massachusetts Press.

——, ed. 1994. *Coming to Light: Contemporary Translations of the Native Literatures of North America.* New York: Random House.

Swann, Brian, and Arnold Krupat, eds. 1987. *Recovering the Word: Essays on Native American Literature.* Berkeley: University of California Press.

Swanton, John R. 1946. *The Indians of the Southeastern United States.* Bureau of American Ethnology Bulletin 137. Washington, D.C.: GPO.

Tedlock, Dennis. 1972. *Finding the Center: Narrative Poetry of the Zuni Indians.* New York: Dial.

——. 1983a. "On the Translation of Style in Oral Narrative." In Swann 1983: 57–77.

——. 1983b. *The Spoken Word and the Work of Interpretation.* Philadelphia: University of Pennsylvania Press.

Thompson, Harold. 1939. *Body, Boots and Britches: Folktales, Ballads and Speech from Country New York.* Philadelphia: J. B. Lippincott.

Thompson, Stith. 1929. *Tales of the North American Indians.* Cambridge: Harvard University Press.

——. 1955–1958. *Motif-Index of Folk-Literature: A Classification of Narrative Elements in Folktales, Ballads, Myths, Fables, Mediaeval Romances, Exempla, Fabliaux, Jest-Books and Local Legends.* 6 vols. Bloomington: Indiana University Press.

——. 1964. "The Star Husband Tale." In Dundes 1964a: 414–459.

Thwaites, Reuben Gold, ed. 1959. *The Jesuit Relations and Allied Documents: Travels and Explorations of the Jesuit Missionaries in New France 1610–1791.* 79 vols. New York: Pageant.

Timberlake, Henry. 1765. *The Memoirs of Lieut. Henry Timberlake, (Who Accompanied the Three Cherokee Indians to England in the Year 1762) Containing Whatever he Observed Remarkable, or Worthy of Public Notice.* London: For the Author.

Titiev, Mischa. 1972. *The Hopi Indians of Old Oraibi: Change and Continuity.* Ann Arbor: University of Michigan Press.

Torgovnick, Marianna. 1990. *Gone Primitive: Savage Intellects, Modern Lives.* Chicago: University of Chicago Press.

Trigger, Bruce G. 1985. *Natives and Newcomers: Canada's "Heroic Age" Reconsidered.* Kingston, Ont.: McGill–Queen's University Press.

Tyler, Stephen. 1985. Review of *Symposium of the Whole,* edited by Jerome and Diane Rothenberg. *American Anthropologist* 87:687–689.

Underhill, Ruth Murray. 1993. *Singing for Power: The Song Magic of the Papago Indians of Southern Arizona.* Tucson: University of Arizona Press.

Untermeyer, Louis, ed. 1931. *American Poetry from the Beginning to Whitman.* New York: Harcourt Brace.

Urban, Greg. 1991. *A Discourse-Centered Approach to Culture: Native South American Myths and Rituals.* Austin: University of Texas Press.

Velie, Alan, ed. 1991. *American Indian Literature: An Anthology*. Rev. ed. Norman: University of Oklahoma Press.

Vico, Giambattista. 1970. *The New Science of Giambattista Vico: Abridged Translation of the Third Edition (1744)*. Trans. Thomas Goddard Bergin and Max Harold Frisch. Ithaca, N.Y.: Cornell University Press.

Vizenor, Gerald. 1984. *The People Named Chippewa: Narrative Histories*. Minneapolis: University of Minnesota Press.

Von Sydow, C. W. 1964. "Folktale Studies and Philology: Some Points of View." In Dundes 1964a: 219–242.

Vorpagel, Becky. 1983. "Daniel Brinton's Concept of Folklore." *New York Folklore* 9(3–4): 31–42.

Wallace, Mark. 1994. "Black Hawk's *An Autobiography*: Production and Use of an 'Indian' Voice." *American Indian Quarterly* 18:481–494.

Walsh, Martin W. 1982. "The Condemnation of Carnival in the *Jesuit Relations*." *Michigan Academician* 15:13–26.

Walton, Eda Lou. 1924. "Navaho Verse Rhythms." *Poetry* 24:40–44.

Ward, Donald, ed. and trans. 1981. *The German Legends of the Brothers Grimm*. Philadelphia: Institute for the Study of Human Issues.

Warren, William W. 1984. *History of the Ojibways, Based Upon Tradition and Oral Statements*. St. Paul: Minnesota Historical Society Press.

Waters, Frank. 1963. *The Book of the Hopi*. New York: Viking.

Weslager, C. A. 1978. *The Delaware Indian Westward Migration with the Texts of Two Manuscripts (1821–22) Responding to General Lewis Cass's Inquiries About Lenape Culture and Language*. Wallingford, Pa.: Middle Atlantic Press.

Whitaker, Alexander. 1613. *Good Newes from Virginia. Sent to the Counsell and Company of Virginia*. London: William Welby.

Wiget, Andrew O. 1986. "Native American Literature: A Bibliographic Survey of American Indian Literary Traditions." *Choice* 23:1503–1512.

———. 1990. "His Life in His Tail: The Native American Trickster and the Literature of Possibility." In Ruoff and Ward 1990: 83–96.

Williams, Samuel Cole. 1927. Introduction to *Lieut. Henry Timberlake's Memoirs 1756–1765*, by Henry Timberlake, 9–17. Johnson City, Tenn.: Watauga Press.

———, ed. 1928. *Early Travels in the Tennessee Country 1540–1800*. Johnson City, Tenn.: Watauga Press.

———, ed. 1930. *Adair's History of the American Indians*. Johnson City, Tenn.: Watauga Press.

Wolf, Eric R. 1982. *Europe and the People Without History*. Berkeley: University of California Press.

Woodbury, Anthony. 1987. "Rhetorical Structure in Central Alaskan Yupik Eskimo Traditional Narrative." In Sherzer and Woodbury 1987: 176–239.

Woodward, Arthur. 1939. "Frank Cushing—'First War-Chief of Zuni.'" *Masterkey* 13:172–179.

Wynter, Sylvia. 1976. "Ethno or Socio Poetics." *Alcheringa/Ethnopoetics* 2(2): 78–94.

Young, M. Jane. 1988. *Signs from the Ancestors: Zuni Cultural Symbolism and Perceptions of Rock Art.* Albuquerque: University of New Mexico Press.

Zahniser, Ed. 1972. Review of *Shaking the Pumpkin,* edited by Jerome Rothenberg. *Living Wilderness* (Autumn): 36–37.

Zitkala-Ša. 1901. *Old Indian Legends.* Boston: Ginn.

Zolbrod, Paul. 1995. *Reading the Voice: Native American Oral Poetry on the Written Page.* Salt Lake City: University of Utah Press.

Zolla, Elémire. 1973. *The Writer and the Shaman: A Morphology of the American Indian.* Trans. Raymond Rosenthal. New York: Harcourt Brace Jovanovich.

Zumwalt, Rosemary. 1976. "Henry Rowe Schoolcraft—1793–1864: His Collection of the Oral Narratives of American Indians." *Kroeber Anthropological Society Papers* 53–54:44–57.

INDEX

ABOUT THE AUTHOR

William M. Clements is Professor of English and Folklore at Arkansas State University. His previous publications on American Indian oral expression include *Native American Folklore, 1879–1979: An Annotated Bibliography* (1984; with Frances M. Malpezzi) and *Native American Folklore in Nineteenth-Century Periodicals* (1986). He has also written *Italian-American Folklore* (1992; with Frances M. Malpezzi).